Documents in Modern History

Roosevelt's peacetime administrations, 1933–41

Published in our
centenary year
2004
MANCHESTER
UNIVERSITY
PRESS

DOCUMENTS IN MODERN HISTORY

Series editor:
Dr G. H. Bennett (University of Plymouth)

Series advisor:
Dr Kevin Jefferys (University of Plymouth)

The *Documents in Modern History* series offers collections of documents on the most widely debated and studied topics in modern British and international history. The volumes place fresh primary material alongside more familiar texts, and provide thought-provoking introductions to place the documents in their wider historical context.

All volumes in the series are comprehensive and broad-ranging. They provide the ideal course textbook for sixth-form students, first-year undergraduates and beyond.

Also available:

Anglo-American relations since 1939
John Baylis

The Labour Party: 'socialism' and society since 1951
Steven Fielding

From Beveridge to Blair: the first fifty years of Britain's welfare state 1948–98
Margaret Jones and Rodney Lowe

Television and the press since 1945
Ralph Negrine

The impact of immigration in post-war Britain
Panikos Panayi

The Vietnam wars
Kevin Ruane

Britain in the Second World War: a social history
Harold L. Smith

British trade unions 1945–95
Chris Wrigley

Documents in Modern History

Roosevelt's peacetime administrations, 1933–41

A documentary history of the New Deal years

Edited by G. H. Bennett

Manchester University Press
Manchester and New York
distributed exclusively in the USA by Palgrave

Published by Manchester University Press
Oxford Road, Manchester M13 9NR, UK
and Room 400, 175 Fifth Avenue, New York, NY 10010, USA
www.manchesteruniversitypress.co.uk

Distributed exclusively in the USA by
Palgrave, 175 Fifth Avenue, New York,
NY 10010, USA

Distributed exclusively in Canada by
UBC Press, University of British Columbia, 2029 West Mall,
Vancouver, BC, Canada V6T 1Z2

British Library Cataloguing-in-Publication Data
A catalogue record for this book is available from the British Library

Library of Congress Cataloging-in-Publication Data applied for

ISBN 0 7190 6564 X *hardback*
EAN 978 0 7190 6564 4
ISBN 0 7190 6565 8 *paperback*
EAN 978 0 7190 6565 1

First published 2004

13 12 11 10 09 08 07 06 05 04 10 9 8 7 6 5 4 3 2 1

Printed in Great Britain
by Bell & Bain Ltd, Glasgow

Contents

Acknowledgements

As is usual in academe, the author finds himself indebted to a large number of institutions and individuals. Now more than ever, academics produce their books in partnership with many individuals and bodies on whom they rely for help, secretarial and library support, and the cold hard cash that drives research on both sides of the Atlantic. In particular I would like to thank the Franklin and Eleanor Roosevelt Institute for awarding me a Lubin-Winant fellowship to facilitate study at the Roosevelt Library. I would also like to thank the staff at the library, particularly Karen Anson, for putting up with endless requests to see material. Also on the funding front I would like to thank the British Academy and the British Association for American Studies. Their awards of grants for other, but related pieces of research incidentally helped to enlarge the range of sources on which this book is based.

Larry DeWitt, the historian at the Social Security Administration, was extremely helpful with material relating to the New Deal and social security, as well as very encouraging about the project as a whole. Staff at the libraries at the University of Plymouth, University of Bristol, University of Exeter, University of Kentucky and the British National Archives were very helpful. Thank you also to the staff at the Greenwood Public Library, South Carolina, for their help with local newspaper sources, and to Gilbert and Susan Guinn of Lander University for providing ongoing help with the New Deal and the South. Staff at state parks in Georgia, South and North Carolina were helpful in identifying some of the legacies of the New Deal. Thank you also to my students and my colleagues, to Roy and Sylvia Bennett, Rachel, Fay, Alice and Poppy Crawshaw (Virginia), and to the staff at the *European Journal of American Culture* who have made the task of simultaneously editing a book and a journal that little bit easier. I must thank Alison Whittle and the staff at Manchester University

Press for giving me the opportunity to edit the series into which this volume fits.

Thanks are also due to Clare Hamling, Nikki Girvin and Becky Stewart, who between them have typed and printed significant chunks of the manuscript. Without their secretarial support the book would not have proceeded as smoothly as it did.

Finally I must offer an apology. While efforts have been made to trace owners of copyright for the material quoted herein, in a few cases that has not been possible. The author offers his apologies to the copyright owners. If they will get in touch with him through the publisher, he will remedy the omission in any future edition.

Introduction

Roosevelt: Dictator or Democrat was the title of Gerald Johnson's study of the President he had observed in the turbulent and traumatic 1930s while working as a journalist. It was a bold title and one that reflected the American public's confusion and unease with some aspects of the work of the Roosevelt administration. To many, Roosevelt was the Democratic dictator, popularly elected by impressive margins on no less than four occasions, gathering more power into his hands at every turn in order to save American democracy. As with his court packing plan in 1937, he seemed willing to subvert the constitution in order to save it. The paradoxes did not end there. Born of privilege, he had the common touch. Saviour of his class, he was accused of being its greatest traitor.[1] Afflicted with polio, he possessed enormous reserves of strength. Unable to walk, he radiated dynamism. In defence of American capitalism he enlarged the federal state as never before. Committed to freedom, he invoked regulation and expanded massively the power of the presidency. Resolute in pursuit of peace, he prepared America for war and oversaw the approach to victory. With Roosevelt the paradoxes abounded. A sense of confusion also surrounded his great New Deal programme, unleashed on America in 1933 as the response of the White House to the problem of the Great Depression which had been born of the Wall Street Crash of October 1929. The billions of dollars thrown at unemployment in a dollar blizzard of scheme creation from the Civilian Conservation Corps (CCC) to the Civil Works Administration (CWA) dazzled many observers. Both agencies, and the Federal Emergency Relief Administration (FERA) which took over the functions of the CWA in 1934, took millions off the streets to plant forests, build roads and control America's rivers. The Public Works Administration (PWA) established under the National Industrial Recovery Act of 1933 employed half a million people on over 34,000 conservation projects between 1933 and 1939 at a total cost of $5 billion. With the New Deal facts and figures and statistics abounded.

While Roosevelt formed the centre and figurehead of this administration, many of his political appointees, backed by the multi-million dollars of the taxpayer, wielded a striking level of political power. The heads of New Deal agencies like Harold Ickes, who as Secretary of the Interior controlled the PWA, and Harry Hopkins who headed the CWA, became national figures. They were the other New Dealers just as much responsible for the New Deal as their political master, Franklin D. Roosevelt. Presidential advisors like Rexford Tugwell, part of the so-called 'Brains Trust', and Frances Perkins, Roosevelt's Secretary of Labor, similarly became national figures.

New Deal innovation did not end with the rise of the federal administrator. In trying to end the depression the Roosevelt administration pioneered new methods of work in an attempt to improve the life of millions. The economy was to be revived through Keynesian economics. The labour codes established by the National Recovery Administration (NRA) would slowly transform American industry and business. In the agricultural sector there was a drive towards environmentally sensitive farming. Propaganda abounded as the New Deal was given an identity in the form of the blue eagle of the NRA, which businesses were encouraged to display as evidence of their patriotic determination to 'do their bit'. The blue eagle was also exhibited at public parades. Parallels with the symbolism of Nazi Germany were not lost on some observers, nor was the alacrity with which the Roosevelt administration strove to dominate the media. Roosevelt developed a very cosy relationship with the American media, and radio listeners thrilled to Roosevelt's fatherly 'fireside chats' in which he addressed the critical issues of the moment in an accessible manner.

The New Deal really did seem 'new', even if some elements of it were clearly borrowed. Some called it revolutionary, but its radicalism was born out of circumstance rather than political expediency or doctrine. The severity of the problem of the Great Depression with which Roosevelt had to grapple is hard to capture adequately. Simple figures convey only part of the hopelessness:

> Over five thousand banks had failed. The total value of the stocks on the New York Stock Exchange had fallen by 89 percent since the crash of 1929. American investors had lost $74 billion. World War 1 itself had cost the country only $25 billion.

> U.S. Steel was still running, barely, with over 80 percent of its productive capacity idle. In Toledo, Ohio, four out of every five workers were unemployed. Over 15 million people were unemployed. According to *Fortune* magazine in October 1932, 34 million Americans – almost a third of the population – had no income whatsoever. In Detroit, the mayor's Unemployment Commission saw 'no possibility of preventing widespread hunger and slow starvation.'[2]

From the security of the twenty-first century we can see that the depression was simply an episode in the economic cycle. From the insecurity of 1932 many wondered whether they were witnessing the end of the capitalist system, which Marx, Engels, Lenin and others had predicted was inevitable. Democracy was undoubtedly in danger, as events in Germany had demonstrated. In July 1932, fearing that revolution was 'in the air', General Douglas MacArthur had led his troops against the so-called bonus army in Washington. The 25,000 men of the bonus army, unemployed First World War veterans who had made their way to Washington to ask for the early payment of their war bonus, scattered in the face of tanks, tear gas and cavalry. Some onlookers feared that they were not just watching the end of capitalist democracy in America, but possibly the beginning of the end of Western civilisation itself. Across broad swathes of the United States law and order seemed in danger of breaking down as the number of destitute and desperate continued to grow.

At the fringe of events in 1932 stood Franklin D. Roosevelt, the Democratic Governor of New York. Born in January 1882 to James and Sara Delano Roosevelt of Hyde Park, New York, Roosevelt came from a landed and wealthy background. Their home, acquired in 1867, has been described as a 'modest country house set in woodland', but a country house it still constituted and the woodland was part of a large estate.[3] Indeed, Franklin Roosevelt would later oversee the planting of 300,000 trees on that estate. The family, from Dutch stock, was an established part of Dutchess County society, and could trace its lineage back to the early settlement of the East Coast. Roosevelt was, in American terms, an aristocrat, and in his youth he was something of a playboy. At Harvard he seemed more interested in social distinction than academic achievement. After marrying his cousin Eleanor Roosevelt in 1905, he left the Law School at Columbia University in 1907 without a degree. In search of a career he entered

Wall Street. However, he quickly grew tired of it, and turned his hand to politics. Propelled by good looks, a sure political instinct, a belief in Christian responsibility, and fine oratorical abilities, at the age of 28 he found himself in the Senate. His rise was rapid, and after allying himself with Woodrow Wilson, in 1920 he was nominated as Democratic vice-presidential candidate for the forthcoming presidential elections. Republican victory in that election stalled his relentless rise, and then in 1921 his political career seemed to be over after he was struck with polio. He would never regain the strength in his legs or the ability to walk unaided. As the Democratic Party endured three successive Republican victories in the presidential elections in the 1920s, Roosevelt struggled to come to terms with, and master, his disability. However, by 1928 he was back, narrowly winning the governorship of New York. From this platform he would go on to secure the Democratic nomination for the 1932 presidential election. He would win that election on the promise of a New Deal for the American public. No one was really sure what it might amount to, but for a majority of the American public the phrase suggested the right instinctive approach. The New Deal, aided by the war, would put the American public back to work, and Roosevelt would die in office having been re-elected in 1936, 1940 and 1944. From the wreckage of a career in 1920–21 he would become the most successful politician America has ever seen.

For the benefit of the high school student a narrative of Roosevelt's life can be constructed along very traditional lines – the rise, fall and rise again model. The contrast between Roosevelt's physical weakness and his political strength is effective and dramatic, as is the image of him as the caring, patrician aristocrat. However, this gilded image requires the addition of a little analytical acid. All heroes are flawed and Roosevelt was no exception. In 1918 Eleanor Roosevelt discovered that her husband was having an extra-marital relationship with Lucy Mercer, her social secretary. From this point on their marriage was a fiction preserved for the sake of their children and for Franklin's political career. It allowed Eleanor to emerge as an important political figure in her own right, championing issues on which she felt more had to be done. Both had later relationships with other people, and in Eleanor's case, of the same sex. Eleanor's relationships with what can euphemistically be referred to as her 'friends' are an aspect of America's political history that some still find hard to face. The Roosevelt marriage was, however, a vital aspect of Franklin's presidential style, as was the disability that he covered up with sympathetic pressmen, leg braces and a specially converted car. Franklin Roosevelt knew how to erect a façade, put on a face, act and work through smoke and mirrors like the best illusionist. The Republicans found him a hard man to pin down. Roosevelt's biographers have subsequently encountered the same problem. Working in the Roosevelt Library at Hyde Park trying to understand the New Deal, the historian feels Franklin's influence in every page, but his presence is ghost-like in more ways than one. On many points, in trying to establish what he thought, and what influenced him, it is impossible to come to definitive answers: the political smoke and the private mirrors obscure the deeper realities. One sees the way in which the President routinely worked through those around him, his advisers putting into words his thoughts and orders, rather than the President acting directly in a way which leaves for posterity the kind of incontrovertible evidence beloved by forensic historians. As James Macgregor Burns has noted on the subject of Roosevelt's 1932 bid for the presidency: 'Roosevelt's method was to leave the actual management of the campaign to Howe and Farley in New York City and to his friends throughout the country, while making the decisions himself'.[4] For the biographer, and there have been many, Roosevelt is one of those characters who can never be known and his policies remain open for debate.

If there is a problem for the historian in the question 'In what did Franklin Roosevelt believe?', at least some enlightenment can be found in his book *Looking Forward*.[5] Published in March 1933, and rapidly proceeding to four printings before the end of the month, it consisted of a compilation of articles and speeches which Roosevelt had given before taking office as President. Together they amounted to a political philosophy which Roosevelt wished to offer to the American public at the start of his administration. It offered hope for the future and affirmed the central role of government in improving the quality of ordinary people's live. Through government, he argued, the socio-economic system could be rebuilt to ensure that a great depression would never again blight the life of the nation.

While he expressed his belief in the capitalist system, he called for planning to prevent over-production. He also asked for the nation's patience, quoting Thomas Jefferson: 'I shall often go wrong through defective judgement. And when right, I shall be thought wrong by those whose positions will not command a view of the whole ground. I ask your support against the errors of others who may condemn what they would not, if seen in all the parts.'[6] Essentially, Roosevelt was reminding the American public of the great maxim of American politics: 'You cannot please all of the people all of the time'. In planning a way out of the depression there would be mistakes, inconsistencies and the potential for unhappy voters. What mattered, thought Roosevelt, was the big picture. The reference to Jefferson was also significant in other ways. Ted Morgan has argued that Roosevelt identified with Jefferson in many ways:

> In Jefferson the gifted amateur, Roosevelt found a model for the protean man, the man of many gifts and disguises, the man with chameleonlike powers of adaptation, the man whose true self is protected by an essential elusiveness, and who rises through his variously altered shapes to great stature – Proteus in Greek mythology being the keeper of the seals, who would foretell the future if anyone could seize and hold him but who would change into other shapes to escape and avoid having to tell the truth. Roosevelt too adopted a stance of deliberate changeability. It allowed him to hold contradictory views simultaneously, juggling apples and oranges until the time was ripe for a decision.[7]

Roosevelt's thoughts and his policies were often carefully camouflaged, because to establish them too precisely was to lay them open to effective attack. Hence, in *Looking Forward* the reader can find the basis for the general lines of policy that the President might like to follow, rather than the intricate details of particular programmes. The nebulous nature of the New Deal was an intentional strategy for its defence.

If it was necessary to camouflage some of the details of particular policies for the sake of the security of the bigger picture, then Roosevelt went to particular trouble to emphasise that the bigger picture did not extend beyond the borders of the United States. There was no international, or even pan-American dimension to the problem of the depression. Roosevelt, it appeared in *Looking Forward*, remained an American nationalist fervently believing in the nation's exceptional qualities: 'America is new. It is in the process of change and development. It has the great potentialities of youth.'[8] For Roosevelt there could be no question of the United States cancelling the debts it was owed as a result of the First World War, and the problems of reconstruction: 'What was loaned by our people through their government must be repaid by foreign governments to our people. It is sound common sense to assist your debtors in every way, but there is neither practicality nor honour nor world safety in cancellation. The stabilisation of world finance can best be achieved by a clear understanding of joint obligations.'[9] Thus in the early days of his administration Roosevelt would do little to address the thorny issue of war debts and reparations which had saddled the international economy since 1919. Eventually, however, the administration would be left with no choice but to write off the debts of other countries to the USA. Likewise, little of Roosevelt's internationalism was evident in his stance on the League of Nations:

> If, today, … I would still favour America's entry into the League … I would go so far as to seek to win over the overwhelming opposition which exists in this country … But the League of Nations today is not the League of Nations conceived by Woodrow Wilson. It might have been had the United States joined. Too often through these years its major function has been not the broad overwhelming purpose of World peace but rather a mere meeting place for the political discussion of strictly European political national difficulties. In these the United States should have no part.[10]

Roosevelt was desperate in the early days of his administration not to come up against the prevailing neo-isolationism which was to characterise American society from 1919 to 7 December 1941.

If Roosevelt's apparent isolationism was to be challenged by later events, then domestic developments would also shape the coming to fruition of the political philosophies contained in *Looking Forward*. On some areas of interest to Roosevelt, such as judicial and panel reform, there would be modest change. In other areas, such as banking reform, change would be more dramatic. Certainly some parts of *Looking Forward* were more rhetoric than substance, but the bigger picture was what truly mattered. Most importantly of all, Roosevelt fashioned himself as a twentieth-century follower of utilitarianism: 'Every Government policy should first be laid against the specification of the greatest number of individual men and women'.[11] Of Dutch stock, this American aristocrat affirmed his faith in the principles of government set down by British philosopher John Stuart Mill. He did this in a way that was particularly relevant to the USA in the 1930s. Government had a responsibility to act in the interests of the majority, but it would act on an individual basis, rather than the collective basis of Fascist Italy or Nazi Germany. Roosevelt was signalling that the days of unfettered rugged individualism, in which the fortunes of individuals depended solely on their own endeavours, were over. In truth such days had ended well before this, although rugged individualism existed still as an American ideal. Now in 1933 Roosevelt was signalling its death as an ideal. Henceforth in the New Deal and beyond Americans would have, and most would enjoy, a new relationship with the federal government. This was something that had been evolving rapidly since the late nineteenth century. Franklin Roosevelt would be the first man to claim it as the rhetorical virtue at the heart of his 'New Deal'.

In scholarly assessments of the New Deal there have been a number of important shifts since the end of the Second World War. Before and shortly after the war the New Deal was written about in partisan terms. In the 1950s Arthur Schlesinger's three-volume study of the New Deal created a benchmark against which subsequent works would be judged. Well researched and well written, while partisan in its praise for Roosevelt, Schlesinger's work created a landmark in the study of the President that has cast a long shadow. The inconsistencies in the New Deal and in the policies pursued by Roosevelt are explained as the result of tactical shifts for political advantage. Despite the fact that Schlesinger's three books only take the reader as far as 1936, he did much to establish the idea that the New Deal consisted of two halves, with the striking down by the Supreme Court of the National Industrial Recovery Act, together with other key legislative elements in the New Deal programme in 1935, forming a divide between the two.

In the 1960s, partly as a result of the rise of the New Left, Schlesinger's portrait of the Roosevelt administration and New Deal began to come under sustained attack. William Leuchtenberg's *Franklin Roosevelt and the New Deal* (1963) extended Schlesinger's picture of the New Deal, arguing that it constituted a kind of social and economic revolution. This revolution extended to the very nature of American government. As a result of the New Deal the federal government concerned itself in the day-to-day life of ordinary Americans to an extent not previously seen. However, Leuchtenberg argues that this was a conservative revolution designed to preserve the socio-economic status quo. Leuchtenberg's questioning of the New Deal was carried further by Paul Conkin's *New Deal* (1967). Conkin attacked the New Deal for its conservatism and timidity.

By the end of the 1960s scholars of Roosevelt and the New Deal had divided into two camps. Some, like Schlesinger, considered Roosevelt to be a great reformer and the saviour of American capitalism. Others, like Conkin, regarded him as the patrician conservative heading off more radical possibilities for social and economic change in the United States. More recent scholarship has continued to show signs of this division and has reflected some of the criticisms of the earlier works. Roger Biles, while acknowledging the difficulties facing Roosevelt as a result of an entrenched conservative elite in places like the Supreme Court, has shown how Roosevelt failed to push harder for reform. Meanwhile, Anthony Badger has sought to redress one of the weaknesses of Schlesinger's study by extending academic analysis to the New Deal at local and regional level. Similar work in extending our understanding of the New Deal by more focused studies has been done by Albert Romasco, who has looked at how the early New Deal affected American business, and James Patterson, whose work has highlighted the importance of Congress in framing the New Deal. Meanwhile Ellis Hawley has analysed the working of the National Industrial Recovery Act, and there have been several useful studies of the evolution of the social security system in the 1930s. Much of the most recent scholarship has examined the New Deal through the lives of New Dealers such as Hugh Johnson, the impact on particular localities, and the impact on the lives of particular, marginalised sections within American society such as African-Americans, first-nation Americans and Hispanics. (All the above-mentioned works can be found in the Guide to Further Reading.)

The scholarship on Roosevelt, meanwhile, has been rather less vibrant. A target for numerous and almost invariably sympathetic biographers, Roosevelt remains the dominating figure of modern American politics. The earliest biographical accounts were written by those within the inner circle of the New Deal. Frances Perkins, his Secretary of Labor, published *The Roosevelt I Knew* in 1946, and Rexford Tugwell, a member of the best and the brightest club of academics appointed to the Brains Trust, brought out *The Democratic Roosevelt: A Biography of Franklin D. Roosevelt* eleven years later.[12] Neither study was hagiographic, but their respect for Roosevelt was apparent on every page. A major problem facing any potential biographer of Roosevelt up until 1962 was the longevity of Eleanor Roosevelt. Not only was the man a politician of mythic proportions, but his wife was still around to ensure that his image was not tarnished. After Eleanor's death in 1962 the task of the potential biographer became a little easier. Indeed, Frank Freidel was already well into the process of writing a multi-volume biography of the President, based on his voluminous papers in the Roosevelt Library at Hyde Park.[13] Freidel's primary concern was to document the life of the President and analysis was sometimes a secondary concern. The first volume of Freidel's biography appeared in 1952, the project finally running out of steam with the fourth volume in 1973. In 1990 he published an overview of his subject in the form of *Franklin Roosevelt: A Rendezvous with Destiny.* A further multi-volume study of Roosevelt has been written by Kenneth Davis, the fifth and penultimate volume of which appeared in 2000 after the first had appeared in 1971.[14] Accessible, and drawing on a wide range of published sources, Davis asks awkward questions of his subject. At the same time his respect for Roosevelt is made plain. What emerges is a well-balanced study.

What is clear from the works of both Freidel and Davis is that study of the life and times of Franklin Roosevelt can become a lifelong task in its own right. A properly researched biography of Roosevelt, surveying the secondary literature as well as the available primary sources, is the work of a lifetime. The mountain of papers which Roosevelt amassed during his life are as formidable in extent as they are rich in their value. Unsurprisingly, many academics from Ted Morgan to Patrick Maney have contented themselves with single-volume studies of the life of Roosevelt.[15] Others have chosen to focus on a particular aspect of the President's life. One particularly interesting area of scholarship has focused on his health, as seen, for instance, in Hugh Gallagher's *FDR's Splendid Deception* and Hugh Evans's *Hidden Campaign.*[16] In the absence of a team of writers to attempt on a collaborative basis a further multi-volume study of Roosevelt's life, such sharply focused volumes will probably be the way in which the scholarship on the life of Roosevelt is taken forward.

To support the burgeoning scholarship on Roosevelt and the New Deal there has been a sub-industry in publishing documents relating to both. The selection of documents in this volume takes into account the fact that texts such as presidential inaugural addresses, while they are important, are freely available in the public domain, especially over the internet. Less public documents are therefore privileged. Impressionistic accounts in memoirs and other documents are also privileged, since they provide good grounds for discussion and understanding. What was particularly surprising to the author was that while the same documents are reproduced in biography after biography of Roosevelt, the Roosevelt Library at Hyde Park, New York, contains masses of unpublished material. To the staff of that library and to those at the Franklin and Eleanor Roosevelt Institute this book is respectfully dedicated.

Notes

1 As James Roosevelt argued: 'Father was a traitor to nobody – the fact is, the class in question might not have survived at all had not the New Deal preserved the entire economy'. James A. Roosevelt and Sidney Shalett, *Affectionately FDR: A Son's Story of a Lonely Man* (New York, Harcourt Brace & Co., 1959), pp. 275–6.

2 M. Walker, *Makers of the American Century* (London, Vintage, 2001), p. 162.

3 M. Simpson, *Franklin D. Roosevelt* (Oxford, Basil Blackwell, 1989), p. 1.

4 J. M. Burns, *Roosevelt: The Lion and the Fox* (New York, Harcourt Brace & Co., 1956), p. 126.

5 F. D. Roosevelt, *Looking Forward* (New York, John Day, 1933).

6 Ibid., p. 12.

7 T. Morgan, *FDR: A Biography* (London, Grafton, 1985), p. 542.

8 Roosevelt, *Looking Forward*, p. 8.

9 Ibid., p. 249.

10 Ibid., p. 25.

11 Ibid., p. 193.

12 F. Perkins, *The Roosevelt I Knew* (New York, Viking, 1946); R. Tugwell, *The Democratic Roosevelt: A Biography of Franklin D. Roosevelt* (New York, Doubleday, 1957).

13 F. Freidel, *Franklin D. Roosevelt*, 4 vols (Boston, Little Brown, 1952–73).

14 K. S. Davis, *F.D.R.*, 5 vols (Vol. 1, New York, Putnam, 1971; Vols 2–5, New York, Random House, 1985–2000).

15 Morgan, *F.D.R.: A Biography*; P. Maney, *The Roosevelt Presence: A Biography of Franklin Delano Roosevelt* (New York,

Twayne, 1992).

16 H. Gallagher, *FDR's Splendid Deception: The Moving Story of Roosevelt's Massive Disability and the Intense Efforts to Conceal it From the Public* (Clearwater FL, Vandamere Press, 1994); H. Evans, *Hidden Campaign: FDR's Health and the Election of 1944* (Armonk NY, M. E. Sharpe, 2002).

1
New Deal rhetoric

The material in the following section is drawn from a variety of public domain sources including *The Public Papers and Addresses of Franklin D. Roosevelt*, sound recordings of presidential addresses and newspaper accounts. Where possible, multiple sources have been checked against each other for authenticity. The documents reproduced represent an amalgam of the various sources. American spelling has been used throughout.

In his inaugural address in 1933 Roosevelt told the American nation that it had 'nothing to fear but fear itself'. This was no empty piece of politician's rhetoric but a shrewd psychological evaluation of the state of the nation's health. A climate of fear had descended on the nation. Consumers were unwilling to spend, investors to invest and depositors to leave their money in the bank. Roosevelt perceived that America needed reassuring. He believed that the American economy was fundamentally sound and that, while individual businesses might fail, the economy would come right again as long as it was carefully handled. He also believed in the reform of the system in order to prevent a further great crash in the future. Roosevelt believed that reform was necessary to save the system, but some of his contemporaries within the American social elite, including some of his neighbours in Dutchess County, New York, firmly believed that Roosevelt was going to destroy it. Thus at all levels America needed reassurance. The most effective weapons in Roosevelt's armoury were the public speech and the radio broadcast.

From 1933 until 1935 he used them to reverse the mood of public panic and to restore a measure of confidence. As Alan Lawson has argued in 'The Cultural Legacy of the New Deal', Roosevelt was the master of vague but 'inspirational generalities'. His 'all-embracing strategy was to appear as the patron of the average American, commanding attention not merely because he was the nation's leader, blessed with a benignly superior, cultivated background, but also by suggesting that he could help define the true average' (A. Lawson, 'The Cultural Legacy of the New Deal', in A. Sitkoff (ed.), *Fifty Years Later: The New Deal Evaluated*, New York, A. A. Knopf, 1985, p. 156). Roosevelt became both Mr Average and the personification of the New Deal. To ordinary Americans he gave a set of government programmes a face and a heart and a life.

One incident, above all, seemed to demonstrate the President's care for the common man. On 19 February 1934 a poor black farmer called Sylvester Harris telephoned the White House to request help to keep his farm. To Harris's surprise Roosevelt himself picked up the telephone, they talked, and Roosevelt promised to help. The President asked the Home Owners Loan Corporation to investigate Harris's difficulties, and they eventually stepped in to save his farm. The President's personal intervention to save Harris's farm was subsequently celebrated in popular song. In January 1935 blues guitarist Lizzie Douglas recorded 'Sylvester and his Mule Blues':

> Sylvester went out in his lot, he looked at his mule.
> And he decided, he'd send the president some news.
>
> Sylvester walked out across his field, begin to play and moan,
> He cried, "Oh, Lord, believe I'm gonna lose my home."
>
> He thought about the president, he got on the wire,
> "If I lose my home, I believe I'll die."
>
> He called to the president, on the telephone,
> "I wanna talk to you, I'm about to lose my home".
>
> First time he called, they get him somebody else,
> "I don't wanna talk to that man, I want to speak to Mr President Roosevelt."
>
> He said, "Now Sylvester, you can rest in ease,
> Catch that big black jackass, and go on by your fields,"
>
> He said, "Sylvester you can rest in ease,
> You can catch that jackass, go and raise all your cotton and seeds."
>
> (G. Van Rijn, *Roosevelt's Blues: African American Blues and Gospel Songs on FDR*, Jackson, University Press of Mississippi, 1997, pp. 96–7)

Roosevelt would undoubtedly have enjoyed the picture of himself personally improving the lot of one of America's poor. If the President could prove so dynamic and effective then there was no limit to what his administration might accomplish.

In the period after Roosevelt secured victory in the 1936 presidential election the New Deal entered a transitional phase. The decisions of the Supreme Court had often gone against the Roosevelt administration. Roosevelt was determined to work around the handicaps set by the Supreme Court and, in time, to ensure that the Supreme Court would no longer thwart the will of the executive. Roosevelt's determination to secure reform threatened fundamental constitutional change, and as he proceeded with his plan to pack the Supreme Court with his own appointees in 1937 he encountered increasing resistance from the Republicans and from within his own party. Again the radio broadcast and public speech were Roosevelt's weapons to attack those who stood in the way of reform, and to reassure those who expressed concerns about his policies. The following year Roosevelt could be found using the radio to reassure the American public about the temporary nature of a downturn in the economy, labelled the Roosevelt recession by the anti-New Dealers.

In addition, after Italy's invasion of Abyssinia in October 1935 and especially after the extent of Hitler's ambitions in Europe became clear in 1938, Roosevelt began to warn the American people about the dangers ahead. Accepting Roosevelt's warnings, the American people re-elected him for an unprecedented third term in 1940, in contravention of the accepted convention established by George Washington that a president would serve for no more than two terms.

A further innovatory aspect of the rhetoric of the New Deal came with the myriad of initials with were used to describe the operation of its key elements. Cumulatively they suggested thorough-going reform, a wide-ranging approach to the problems of poverty and unemployment, and above all dynamism. Perhaps the most important were the following:

NIRA The National Industrial Recovery Act, leading to the creation of the NRA (the National Recovery Administration). The NIRA and the NRA aimed to improve business conditions by getting industry to self-regulate on issues such as fair competition and labour.

AAA	The Agricultural Adjustment Acts of 1933 and 1938. They aimed to improve farm incomes and security by controlling over-production.
HOLC	The Home Owners Loan Corporation. This was set up in 1933 to give money to allow non-farm owners to refinance their mortgages. Farmers were covered by the Farm Credit Act of June 1933.
TVA	The Tennessee Valley Authority. This embodied a wide-ranging approach to rural poverty in the South of the United States. It aimed to improve farm incomes, encourage economic diversification away from staple agricultural crops and improve living conditions across a wide area.
FHA	The Federal Housing Act. This insured mortgages for home owners.
CCC	The Civilian Conservation Corps. Unemployed young men were put to work on land improvement projects like re-afforestation.
CWA	The Civil Works Administration. Unemployed men were put to work on projects such as road repair. The CWA was disbanded in 1934 and its functions assumed by the FERA.
FERA	The Federal Emergency Relief Administration. This undertook projects for the relief of unemployment in partnership with municipal and state governments.
PWA	The Public Works Administration. Established under NIRA, this employed people on large-scale construction projects such as dams and roads.
NYA	The National Youth Administration. This was established in June 1935 to encourage young people to remain in education.
WPA	The Works Progress Administration. This was established in 1935 to provide further schemes to help the unemployed.

Some of the agencies and acts overlapped, and some were replaced by others, but the total effect in rhetorical terms was spectacular. No one could suggest that Roosevelt was a do-nothing president.

THE KEYNOTE SPEECHES

1.1 Roosevelt's nomination address, Chicago, 2 July 1932

In accepting the 1932 nomination of the Democratic Party for the presidential election, Franklin Delano Roosevelt, the Governor of New York since 1929, promised a New Deal for ordinary Americans. Precisely what the New Deal involved was not made clear in his nomination address, but the political situation meant that he didn't have to. The state of the national economy meant that there was little chance that Republican incumbent Herbert Hoover would retain the presidency. Roosevelt could thus afford to talk in generalities rather than the specifics of policies. Nevertheless with the rhetoric of dynamism and change Roosevelt rallied members of his party, warning them and the country that radical action was required to bring the economy back to prosperity. To do too little might have meant the dispossessed turning to political extremes to find a solution to the nation's problems. Roosevelt also made it clear that if he was elected he would be prepared to work with moderate Republicans in Congress to tackle the problem of the depression. In his rhetoric he regarded the nation's economic problems as a national emergency calling for extraordinary measures. His rhetoric echoed developments in Europe. In Britain a coalition government had been formed, and the image of dynamism was central to the rhetoric of Mussolini's Fascist Italy.

The great social phenomenon of this depression, unlike others before it, is that it has produced but a few of the disorderly manifestations that too often attend upon such times.

Wild radicalism has made few converts, and the greatest tribute that I can pay to my countrymen is that in these days of crushing want there persists an orderly and hopeful spirit on the part of the millions of our people who have suffered so much. To fail to offer them a new chance is not only to betray their hopes but to misunderstand their patience.

To meet by reaction that danger of radicalism is to invite disaster. Reaction is no barrier to the radical. It is a challenge, a provocation.

The way to meet that danger is to offer a workable program of reconstruction, and the party to offer it is the party with clean hands.

This, and this only, is a proper protection against blind reaction on the one hand and an improvised, hit-or-miss, irresponsible opportunism on the other.

There are two ways of viewing the Government's duty in matters affecting economic and social life. The first sees to it that a favored few are helped and hopes that some of their prosperity will leak through, sift through, to labor, to the farmer, to the small business man. That theory belongs to the party of Toryism, and I had hoped that most of the Tories left this country in 1776.

But it is not and never will be the theory of the Democratic Party. This is no time for fear, for reaction or for timidity. Here and now I invite those nominal Republicans who find that their conscience cannot be squared with the groping and the failure of their party leaders to join hands with us; here and now, in equal measure, I warn those nominal Democrats who squint at the future with their faces turned toward the past, and who feel no responsibility to the demands of the new time, that they are out of step with their Party.

Yes, the people of this country want a genuine choice this year, not a choice between two names for the same reactionary doctrine. Ours must be a party of liberal thought, of planned action, of enlightened international outlook, and of the greatest good to the greatest number of our citizens.

New York Times, 3 July 1932.

1.2 The significance of Roosevelt's acceptance speech to his campaign

The battle to secure the nomination of the Democratic Party in 1932 had been hard. However, the fight to secure the nomination had ensured excellent press coverage for Governor Roosevelt's campaign, and his acceptance speech was given massive publicity. Roosevelt's campaign manager in 1932, James A. Farley, considered it to be a decisive moment in the campaign.

The intensity of the struggle which had to be waged to capture the Democratic presidential nomination for Franklin D. Roosevelt in 1932 was in reality a tremendous piece of good fortune – far more effective than if he had won the honor without a battle in a drab convention. The love of drama is age-old in the human heart, and by the time the Governor of New York was flying to Chicago to accept the nomination, the attention of every voter in America was turned his way.

Roosevelt played the role with consummate skill, and the country caught the picture of a smart and daring man who knew what was wrong with the economic machine and what was needed to set it right. His ability to discuss political issues in short, simple sentences also made a powerful impression. We noticed shortly after his acceptance speech, from reports of state and local leaders, that he had gotten away to a flying start. He never lost that advantage.

James A. Farley, *Behind the Ballots: The Personal History of a Politician* (New York, Harcourt Brace & Co., 1938), p. 155.

1.3 Roosevelt's first inaugural address, 4 March 1933

Roosevelt won the 1932 presidential election by 22,809,638 popular votes to Republican Herbert Hoover's 15,758, 901. In the electoral college Roosevelt's victory was still more sweeping: 472 votes to Hoover's 59. Victory meant that he had to deliver on his promises of a New Deal. On his inauguration in Washington on a cold winter's day in March 1933, Roosevelt amplified his earlier warnings about the severity of the depression and the steps that he was prepared to take in order to deal with the national emergency. The calmness and certainty with which he spoke, relayed across the United States by radio stations, helped to raise the morale of a nation in which 13 million were unemployed. To the unemployed his address promised a new kind of federal government: one which would take responsibility for the lives of its citizens. Roosevelt's opponents in Congress meanwhile were alarmed at the President's warning that it might be necessary for him to assume broad executive power. They wondered what this might mean, and whether it suggested that Roosevelt was willing to subvert or overthrow elements of the constitution in order to get through the legislation which he felt was vital to address the emergency of the depression.

Our greatest primary task is to put people to work. This is no unsolvable problem if we face it wisely and courageously. It can be accomplished in part by direct recruiting by the Government itself, treating the task as we would treat the emergency of a war, but at the same time, through this employment, accomplishing greatly needed projects to stimulate and reorganize the use of our natural resources.

Hand in hand with this we must frankly recognize the overbalance of population in our industrial centers and, by engaging on a national scale in a redistribution, endeavor to provide a better use of the land for those best fitted for the land. The task can be helped by definite efforts to raise the values of agricultural products and with this the power to purchase the output of our cities. It can be helped by preventing realistically the tragedy of the growing loss through foreclosure of our small homes and our farms. It can be helped by insistence that the Federal, State, and local governments act forthwith on the demand that their cost be drastically reduced. It can be helped by the unifying of relief activities which today are often scattered, uneconomical, and unequal. It can be helped by national planning for and supervision of all forms of transportation and of communications and other utilities which have a definitely public character. There are many ways in which it can be helped, but it can never be helped merely by talking about it. We must act and act quickly … With this pledge taken, I assume unhesitatingly the leadership of this great army of our people dedicated to a disciplined attack upon our common problems.

Action in this image and to this end is feasible under the form of government which we have inherited from our ancestors. Our Constitution is so simple and practical that it is possible always to meet extraordinary needs by changes in emphasis and arrangement without loss of essential form. That is why our constitutional system has proved itself the most superbly enduring political mechanism the modern world has produced. It has met every stress of vast expansion of territory, of foreign wars, of bitter internal strife, of world relations.

It is to be hoped that the normal balance of Executive and legislative authority may be wholly adequate to meet the unprecedented task before us. But it may be that an unprecedented demand and need for undelayed action may call for temporary departure from that normal balance of public procedure.

I am prepared under my constitutional duty to recommend the measures that a stricken Nation in the midst of a stricken world may require. These measures, or such other measures as the Congress may build out of its experience and wisdom, I shall seek, within my constitutional authority, to bring to speedy adoption.

But in the event that the Congress shall fail to take one of these two courses, and in the event that the national emergency is still critical, I shall not evade the clear course of duty that will then confront me. I shall ask the Congress for the one remaining instrument to meet the crisis – broad Executive power to wage a war against the emergency, as great as the power that would be given to me if we were in fact invaded by a foreign foe.

For full speech see *The Public Papers and Addresses of Franklin D. Roosevelt*, Vol. 2 (New York, Random House, 1938), pp. 11–16. See also www.bartleby.com/124/pres49.html.

1.4 Arthur Krock for the *New York Times* comments on Roosevelt's inaugural address, 5 March 1933

Roosevelt was a consummate actor. He knew that words mattered, and he realised that how they were delivered was perhaps even more important. Thanks to the newspapers the words of his inaugural address would be read all over the United States, but they would also be carried to the millions searching for hope by radio and newsreel. The style of the address was crucially important. Roosevelt created an image of gravitas and determination that was well received by the thousands who watched and listened to the event live, and the millions who would later see and hear recordings of it. However, Roosevelt's inaugural address was not uniformly welcomed. One newspaper's headline ran 'ROOSEVELT ASKS FOR DICTATOR'S ROLE'.

WASHINGTON, March 4 – With solemn mien, Franklin D. Roosevelt of New York took the oath of office and became the thirty-second President of the United States on the main steps of the Capitol at eight minutes after 1 o'clock this afternoon.

A deep consciousness of the task before him was patent in his usual demeanour as his face stern, his voice grave, he repeated after Chief Justice Hughes the historic words of the oath. This realization animated also the inaugural address which Mr. Roosevelt then delivered in the presence of at least a hundred thousand persons who gathered in the Capitol grounds.

The sense of the administration's burdens was apparent, too, in the manner and speech of Vice President Garner, who, an hour before the President took the oath, laid down his gavel of Speaker of the House of Representatives and was inducted into his new office in the Senate chamber, where he will henceforth preside.

Action was the promise of Mr. Roosevelt's speech, and action was immediately forthcoming. The first moment after the ceremonies were over, the President swore in the Cabinet, summoned the party leaders to a Sunday conference to work out the plan for banking relief and arranged to call an extra session of the Seventy-third Congress, probably on Wednesday, to legislate the plan into law.

New York Times, 5 March 1933.

1.5 Roosevelt's second inaugural address, 20 January 1937

In his second inaugural address Roosevelt signalled that there could be no let-up in the pace of reform. Millions of dollars had been spent on relief projects and millions given employment and yet the number of jobless remained high. The depression was proving more resilient than most had expected. Poverty remained endemic in some parts of the United States, particularly the South, and the New Deal had run into serious opposition from a number of quarters. The striking down of the National Recovery Act by the Supreme Court in 1935 was a serious blow, and Roosevelt's critics charged that despite the millions spent the real economic progress of the nation was minimal. Roosevelt urged the American people not to give up or to seek more radical solutions to the problem of the depression.

Shall we pause now and turn our back upon the road that lies ahead? Shall we call this the promised land? Or, shall we continue on our way? For "each age is a dream that is dying, or one that is coming to birth."

Many voices are heard as we face a great decision. Comfort says, "Tarry a while." Opportunism says, "This is a good spot." Timidity asks, "How difficult is the road ahead?"

True, we have come far from the days of stagnation and despair. Vitality has been preserved. Courage and confidence have been restored. Mental and moral horizons have been extended.

But our present gains were won under the pressure of more than ordinary circumstances. Advance became imperative under the goad of fear and suffering. The times were on the side of progress.

To hold to progress today, however, is more difficult. Dulled conscience, irresponsibility, and ruthless self-interest already reappear. Such symptoms of prosperity may become portents of disaster! Prosperity already tests the persistence of our progressive purpose.

Let us ask again: Have we reached the goal of our vision of that fourth day of March 1933? Have we found our happy valley?

I see a great nation, upon a great continent, blessed with a great wealth of natural resources. Its hundred and thirty million people are at peace among themselves; they are making their country a good neighbor among the nations. I see a United States which can demonstrate that, under democratic methods of government, national wealth can be translated into a spreading volume of human comforts hitherto unknown, and the lowest standard of living can be raised far above the level of mere subsistence.

But here is the challenge to our democracy: In this nation I see tens of millions of its citizens – a substantial part of its whole population – who at this very moment are denied the greater part of what the very lowest standards of today call the necessities of life.

I see millions of families trying to live on incomes so meager that the pall of family disaster hangs over them day by day.

I see millions whose daily lives in city and on farm continue under conditions labeled indecent by a so-called polite society half a century ago.

I see millions denied education, recreation, and the opportunity to better their lot and the lot of their children.

I see millions lacking the means to buy the products of farm and factory and by their poverty denying work and productiveness to many other millions.

I see one-third of a nation ill-housed, ill-clad, ill-nourished.

It is not in despair that I paint you that picture. I paint it for you in hope – because the Nation, seeing and understanding the injustice in it, proposes to paint it out. We are determined to make every American citizen the subject of his country's interest and concern; and we will never regard any faithful law-abiding group within our borders as superfluous. The test of our progress is not whether we add more to the abundance of those who have much; it is whether we provide enough for those who have too little.

If I know aught of the spirit and purpose of our Nation, we will not listen to Comfort, Opportunism, and Timidity. We will carry on.

For full text see www.bartleby.com/124/pres50.html.

1.6 Roosevelt's third inaugural address, 20 January 1941

In 1940 Roosevelt decided to break the convention set down by George Washington that a president would stand for only two terms of office. The war situation called for a continuation of the leadership that had served America since 1933. In 1940 the American people agreed with him, especially because economic progress continued to be made. In 1944 they would agree to re-elect Roosevelt for a fourth and final time.

Eight years ago, when the life of this Republic seemed frozen by a fatalistic terror, we proved that this is not true. We were in the midst of shock – but we acted. We acted quickly, boldly, decisively.

These later years have been living years – fruitful years for the people of this democracy. For they have brought to us greater security and, I hope, a better understanding that life's ideals are to be measured in other than material things.

Most vital to our present and our future is this experience of a democracy which successfully survived crisis at home; put away many evil things; built new structures on enduring lines; and, through it all, maintained the fact of its democracy.

For action has been taken within the three-way framework of the Constitution of the United States. The coordinate branches of the Government continue freely to function. The Bill of Rights remains inviolate. The freedom of elections is wholly maintained. Prophets of the downfall of American democracy have seen their dire predictions come to naught.

Democracy is not dying.

We know it because we have seen it revive – and grow.

We know it cannot die – because it is built on the unhampered initiative of individual men and women joined together in a common enterprise – an enterprise undertaken and carried through by the free expression of a free majority.

We know it because democracy alone, of all forms of government, enlists the full force of men's enlightened will.

We know it because democracy alone has constructed an unlimited civilization capable of infinite progress in the improvement of human life.

We know it because, if we look below the surface, we sense it still spreading on every continent – for it is the most humane, the most advanced, and in the end the most unconquerable of all forms of human society.

A nation, like a person, has a body – a body that must be fed and clothed and housed, invigorated and rested, in a manner that measures up to the objectives of our time.

A nation, like a person, has a mind – a mind that must be kept informed and alert, that must know itself, that understands the hopes and the needs of its neighbors – all the other nations that live within the narrowing circle of the world.

And a nation, like a person, has something deeper, something more permanent, something larger than the sum of all its parts. It is that something which matters most to its future – which calls forth the most sacred guarding of its present.

It is a thing for which we find it difficult – even impossible – to hit upon a single, simple word.

And yet we all understand what it is – the spirit – the faith of America. It is the product of centuries. It was born in the multitudes of those who came from many lands – some of high degree, but mostly plain people, who sought here, early and late, to find freedom more freely ...

In the Americas its impact has been irresistible. America has been the New World in all tongues, to all peoples, not because this continent was a new-found land, but because all those who came here believed they could create upon this continent a new life – a life that should be new in freedom ...

The hopes of the Republic cannot forever tolerate either undeserved poverty or self-serving wealth.

We know that we still have far to go; that we must more greatly build the security and the opportunity and the knowledge of every citizen, in the measure justified by the resources and the capacity of the land.

But it is not enough to achieve these purposes alone. It is not enough to clothe and feed the body of this Nation, and instruct and inform its mind. For there is also the spirit. And of the three, the greatest is the spirit.

Without the body and the mind, as all men know, the Nation could not live.

But if the spirit of America were killed, even though the Nation's body and mind, constricted in an alien world, lived on, the America we know would have perished.

That spirit – that faith – speaks to us in our daily lives in ways often unnoticed, because they seem so obvious. It speaks to us here in the Capital of the Nation. It speaks to us through the processes of governing in the sovereignties of 48 States. It speaks to us in our counties, in our cities, in our towns, and in our villages. It speaks to us from the other nations of the hemisphere, and from those across the seas – the enslaved, as well as the free. Sometimes we fail to hear or heed these voices of freedom because to us the privilege of our freedom is such an old, old story.

For full text see www.bartleby.com/124/pres51.html. Also recorded in the British National Archives (Public Record Office) TNA: PRO FO371/ 26145.

RELATIONS WITH THE PRESS

1.7 The first press conference, 8 March 1933

Roosevelt identified confidence building as the most essential task of the New Deal. If the confidence of the American worker and consumer could be restored, the economy would, he hoped, start to revive. Fireside chats were one weapon in his armoury against public despair, as were the American newspapers. The rapport which he enjoyed with journalists was one of the great assets of the administration. He was determined to break down some of the barriers between the presidency and the media and to foster trust and openness between the two. The closeness between President and journalistic establishment was evident at his first presidential press conference.

THE PRESIDENT: It is very good to see you all. My hope is that these conferences are going to be merely enlarged editions of the kind of very delightful family conferences I have been holding in Albany for the last four years.

I am told that what I am about to do will become impossible, but I am going to try it. We are not going to have any more written questions; and, of course, while I cannot answer seventy-five or a hundred questions because I simply haven't got the time, I see no reason why I should not talk to you ladies and gentlemen off the record in just the way I have been doing in Albany and in the way I used to do in the Navy Department down here. Quite a number of you, I am glad to see, date back to the days of the previous existence which I led in Washington.

And so I think we shall discontinue the practice of compelling the submitting of questions in writing before the conference in order to get an answer. There will be a great many questions, of course, that I won't answer, either because they are "if" questions – and I never answer them – and Brother Stephenson will tell you what an "if" question is –

MR. STEPHENSON (Reporter): I ask forty of them a day.

THE PRESIDENT: And the others, of course, are the questions which for various reasons I do not want to discuss, or I am not ready to discuss, or I do not know anything about. There will be a great many questions you will ask that I do not know enough about to answer.

Then, in regard to news announcements, Steve (Early, Assistant Secretary to the President) and I thought that it would be best that straight news for use from this office should always be without direct quotations. In other words, I do not want to be directly quoted, unless direct quotations are given out by Steve in writing. That makes that perfectly clear.

Then there are two other matters we will talk about: The first is "background information", which means material which can be used by all of you on your own authority and responsibility, not to be attributed to the White House ... Then the second thing is the "off the record" information which means, of course, confidential information which is given only to those who attend the conference ... I want to ask you not to repeat this "off the record" confidential information either to your own editors or to your associates who are not here; because there is always the danger that, while you people may not violate the rule, somebody may forget to say, "This is off the record and confidential," and the other party may use it in a story ...

Now, as to news, I don't think there is any. (Laughter)

For full speech see *The Public Papers and Addresses of Franklin D. Roosevelt*, Vol. 2 (New York, Random House, 1938), pp. 30–45.

THE FIRESIDE CHATS

1.8 Fireside chat on the bank crisis, 12 March 1933

By late 1932 the banks were coming under mounting pressure as investors withdrew their deposits. In many cases these withdrawals were necessitated by the financial need of the depositors. In other cases withdrawals were prompted by rumours that particular banks were about to fail and that depositors would lose all their money. Such rumours prompted runs on particular banks as worried depositors withdrew all their funds. By January and February runs on banks threatened a complete collapse of the American banking system. One of Roosevelt's first acts as President was to declare a bank holiday, to strengthen the banking system and to get the banks to reopen. In addition to federal action to strengthen the banks Roosevelt used the radio to reassure the American nation that the banking system was sound.

We had a bad banking situation. Some of our bankers had shown themselves either incompetent or dishonest in their handling of the people's funds. They had used the money entrusted to them in speculations and unwise loans. This was of course not true in the vast majority of our banks but it was true in enough of them to shock the people for a time into a sense of insecurity and to put them into a frame of mind where they did not differentiate, but seemed to assume that the acts of a comparative few had tainted them all. It was the Government's job to straighten out this situation and do it as quickly as possible – and the job is being performed.

I do not promise you that every bank will be reopened or that individual losses will not be suffered, but there will be no losses that possibly could be avoided; and there would have been more and greater losses had we continued to drift. I can even promise you salvation for some at least of the sorely pressed banks. We shall be engaged not merely in reopening sound banks but in the creation of sound banks through reorganization.

It has been wonderful to me to catch the note of confidence from all over the country. I can never be sufficiently grateful to the people for the loyal support they have given me in their acceptance of the judgment that has dictated our course, even though all of our processes may not have seemed clear to them.

After all there is an element in the readjustment of our financial system more important than currency, more important than gold, and that is the confidence of the people. Confidence and courage are the essentials of success in carrying out our plan. You people must have faith; you must not be stampeded by rumors or guesses. Let us unite in banishing fear. We have provided the machinery to restore our financial system; it is up to you to support and make it work.

It is your problem no less than it is mine. Together we cannot fail.

For full speech see *The Public Papers and Addresses of Franklin D. Roosevelt*, Vol. 2 (New York, Random House, 1938), pp. 61–6. See also www.mhric.org/fdr/chat1.html and www.fdrlibrary.marist.edu/031233.html.

1.9 James Farley's comments on the banking address

In his memoirs James A. Farley, Roosevelt's campaign manager in 1932, commented on the significance and effect of his first fireside chat.

In my opinion, Roosevelt's banking address will go in history as one of the greatest utterances of an American President. If we are to measure the effectiveness and worth of an address by the response which it calls forth, it may be the greatest of all because no other talk in history ever called forth such a wave of spontaneous enthusiasm and co-operation. He risked tremendous odds in following such a course. We know how successful it was, but it is just as easy to imagine the economic and financial chaos that would have resulted if the people had given way to fear and panic instead of resolutely regaining their lost confidence. With a flash of inspiration, he accomplished a miracle of wise government.

James A. Farley, *Behind the Ballots: The Personal History of a Politician* (New York, Harcourt Brace & Co., 1938), p. 210.

1.10 Fireside chat outlining the New Deal programme, 7 May 1933

The New Deal had been the great election slogan in 1932. In May 1933 Roosevelt set down for the American public a sketch of what it would involve. The emphasis would be on relieving distress and finding jobs for the unemployed.

First, we are giving opportunity of employment to one-quarter of a million of the unemployed, especially the young men who have dependents, to go into the forestry and flood prevention work. This is a big task because it means feeding, clothing and caring for nearly twice as many men as we have in the regular army itself. In creating this civilian conservation corps we are killing two birds with one stone. We are clearly enhancing the value of our natural resources and second, we are relieving an appreciable amount of actual distress. This great group of men have entered upon their work on a purely voluntary basis, no military training is involved and we are conserving not only our natural resources but our human resources. One of the great values to this work is the fact that it is direct and requires the intervention of very little machinery.

Second, I have requested the Congress and have secured action upon a proposal to put the great properties owned by our Government at Muscle Shoals to work after long years of wasteful inaction, and with this a broad plan for the improvement of a vast area in the Tennessee Valley. It will add to the comfort and happiness of hundreds of thousands of people and the incident benefits will reach the entire nation.

Next, the Congress is about to pass legislation that will greatly ease the mortgage distress among the farmers and the home owners of the nation, by providing for the easing of the burden of debt now bearing so heavily upon millions of our people.

Our next step in seeking immediate relief is a grant of half a billion dollars to help the states, counties and municipalities in their duty to care for those who need direct and immediate relief.

In addition to all this, the Congress also passed legislation authorizing the sale of beer in such states as desired. This has already resulted in considerable reemployment and, incidentally, has provided much needed tax revenue.

For full text see www.mhric.org/fdr/chat2.html and www.fdrlibrary.marist.edu/050733.html.

1.11 Fireside chat reviewing the achievements of the 73rd Congress, 28 June 1934

The achievements of the Roosevelt administration were trumpeted regularly in the battle to restore the confidence of the American consumer and the morale of the American worker. In his first fireside chat of 1934, delivered from the White House, Roosevelt outlined the work of his administration over the previous year. He asked his listeners to focus on the question 'Are you better off than you were last year?'.

I mention only a few of the major enactments. It provided for the readjustment of the debt burden through the corporate and municipal bankruptcy acts and the farm relief act. It lent a hand to industry by encouraging loans to solvent industries unable to secure adequate help from banking institutions. It strengthened the integrity of finance through the regulation of securities exchanges. It provided a rational method of increasing our volume of foreign trade through reciprocal trading agreements. It strengthened our naval forces to conform with the intentions and permission of existing treaty rights. It made further advances towards peace in industry through the labor adjustment act. It supplemented our agricultural policy through measures widely demanded by farmers themselves and intended to avert price destroying surpluses. It strengthened the hand of the Federal Government in its attempts to suppress gangster crime. It took definite steps towards a national housing program through an act which I signed today designed to encourage private capital in the rebuilding of the homes of the Nation. It created a permanent Federal body for the just regulation of all forms of communication, including the telephone, the telegraph and the radio. Finally, and I believe most important, it reorganized, simplified and made more fair and just our monetary system, setting up standards and policies adequate to meet the necessities of modern economic life, doing justice to both gold and silver as the metal bases behind the currency of the United States.

For full text see *The Public Papers and Addresses of Franklin D. Roosevelt*, Vol. 3 (New York, Random House, 1938), pp. 312–18. See also www.mhric.org/fdr/chat5.html and www.fdrlibrary.marist.edu/062834.html.

1.12 Fireside chat on the Works Relief Program, 28 April 1935

Social security and the continuing struggle for jobs were again the focus of Roosevelt's fireside chat to the nation in April 1935. It was a further signal that the process of reforming the United States would take place alongside continuing efforts to relieve unemployment and its related ills and to secure recovery in industry and agriculture.

My most immediate concern is in carrying out the purposes of the great work program just enacted by the Congress. Its first objective is to put men and women now on the relief rolls to work and, incidentally, to assist materially in our already unmistakable march toward recovery. I shall not confuse my discussion by a multitude of figures. So many figures are quoted to prove so many things. Sometimes it depends upon what paper you read and what broadcast you hear. Therefore, let us keep our minds on two or three simple, essential facts in connection with this problem of unemployment. It is true that while business and industry are definitely better our relief rolls are still too large. However, for the first time in five years the relief rolls have declined instead of increased during the winter months. They are still declining. The simple fact is that many million more people have private work today than two years ago today or one year ago today, and every day that passes offers more chances to work for those who want to work. In spite of the fact that unemployment remains a serious problem here as in every other nation, we have come to recognize the possibility and the necessity of certain helpful remedial measures. These measures are of two kinds. The first is to make provisions intended to relieve, to minimize, and to prevent future unemployment; the second is to establish the practical means to help those who are unemployed in this present emergency. Our social security legislation is an attempt to answer the first of these questions; our work relief program the second.

The program for social security now pending before the Congress is a necessary part of the future unemployment policy of the government. While our present and projected expenditures for work relief are wholly within the reasonable limits of our national credit resources, it is obvious that we cannot continue to create governmental deficits for that purpose year after year. We must begin now to make provision for the future. That is why our social security program is an important part of the complete picture. It proposes, by means of old age pensions, to help those who have reached the age of retirement to give up their jobs and thus give to the younger generation greater opportunities for work and to give to all a feeling of security as they look toward old age.

The unemployment insurance part of the legislation will not only help to guard the individual in future periods of lay-off against dependence upon relief, but it will, by sustaining purchasing power, cushion the shock of economic distress. Another helpful feature of unemployment insurance is the incentive it will give to employers to plan more carefully in order that unemployment may be prevented by the stabilizing of employment itself.

Provisions for social security, however, are protections for the future. Our responsibility for the immediate necessities of the unemployed has been met by the Congress through the most comprehensive work plan in the history of the Nation. Our problem is to put to work three and one-half million employable persons now on the relief rolls. It is a problem quite as much for private industry as for the government.

For full text see www.mhric.org/fdr/chat7.html and www.fdrlibrary.marist.edu/042835.html.

1.13 Radio speech, 2 November 1936

> The 1936 election promised to be a severe test of Roosevelt's administration. The New Deal had achieved much but the depression continued to defy the best efforts of his administration. In a radio address to the American public on the eve of the poll Roosevelt showed that after three and a half years in the White House he continued to identify with ordinary citizens, and knew how to get them to identify with him.

I have come home to my own county to vote with my fellow townsmen. My people have voted here in Dutchess County for more than a century. I cast my first vote here in 1903.

Tomorrow fifty-five million Americans are eligible to vote. I hope that all of those fifty-five millions will vote.

I like to think of these millions as individual citizens from Maine to the southern tip of California, from Key West to Puget Sound – farmers who stop their fall plowing long enough to drive into town with their wives – wage earners stopping on the way to work or the way home – business and professional men and women – town and city housewives – and that great company of youth for whom this year's first vote will be a great adventure.

Americans have had to put up with a good many things in the course of our history. But the only rule we have ever put up with is the rule of the majority. That is the only rule we ever will put up with. Spelled with a small "d" we are all democrats.

In some places in the world the tides are running against democracy. But our faith has not been unsettled. We believe in democracy because of our traditions. But we believe in it even more because of our experience.

Not only are people voting in larger numbers this year. They also know more this year than ever before about the real issues. They are thinking for themselves. They listen to both sides. They no longer accept at face value opinions or even statements from newspapers, from political spokesmen and from so-called leaders of their communities. They insist on checking up.

For full text see *The Public Papers and Addresses of Franklin D. Roosevelt*, Vol. 5 (New York, Random House, 1938), pp. 577–81.

1.14 Fireside chat on the current recession, 14 April 1938

In 1937, as it looked as though the United States was coming out of recession, the administration began slowly to turn off the flow of public money so as to prevent a boom. As the flow of public funds into the economy began to slow, the economy once again entered recession. It was a serious blow to the administration and to faith in the Keynesian model of economics. The recession proved short-lived as the flow of public funds resumed at its previous rate.

This recession has not returned to us the disasters and suffering of the beginning of 1933. Your money in the bank is safe; farmers are no longer in deep distress and have greater purchasing power; dangers of security speculation have been minimized; national income is almost 50% higher than it was in 1932; and government has an established and accepted responsibility for relief.

But I know that many of you have lost your jobs or have seen your friends or members of your families lose their jobs, and I do not propose that the Government shall pretend not to see these things. I know that the effect of our present difficulties has been uneven; that they have affected some groups and some localities seriously but that they have been scarcely felt in others. But I conceive the first duty of government is to protect the economic welfare of all the people in all sections and in all groups. I said in my Message opening the last session of the Congress that if private enterprise did not provide jobs this spring, government would take up the slack – that I would not let the people down. We have all learned the lesson that government cannot afford to wait until it has lost the power to act.

For full text see www.mhric.org/fdr/chat12.html and www.fdrlibrary.marist.edu/041438.html.

1.15 Fireside chat on the Democratic Party primaries, 24 June 1938

1938 was a bad year for Roosevelt as the economy slipped back into recession. In his fireside chat on 24 June he acknowledged frankly that mistakes had been made.

One word about our economic situation. It makes no difference to me whether you call it a recession or a depression. In 1932 the total national income of all the people in the country had reached the low point of thirty-eight billion dollars in that year. With each succeeding year it rose. Last year, 1937, it had risen to seventy billion dollars – despite definitely worse business and agricultural prices in the last four months of last year. This year, 1938, while it is too early to do more than give a mere estimate, we hope that the national income will not fall below sixty billion dollars, and that is a lot better than thirty-eight billion dollars. We remember also that banking and business and farming are not falling apart … as they did in the terrible winter of 1932 to 1933.

Last year mistakes were made by the leaders of private enterprise, by the leaders of labor and by the leaders of Government – all three.

Last year the leaders of private enterprise pleaded for a sudden curtailment of public spending, and said they would take up the slack. But they made the mistake of increasing their inventories too fast and setting many of their prices too high for their goods to sell.

Some labor leaders goaded by decades of oppression of labor made the mistake of going too far. They were not wise in using methods which frightened many well-wishing people. They asked employers not only to bargain with them but to put up with jurisdictional disputes at the same time.

Government too made mistakes – mistakes of optimism in assuming that industry and labor would themselves make no mistakes – and Government made a mistake of timing in not passing a farm bill or a wage and hour bill last year.

As a result of the lessons of all these mistakes we hope that in the future private enterprise – capital and labor alike – will operate more intelligently together, [and] operate in greater cooperation with their own Government than they have in the past. Such cooperation on the part of both of them will be very welcome to me. Certainly at this stage there should be a united stand on the part of both of them to resist wage cuts which would further reduce purchasing power.

This afternoon, only a few hours ago, I am told that a great steel company announced a reduction in prices with a view to stimulating business recovery. And I was told, and I am gratified to know, that this reduction in prices has involved no wage cut. Every encouragement ought to be given to industry which accepts the large volume and high wage policy.

If this is done throughout the Nation, it ought to result in conditions which will replace a great part of the Government spending which the failure of cooperation has made necessary this year.

For full text see www.mhric.org/fdr/chat13.html and www.fdrlibrary.marist.edu/062438.html.

MESSAGES TO CONGRESS AND OTHER BODIES

1.16 Annual message to Congress, 3 January 1934

The President's annual address to Congress provided him with the opportunity to talk to both congressmen and the wider public. Roosevelt's 1934 address reviewed the state of the nation, trumpeted success and set forward a programme for the year ahead. Great strides had indeed been made but the recovery of American industry and agriculture remained a distant dream. Roosevelt's speeches conveyed the continuing dynamism of his administration and his unshakable belief that the depression would yield to the sustained attack being mounted against it.

We have made great strides toward the objectives of the National Industrial Recovery Act, for not only have several millions of our unemployed been restored to work, but industry is organizing itself with a greater understanding that reasonable profits can be earned while at the same time protection can be assured to guarantee to labor adequate pay and proper conditions of work. Child labor is abolished. Uniform standards of hours and wages apply today to 95 percent of industrial employment within the field of the National Industrial Recovery Act. We seek the definite end of preventing combinations in furtherance of monopoly and in restraint of trade, while at the same time we seek to prevent ruinous rivalries within industrial groups which in many cases resemble the gang wars of the underworld and in which the real victim in every case is the public itself.

Under the authority of this Congress, we have brought the component parts of each industry together around a common table, just as we have brought problems affecting labor to a common meeting ground. Though the machinery, hurriedly devised, may need readjustment from time to time, nevertheless I think you will agree with me that we have created a permanent feature of our modernized industrial structure and that it will continue under the supervision but not the arbitrary dictation of Government itself.

You recognized last spring that the most serious part of the debt burden affected those who stood in danger of losing their farms and their homes. I am glad to tell you that refinancing in both of these cases is proceeding with good success and in all probability within the financial limits set by the Congress.

But agriculture had suffered from more than its debts. Actual experience with the operation of the Agricultural Adjustment Act leads to my belief that thus far the experiment of seeking a balance between production and consumption is succeeding and has made progress entirely in line with reasonable expectations toward the restoration of farm prices to parity. I continue in my conviction that industrial progress and prosperity can only be attained by bringing the purchasing power of that portion of our population which in one form or another is dependent upon agriculture up to a level which will restore a proper balance between every section of the country and between every form of work.

In this field, through carefully planned flood control, power development and land-use policies in the Tennessee Valley and in other great watersheds, we are seeking the elimination of waste, the removal of poor lands from agriculture and the encouragement of small local industries, thus furthering this principle of a better balanced national life. We recognize the great ultimate cost of the application of this rounded policy to every part of the Union. Today we are creating heavy obligations to start the work because of the great unemployment needs of the moment. I look forward, however, to the time in the not distant future, when annual appropriations, wholly covered by current revenue, will enable the work to proceed under a national plan. Such a national plan will, in a generation or two, return many times the money spent on it; more important, it will eliminate the use of inefficient tools, conserve and increase natural resources, prevent waste, and enable millions of our people to take better advantage of the opportunities which God has given our country.

For full text see *The Public Papers and Addresses of Franklin D. Roosevelt*, Vol. 3 (New York, Random House, 1938), pp. 8–14.

1.17 Message to Congress reviewing the broad objectives and accomplishments of the administration, 8 June 1934

Messages to Congress, which would be reported by the leading newspapers, provided another way for Roosevelt to get his message across, and to reassure the nation.

On the side of relief we have extended material aid to millions of our fellow citizens.

On the side of recovery we have helped to lift agriculture and industry from a condition of utter prostration.

But, in addition to these immediate tasks of relief and of recovery we have properly, necessarily and with overwhelming approval determined to safeguard these tasks by rebuilding many of the structures of our economic life and reorganizing it in order to prevent a recurrence of collapse.

It is childish to speak of recovery first and reconstruction afterward. In the very nature of the processes of recovery we must avoid the destructive influences of the past ...

Our task of reconstruction does not require the creation of new and strange values. It is rather the finding of the way once more to known, but to some degree forgotten, ideals and values. If the means and details are in some instances new, the objectives are as permanent as human nature.

Among our objectives I place the security of the men, women and children of the Nation first.

This security for the individual and for the family concerns itself primarily with three factors. People want decent homes to live in; they want to locate them where they can engage in productive work; and they want some safeguard against misfortunes which cannot be wholly eliminated in this man-made world of ours ...

These three great objectives – the security of the home, the security of livelihood, and the security of social insurance – are, it seems to me, a minimum of the promise that we can offer to the American people. They constitute a right which belongs to every individual and every family willing to work. They are the essential fulfilment of measures already taken toward relief, recovery and reconstruction.

This seeking for a greater measure of welfare and happiness does not indicate a change in values. It is rather a return to values lost in the course of our economic development and expansion.

Ample scope is left for the exercise of private initiative. In fact, in the process of recovery, I am greatly hoping that repeated promises of private investment and private initiative to relieve the Government in the immediate future of much of the burden it has assumed, will be fulfilled. We have not imposed undue restrictions upon business ... It is true that there are a few among us who would still go back. These few offer no substitute for the gains already made, nor any hope for making future gains for human happiness. They loudly assert that individual liberty is being restricted by Government, but when they are asked what individual liberties they have lost, they are put to it to answer.

For full text see *The Public Papers and Addresses of Franklin D. Roosevelt*, Vol. 3 (New York, Random House, 1938), pp. 287–93.

1.18 Annual message to Congress, 4 January 1935

In January 1935 Roosevelt returned to Congress to proclaim again the year's achievements, and he used the occasion to signal that his administration was about to embark on a crusade for social security. He proposed fundamental reforms to ensure that in the future there could be no repeat of the individual human suffering involved in the Great Depression. The move towards social security had partly been forced upon the administration by Dr Francis Townsend and his old age pension plan.

I recall to your attention my message to the Congress last June in which I said: "among our objectives I place the security of the men, women and children of the Nation first." That remains our first and continuing task; and in a very real sense every major legislative enactment of this Congress should be a component part of it.

In defining immediate factors which enter into our quest, I have spoken to the Congress and the people of three great divisions:

1. The security of a livelihood through the better use of the national resources of the land in which we live.

2. The security against the major hazards and vicissitudes of life.

3. The security of decent homes.

I am now ready to submit to the Congress a broad program designed ultimately to establish all three of these factors of security – a program which because of many lost years will take many future years to fulfil.

For full text see *The Public Papers and Addresses of Franklin D. Roosevelt*, Vol. 4 (New York, Random House, 1938), pp. 15–25.

1.19 Annual message to Congress, 6 January 1937

Soon after the 1936 election Roosevelt began to move against the Supreme Court, which he regarded as a brake on the process of reform. He further believed that it was unrepresentative and was incapable of meeting the needs of the American people in the ongoing crisis of the depression.

During the past year there has been a growing belief that there is little fault to be found with the Constitution of the United States as it stands today. The vital need is not an alteration of our fundamental law, but an increasingly enlightened view with reference to it. Difficulties have grown out of its interpretation but rightly considered, it can be used as an instrument of progress, and not as a device for prevention of action.

It is worth our while to read and reread the preamble of the Constitution, and Article I thereof which confers the legislative powers upon the Congress of the United States. It is also worth our while to read again the debates in the Constitutional Convention of one hundred and fifty years ago. From such reading, I obtain the very definite thought that the members of that Convention were fully aware that civilization would raise problems for the proposed new Federal Government, which they themselves could not even surmise; and that it was their definite intent and expectation that a liberal interpretation in the years to come would give to the Congress the same relative powers over new national problems as they themselves gave to the Congress over the national problems of their day.

In presenting to the Convention the first basic draft of the Constitution, Edmund Randolph explained that it was the purpose "to insert essential principles only, lest the operation of government should be clogged by rendering those provisions permanent and unalterable which ought to be accommodated to times and events."

With a better understanding of our purposes, and a more intelligent recognition of our needs as a Nation, it is not to be assumed that there will be prolonged failure to bring legislative and judicial action into closer harmony. Means must be found to adapt our legal forms and our judicial interpretation to the actual present national needs of the largest progressive democracy in the modern world.

For full text see *The Public Papers and Addresses of Franklin D. Roosevelt*, Vol. 5 (New York, Random House, 1938), pp. 13–24.

OTHER NEW DEALERS

1.20 Louisville is an NRA town: newspaper column by Hugh S. Johnson

The New Deal did not rest solely on the oratorical abilities of Roosevelt. Other members of his administration were just as skilled propagandists as the President. In addition to his political activities as head of the National Recovery Administration in the 1930s Hugh S. Johnson also wrote regularly for the Scripps-Howard group of newspapers. This gave him a platform from which to proclaim the achievements of the NRA and the New Deal more generally.

The more you travel around this nation the brighter things look. I have found another important community where, if the depression isn't broken, it is at least badly bent.

Nearly all the businesses in Louisville [Kentucky] are making money for the first time in several years. The outlook is generally bright. More people have new business plans. There is a better balance. Banks are in excellent shape. Everybody is beginning to fight again.

Louisville is an NRA town. It staged one of the first big NRA parades. Both its people and its businesses remained enthusiastic and faithful even during the Blue Eagle's darkest days.

When the Blue Eagle got the ax, one important employer – whose name was not Uriah Heep – called his workers together. "You've had me for two years," he told them, "now I've got you."

He added 25 per cent to the hours of their work week. He cut all wages and salaries. He fired everybody thus rendered surplus. Then he advertised a lot of cut prices, among which was a cut of about 30 per cent in the price of a standard advertised Kentucky product.

On the same day most of the other employers in Louisville published a pledge to maintain NRA principles permanently.

Next day Uriah Heep's place of business didn't have any customers in it. Day after day passed with no sales. The business leaders of the town gave out some statements about Uriah's policy, without mentioning him by name, and the atmosphere became frigid or outright torrid wherever he encountered acquaintances – he had few friends.

After about 10 days of this, Uriah took a full page for an advertisement. He changed to another Dickens character. He was now old scrooge at Christmas. The advertisement was a Christmas carol in the month of June. He had raised all wages, shortened all hours, hired his people back and announced that it was not good to sell the products of Kentucky short. "God bless us all," said Tiny Tim.

But as yet his counting houses are not humming. You can believe it when Dickens tells about how old Scrooge stopped the habits of a lifetime and ceased pinching pennies overnight, but in this more realistic age and clime all the Tiny Tims down in Louisville, in their soft southern elegance, just say "Baloney."

Hugh S. Johnson, *Washington Daily News*, 28 June 1935, Hugh Johnson Papers 1, Roosevelt Library.

1.21 Harry Hopkins: dominating the media

In the lead-up to the 1936 presidential election Harry Hopkins was highly active in mobilising his extensive contacts in support of Roosevelt's campaign. Here in a telephone conversation with David Niles, Director of the liberal Ford Hall forum in Boston, the frantic nature of the 1936 campaign is evident, as are some of the animosities in the Democratic Party.

Niles: Got a speech in your system you want to get off on the air tonight?

Hopkins: I thought La Guardia was going to talk tonight?

Niles: No, he has changed his mind.

Hopkins: No, I don't think I want to talk. My feeling is this – that unless they are going to attack relief pretty hard, I had better pipe down.

Niles: Well of course they did yesterday.

Hopkins: I could get up a speech, but I wonder if you would not be better off by putting some other person on the air tonight.

Niles: How about Aubrey?

Hopkins: You mean about the [National] Youth [Administration]?

Niles: Yes, I put Ed Casey on last night about the Youth. I think you ought to do it yourself if you've got something.

Hopkins: I can do it; there is no reason why I can't do it, but I was just wondering about the tactics. Are you stuck for a speaker?

Niles: I haven't tried anyone but you.

Hopkins: What did La Guardia to [*sic*] – go temperamental on you?

Niles: Yes. He said he did not get any publicity in the papers this morning.

Hopkins: That's ridiculous!

Niles: It's worse than ridiculous; it is the third time he has done it.

[Hopkins eventually declined to speak, but a replacement was found.]

Hopkins telephone conversation with Mr Niles, 26 October 1936, Hopkins Papers 24/178, Roosevelt Library.

1.22 Radio interview on the future of labour between Senator Pope and the Secretary of Labor, Frances Perkins, April 1937

More usually associated with the television age, even in the days of radio the broadcast political interview offered plentiful opportunity to get the administration's message across.

SENATOR: I am glad indeed to have this opportunity to discuss some of the problems of the nation's wage earners and what the United States Department of Labor is doing in their interest. It is an added pleasure to have with me, Secretary of Labor, Frances Perkins whose department has achieved such fine results since March 1933, not only as they affect wage earners, but as they affect the general welfare of all the people. Right now, Miss Perkins, many people are interested in industrial relations and perhaps you will tell us something as to how the situation sizes up from your viewpoint.

SECRETARY: Yes, Senator, I agree with you that many people are interested in industrial relations and it is right that they should be because it is in the interest of wage earners, employers and the general public that such relations should be stabilized.

SENATOR: Have you any plan in mind by which this desired condition can be brought about.

SECRETARY: I have already held conferences in Washington to discuss collective bargaining, which as you all know, is established as the law of the land by the recent decision of the Supreme Court. Others are planned and at each of them will be present, leaders of workers and employers and representatives of the Government and the public. I hope that out of these meetings a program will emerge which will help to stabilize industrial relations.

SENATOR: Specifically what do you propose to discuss.

SECRETARY: It is proposed to discuss, at the outset at least, just how the two great partners in industry can op-operate in making use of the effective technique of conciliation and mediation under the National Labor Relations Act. The United States Department of Labor has available the services of officials skilled in conciliation and mediation work and representatives of workers and employers will find we are always ready to lend expert assistance in working out agreements which will insure industrial peace for extended periods.

SENATOR: Do you think there will be a reduction in the number of industrial disputes now that the Supreme Court has upheld the validity of the National Labor Relations Act?

SECRETARY: That would seem to be likely, Senator, and for this reason – The Court ruling has certainly done away with the principal cause of industrial unrest in America today. Not only have the most bitter strikes in recent months centred around the issue of union organisation but more strikes have arisen from this cause than from all other causes combined. Of the 1,015 strikes reported during the six month period ending February 1, 1937, 524 were for union organisation and 491 for all other causes.

SENATOR: Won't you tell us what in your opinion the Court rulings will mean to workers and employers?

SECRETARY: The decisions mean that employers in the basic interstate industries will now recognize the established right of their employees to bargain collectively and will not interfere with the attempt of their workers to organize for this purpose. The decisions mean that the legal machinery which the Federal Government has provided, in the National Labor Relations Board, for the protection of this right is now available. In recent months when lower court injunctions had created doubts as to the validity of this machinery and greatly impaired its effectiveness there had been a tendency on the part of both employers and employees to ignore the Labor Relations Act.

SENATOR: There is another side of the industrial picture in which we are all vitally interested, Miss Perkins, and this is – how the lot of wage earners has improved since the low point of the depression in March 1933.

SECRETARY: More than 7,000,000 men and women, who were jobless and panic stricken then are working again in private and regular government employment and drawing their weekly pay regularly. Factory pay rolls alone were $117,413,000 greater weekly in February of this year than they were in the corresponding month in 1933. Outside of private employment over 2,800,000 men and women are engaged in useful work provided or assisted by Government.

SENATOR: How do these figures compare with those of years of prosperity?

SECRETARY: The total number of persons employed in non-agricultural work in the United States, exclusive of Works Progress Administration, is approximately the same as the number of persons who were employed in the United States in July 1930. If to these are added those employed in the agriculture and on the Federal Works program, that total will approximate the average employment of 1929.

SENATOR: Some industries are employing more people now than even in the boom period, I have learned through your reports.

SECRETARY: Yes. We now find ourselves in a situation where many of our industries are employing more people than at any other time in American history. Thus, for example, the employment rate in the blast-furnace – steel work and rolling mill industry is the highest on record. The same is true of the manufacture of engines, turbines and tractors. A similar situation prevails in glass manufacture, in knitted goods, in men's clothing, women's clothing, shirts and collars, baking, and paper and pulp.

With the exception of November and December of 1936, and two months in the Spring of 1929 the automobile industry is employing more people than at any other time for which records are available.

In the manufacture of wire, the employment level exceeds the averages of all years back to 1923. A similar situation prevails in the cash register industry, the manufacture of typewriters, clocks and watches. In the carpet and rug industry, and the cotton goods industry employment exceeds the level of any period since the early part of 1927.

In woollen and worsted goods, employment is above the average for any period since April 1925. Chemicals are back to the level of January 1929 and exceed the averages of all years for which data is available.

In the manufacture of hardware we are at the highest level since February 1930. Other industries which are back to the levels of the early days of 1930 are agricultural implements, electrical machinery, machine tools, and foundries and machine shops.

SENATOR: I know that the lot of the farmer and employer has been greatly improved since the low point of the depression.

SECRETARY: They too have reaped benefits during the last few years. For instance, the cash income of the nation's farmers from the scale of their principal product rose from $4,328,000 in 1932 to $7,578,000 in 1936 and while 1,925 reporting corporations showed profits of only $151,000,000 in 1932, 2,140 reporting corporations showed profits of $3,622,000,000 in 1936.

SENATOR: We have passed such legislation which has been of special importance to wage earners and the most important in the opinions of many of us is Social Security.

SECRETARY: Surely the Social Security Act is a truly forward looking measure for the protection of millions of our people, providing as it does for unemployment compensation, when a worker loses a job through no fault of his own, old-age insurance, assistance for the needy aged and for crippled and needy children and the bling [*sic*, for blind]. It means that our people can now look forward to a real measure of security against the hazards with which we became so heartbreakingly familiar during the depression period. It means that here in the United States we have begun, through the leadership of President Roosevelt, an effort to level the economic peaks and valleys in the interest of all our people.

SENATOR: I have been greatly interested in other helpful progress designed to aid the youth of the nation such as the CCC and the National Youth Administration. They have both accomplished big things.

SECRETARY: Yes indeed. The Civilian Conservation Corps and the National Youth Administration have been important parts of President Roosevelt's program to help young Americans through a depression which was not of their making and about which so many of them could do nothing. Before his inauguration thousands of our young people were roaming about the country in dire need and with the spectre before them of becoming permanently homeless wanderers. Now they have been and will continue to add to the national wealth by constructive work in the Civilian Conservation Corps and have been enabled to continue their education in schools and colleges through the National Youth Administration.

SENATOR: Many people are interested in what the United States Employment Service is doing in finding jobs.

SECRETARY: The United States Employment Service, as set up by the Wagner ... Act in 1933, is performing a most useful service in the interest of the jobless. Approximately 9,000,000 job placements have been made by this agency and the re-employment Service in connection with it, in the last two fiscal years. Of these more than two and one-quarter million were placements in private industry. Private placements in March reached the highest level in the past 33 months which is another indication of improving conditions.

SENATOR: What do you think would be helpful to make possible a continuation of this condition in the interest of wage earners?

SECRETARY: It is highly important that the purchasing power of low income groups be increased so as to make it possible for them to purchase the very goods which they and their brothers and well organized industries manufacture and sell to the people of the United States. The raising and stabilizing of the wage earner's income, the raising of the farmer's income and the raising of the agricultural laborer's income is a part of the responsibility of those who are responsible for the promotion of the welfare of the workers to the United States. We need to build up constantly a purchasing power of the Country.

SENATOR: We need continuation of efforts to bring the purchasing power of wage earners and farmers up to a level with the production powers of the Country.

SECRETARY: Reasonably short hours, no child labor, first-class working conditions, wages commensurate with the value of the services and wages commensurate with the American standard of living are indeed needed, Senator. It is in the increase of the standard of living, as well as in the maintenance of a living wage, that the true future development of labor's income lies. The American standard of living is a very high standard, and most wage earners are not able to approximate it in the course of their working life. As a result, we need not only to fix minimum wages for those who are in the lowest income groups and most subject to exploitation, but we have to think continuously of the improvement of other wages up to the American standard of living.

SENATOR: What else do you think might be needed to help improve the condition of wage earners?

SECRETARY: We need assurance of protection of workers against the major hazards of modern industry – lack of earning power due to accidents, due to unemployment, and due to old age and untimely death. These are partially provided for in the present social security act.

SENATOR: Surely we might do something in this country to aid those who are still victims of the depression.

SECRETARY: There ought to be a permanent activity in the United States for the rehabilitation of the victims of the depression and of old-age poverty. Let us not call it relief any more – let's call it rehabilitation and reconstruction. If we had had a great war or a great earthquake, we should cease to think in terms of relief and begin to think in terms of rehabilitation and reconstruction of the victims of these disasters.

SENATOR: The Administration is developing a fine program in the interest of wage earners. It will benefit the farmer and business as well.

SECRETARY: I agree with you, Senator, and think the following points will cover it:

1. The protection of the great mass of workers by legislation on minimum working conditions.

2. Protection and promotion by legal enactment and machinery of right to organize and bargain collectively for those who wish to do so as a method of improving the standard of living and securing status and importance for wage earners who are willing and able to make this effort.

3. Utilisation of effective techniques of conciliation and mediation to ease the strain of collective bargaining and to see that fairness and justice prevails between the great partners in industry.

4. Provision for workers and employers alike of economic and financial information relating to industries where collective bargaining is under way.

Radio interview between Senator Pope and the Secretary of Labor, Frances Perkins, April 1937, Frances Perkins Papers, Roosevelt Library.

1.23 Radio speech on the reasons for resettlement by Rexford G. Tugwell

The radio speech offered New Dealers the chance to speak directly to millions of Americans sitting at home in their front parlour. During the 1920s radio had grown massively in the United States and by the 1930s most homes had a set. Radio speeches were often couched in homely terms to maximise their impact and to ensure that they were not out of place with the surroundings in which they were listened to.

Just after the war, alluring advertisements appeared in the larger newspapers of the Middle West. They ran about as follows:

> "FOR SALE – Excellent Wisconsin farm lands. Buy now and assure your future. Small down payment, easy terms. No previous farm experience needed. Hundreds have made good."

Barbers, mechanics, steel workers, school teachers and tailors saw in these advertisements the opportunity to realise a life-long dream. Here was a chance to establish a home on the traditional American pattern, to become well-off and to provide for their children's future.

It seemed easy and safe. Farm prices were high; even banks and insurance companies were investing heavily. What safer place could be found for savings? Many borrowed money and added it to their own savings in order to make first payments. The earnings of years were transferred to the bank accounts of farm land speculators. So great were hopes and so artistic were the illustrated booklets that some purchases were made sight unseen. Other buyers, more cautious but still afire with enthusiasm, asked to be shown the land before parting with their life savings.

The speculators were ready for them. A few model farms had been fixed up on the best land. Drainage ditches were in operation. Fields were under cultivation. Families were living in pretty little farm houses and the barns were filled with sleek cattle. The picture was so serene that even the doubtful, after viewing its pastoral charm, dug into their pockets for the cash payments.

That was sixteen or seventeen years ago. Let's see what these people got for their money. Of course they didn't get the model farms. Instead of rich soil, they got land which had been part of the sandy bottom of an ancient glacial lake or was filled with rocky outcroppings. Instead of lush, green pastures, they got a crop of blackened tree stumps which had to be dug and dynamited out of the way before a plough could be used. Instead of an attractive cottage, they had to patch together a rough cabin and barn out of raw planks and tar paper. They and not the land had been sold.

Courage failed a few in this wilderness of sand and stumps and peat bogs and they were glad to get out with the loss of their down payments. However, it was not long before a slick salesman had lured another family into the same predicament.

Long before the Federal Government stepped in, many of those who stuck it out were being supported by charity. Many still are. For all of them living is desperately hard. Children are underfed and badly clothed. Not long ago a Resettlement man called at the home of one of these poor land farmers. His young daughter said: "Dad ought to be in bed. He's almost got pneumonia." But he wasn't in bed. He was standing almost knee-deep in a swamp cutting marsh grass for the few cows and horses he had left. Malnutrition had worn down his resistance and overwork had sapped his energy. He was helpless and hopeless.

These people are stranded. Their resources have been swept away and they are unable to move. No one will buy their land. It never should have been put under the plough in the first place. No one but a slick salesman could sell it and these gentlemen are having a hard time now.

Our Resettlement people are now trying to help. We are buying up land in this old glacial lake bottom and in other badly used areas and shall put it back to uses nature will allow. Some 150,000 acres in this particular section will be turned into recreational areas and wildlife refuges. More than two hundred families in this one project alone will be offered a chance to move to good land nearby. After nearly a generation of frustration and disappointment, hope is again restored to them.

More is involved than relief of human misery and suffering. Taxpayers will be saved thousands of dollars each year. Roads and schools in the purchase areas will be closed down. The families moving out of the area will become self-supporting taxpayers, whereas now in some of the townships involved more than half of the land has been tax delinquent. The land is being changed from a public liability into a public asset.

This is only one type of Resettlement problem. Let me tell you what has happened in another area, in what is sometimes called the "Dust Bowl." Some years ago a prosperous farmer from the Corn Belt bought a large tract on the south western plains. He invested several thousand dollars in land and equipment and had one of the best farming lay-outs in the region. He thought he had every chance of success. Prices were good and neighboring farms in the same region had produced bumper crops in the previous few years. He, too, had a dream. He thought that, after a few years of large-scale farming, he could have retired with a competence, and he was a practical and successful farmer who knew what he was about.

That was several years ago. No sooner had he plowed under the wild prairie grass than the wind began its destruction. It was a drought year – and practically every year since has been a drought year. The wind has lifted the top soil – his capital – and blown it away in black, choking clouds. It now lies in drifts and dunes on once grassy fields. Continued failure has wiped out his investment and today he too, is stranded. He recently told one of our Resettlement Administration people: "Our one hope is to get away but we can't get away unless the government helps us."

This is not an exceptional case. There are thousands of families in a similar situation throughout the whole of the Great Plains. Like the Wisconsin lake bottom, much of this land should never have been plowed. But it makes excellent range for livestock and the Resettlement Administration is helping to restore it to that productive use. This is the country where grass grew waist high, where the great herds of buffalo lived and where the traditional prairie fires menaced the early settlers.

To make a change now is less costly than it would be to wait. Few people realise how wasteful it is to misuse land. Let me illustrate. A study made in one county of the Northwest shows that the public is paying $185.61 per family to transport children in a poor land area to school. The actual tax collected from each farm concerned averaged six dollars – less than 4% of each family's transportation bill. The other citizens in the county had to dig into their pockets for the difference.

By restoring misused lands to a better use, the Resettlement Administration is helping to plug this economic leak. At the same time, we are adding directly to the wealth of the nation, for land which is a public liability if wrongly used, becomes a national asset if it is rightly used.

We will have bought about ten million acres of such misused land by the end of this year. These acres are located in 208 different projects throughout the country. About 22,000 farm families are in this way being given a chance to move to better lands. The tracts we are buying are being developed as forests, parks, grazing areas and wildlife refuges. The mere task of preparing them for these other uses will give employment to a daily average of more than 75,000 men under the work relief program.

This process of land adjustment is the basis of a long-time program and must be judged as such, and not as an emergency relief measure to be abandoned with the first economic upturn. But more than a million rural families have been on relief. This means that nearly five million people, living on the land, have had to depend upon outside sources to provide them with food; and helping them is our emergency task. Many of these were farmers on land which ordinarily would support them. Depression, drought, flood, foreclosure had robbed them of their livestock and equipment, often forcing them into tenancy and sharecropping. It was obvious that a small amount of financial aid would tide them over their emergency and prevent them from becoming permanently dependent on relief.

For example, a farmer with a good record behind him – let's call him Homer Grant – lived in a corn and hog country. His small farm had supported himself and his family. There was a mortgage on the place but he had being paying interest regularly and, until 1930–31, had often been able to lay a little money aside. He was counting on sending his children to the State University. But farm prices fell disastrously and Grant had to go to the bank, not to deposit money but to withdraw his savings. Soon his money was exhausted and the mortgage holder began prodding him for overdue payments. You know the rest of his familiar story. It has been re-enacted in hundreds of thousands of farm homes in the United States. His resources became completely exhausted and he had to ask for public relief.

A visit from the county rehabilitation agent prevented his misfortune from becoming a tragedy. Sitting down with Grant, this Resettlement agent worked out a budget and farm management plan, and recommended him for a rehabilitation loan of $600. With this money, Grant was able to buy live-stock, tools, fertiliser and seed. Resettlement gave him a chance to get back on his feet. Once more his farm is yielding him a profit and he is repaying, not only his rehabilitation loan, but his mortgage as well. Incidental to his economic rehabilitation, he has learned better methods of farming and his wife has learned more economical methods of home management. A good farmer has been saved to continue the efficient cultivation of his own farm by a small loan which will be repaid to the government, as a result of this typical case of Resettlement activity.

For, through the Resettlement Administration, the Federal Government is extending similar help to half a million farm families. They are off relief. They are becoming self-supporting. They have regained their self-respect. They are once more useful members of the community. They are already paying back to the Government their rehabilitation loans and the only cost to the country is the cost of administering and supervising this program for individual recovery.

How is this program working? Let me read you what some of the farm families say:

> "When you found me I was crawlin'. Now I'm walkin'."
> "We would have had a bare existence from hand to mouth."
> "We would have lived, but food would have been scarce."
> "My family would have probably gone hungry."
> "We just couldn't have lived and kept our self-respect."
> "I guess we would have gone to the dogs."
> "I have more faith in Uncle Sam than ever before."

This rehabilitation program is not a relief program. Instead it is designed to take farmers off relief and to make them permanently independent. It is also helping other farmers to avoid the necessity of asking for relief. One way in which we do this is through our voluntary debt adjustment committees. More than 15,000 volunteer workers, under the direction of the Resettlement Administration, are seeking to prevent farm bankruptcy and foreclosure by settling the differences between debtors and creditors. Already 150,000 farm homes have been saved to their present owners in this way.

The Resettlement Administration is, as you see, doing precisely the opposite to relief as it is generally considered. We are preventing farm families from going on the relief rolls and are taking them off the relief rolls. Under our present program of rehabilitation we expect to provide for more than 525,000 farm families, two and a half million men, women and children.

In addition to this program of rehabilitation and land adjustment, we have a third activity – the improvement of rural and of suburban housing. At the present time we have completed or are completing sixty one community projects. These are of various types. Some are in agricultural areas, where the families engage in farming. Others are near industrial centers and afford low-income workers an opportunity to have decent housing.

Slums are generally associated with the tenement districts of our larger cities and most of us do not realise that in poverty-stricken parts of our countryside, families with seven and eight children live in bleak one and two-room shacks. Rags are stuffed in holes in the walls and windows. Poverty, as expressed in bad housing, is just as detrimental to health in the country as it is in the city. So we are now utilizing workers from the relief rolls to help families acquire better homes both in agricultural and suburban communities. Often it is possible to group farms together in such a way that schools, electricity, roads and other public services can be more economically provided. We are developing a number of these agricultural communities and are in addition building four large suburban housing projects, accommodating a total of five thousand low-income families. These projects are located near large industrial centers where steady employment is assured.

Of the need for better housing there can be no dispute, for it has been estimated that we shall have to build 14,000,000 new dwellings in this country in the next ten years; and studies show that over a third of all our present houses are obsolete. The suburban housing projects which we have started obviously cannot do more than demonstrate the possibility of providing employed workers in the low-income groups with decent housing and to point the way to future housing developments. Our projects, for example, should show, first of all, the advantage of locating in suburban areas where land prices are lower and where the absence of other buildings makes it possible to develop complete communities. Each project will be enclosed by a protective strip of woodland or a "greenbelt" to save the residential area from undesirable encroachments. Parks and other recreational facilities will be thus provided and garden plots will be available to those desiring them. Schools, community centres, stores, shops and other public buildings are included in the plan to provide self-contained suburban towns. Work is progressing rapidly on the first of these projects, located at Berwyn, in Maryland, ten miles from Washington, and the others will be started soon.

Because our program involves the moving of some families to new places, it is called the Resettlement program. It is designed to create a better readjustment, we are called upon to end the physical abuse of our soil and the resulting erosion of our land. Still more important is our duty to end what might be called human erosion – the wasting away of millions of our people in a hopeless struggle to earn a living from lands which will not support life.

Throughout our program runs a single clear pattern which marks it as a part of our national tradition. We are moving in the wake of our dreams and trying to bring reality a little closer. The free lands of the boundless West were a national dream from the dawn of our history on this continent. Men struggled, fought, faced torture, starvation and death to win the right of our people to the lands which lay beyond the Alleghanies. Although for forty years the frontier has gone, its memory and its motives still control our national feeling about the land and the people who make their living from the land. For the land, in part, we revolted against the English King and for the land our own people waged a bitter four-year war, on the issue of whether slave or free labor should develop our national heritage. Land use is, you see, a fighting question and has been since the dawn of time. The victorious sweep of our people across the continent was as complete and as unplanned as most victories.

Another dream – perhaps the most tragically frustrated in our history – centers around the Great Valley and the Father of Waters which gives it its name. The Mississippi River provided an artery north and south which has marked out its basin as the seat of power and civilization in our national future. To secure the mouth of the Mississippi, even the pacific Jefferson was ready to ally himself with England and the belligerent Jackson led the men of the West to battle at New Orleans in order that the river might remain in American hands. Spaniard, Frenchman and Englishman have fought us to control this gigantic artery of wealth and commerce. The issue of whether the West would join the North in the war between the States was decided when the Confederates barred traffic on the Mississippi before ever Fort Sumter was fired upon. The war was fought to free the river and when Lincoln was able to say "The Father of Waters flows unvexed to the sea," he was announcing the success of more than the Union Armies. He was giving voice to a national dream, which seemed to have achieved reality.

Yet for seventy years, that Great Valley, which could and should be the controlling force in our economic and political life, has been divided by sectional and emotional antipathies, while the farmers of that valley face actual destitution and hopelessness in what should be the granary of the world. The Northern farmer who works for a mortgage and the Southern agriculturist who works for a landlord alike are tenants and sharecroppers in a region where, if anywhere, every man *should* be a king. The traffic which should flow easily and economically from north to south, out through the Lakes or through the Gulf, has been warped and chained to swell the profits and importance of distant cities. Banks and insurance companies hold title to provinces where wealth and power and freedom should accumulate as a heritage for our people. And year after year the people of the valley are pitted against each other in political conflict where they should stand shoulder to shoulder in defence of their birth right. This peonage has gone on too long. We must as a nation face the supreme reality of geography and give to the people who live in the Great Valley the heritage which Jefferson and Jackson and Lincoln sought to assure to them.

And then there is that other recent dream, whose smoking ruins lie everywhere around us. The dream of the "New Era," the dream of a nation whose industries would make us all rich, through the high wages and low costs possible as a result of technological advance. This was the dream which drained our best people from the farms, from all over the world, into the metropolitan and industrial areas. For forty years and more we invested our wealth, our men and our energy in the most marvellous flowering of human ingenuity applied to industry within our history. That dream all but destroyed itself in 1929 and the years which followed, leaving behind it men and women without employment, hope, shelter or food – beyond a niggardly dole or charity. Yet the dream had substance for it represented what was practically possible if we could only master the techniques of living and working together, in order to give every man his due and special privilege to neither capital, labor nor consumer. It *is* possible to have a New Era in terms of assured income, security and contentment at a high standard of living. It is possible if we learn to adapt ourselves to the realities of the power age and cease to rely upon the outworn shibboleths of international finance and the pat formulas of 19th century economists who thought in terms of feudal privilege and vested interests. This, the most recent and most hopeful of our great dreams, must not be allowed to lapse into industrial serfdom, in which the only right a worker has is to sell his labor if another man desires to hire him; and the farmer labors in perpetual slavery to a landlord or a mortgage. And it will not if such a program as we have begun can go on over the years. It is the least controversial job I know. Everyone agrees that it needs doing. For myself and my fellow workers, I can only say that we hope to do our share of it wisely and well.

Address on the National Radio Forum, arranged by the *Washington Star*, and broadcast over the network of the National Broadcasting Company, 10.30 p.m., Monday 2 December 1935, Official Files OF 1568/2, Roosevelt Library.

THE RHETORIC OF DYNAMISM

1.24 Press release on the first meeting of the Executive Council, 18 July 1933

Press releases were one of the principal weapons of the administration in trying to get its message of hope across to the public. This press release was issued after the first meeting of the Executive Council, a body which helped the President in the formulation of policy, on 18 July 1933. It was intended to show the businesslike and dynamic way in which the government was trying to tackle the depression.

The Executive Council held its first official session today. Attorney General Cummings, being the senior cabinet officer present, presided. Reports were received from all the Departments in regard to their activities, and a number of matters were brought up for general discussion without action.

The most important function of the Conference is to keep each Department, including the newly created agencies of the Government in touch with all that is being done towards the main objectives of the Administration. Where it is found that several agencies are interested in the same problems, this Council will also arrange for conferences and committees of co-ordination in each instance as it comes up. Several such informal committees were appointed this afternoon.

The reports received today were very full, and as the result, every Department at the close of the meeting was fully appraised of what is being done in every line of governmental activity. This will be helpful in securing quick action and close co-ordination.

Press release following the first meeting of the Executive Council, Washington, 18 July 1933, Official Files OF 70/1, Roosevelt Library.

2
New Deal domestic policy

Relief, recovery and reform were the alliterative headings for the New Deal battleplan to combat the depression: relief to preserve human life and the fabric of society; recovery to reinvigorate the economy and create real jobs; and reform to prevent such a cataclysm from happening again. Unsurprisingly events forced a deviation from the plan. Roosevelt's inauguration coincided with the near collapse of the banking system. Banks closed their doors as panicked investors, spurred by events at other banks, rushed to withdraw their funds. Roosevelt found that his first task in trying to bring order out of chaos was to reform the banking system. After the banking emergency, which dominated the first few days of his administration, radical steps would be taken to relieve distress and provide employment. Jobs were created by the million as federal money was poured into the economy. In the longer term industry and business were reformed under the National Industrial Recovery Act, and the problems of agriculture were tackled under a series of Agricultural Adjustment Acts which sought to raise farm incomes by reducing over-production. In the mid-1930s, in an effort to ensure that the nation would never again face such hardship, and in a move to outflank the political opponents of the administration, a social security system was introduced.

However, the evolution of the New Deal was not straightforward. The National Industrial Recovery Act was struck down by the Supreme Court in 1935 and other key components of the New Deal came under legal challenge. As a result some historians have argued that there were in fact two New Deals: 1933–35 and 1935–40. Such a division is suggestive of careful planning and organisation. In reality, New Deal policy resists such easy boxing and division. It evolved, having deep roots in the progressive era thinking of the late nineteenth and early twentieth centuries. With the onset of war there was no swift change from New Deal to war. Instead, New Deal evolved into war, the requirements of war feeding into the requirements of the New Deal. Twenty years after the death of Roosevelt the New Deal had become President Johnson's New Society: the labels and degree of radicalism had changed but the policies were recognisably similar.

EMERGENCY MEASURES, 1933–34

2.1 The 'terror' of 1933

From the perspective of the twenty-first century it is hard to truly appreciate the depth of 'terror' felt in 1933. To some observers it appeared as though the capitalist system itself was on the verge of collapse. Endemic unemployment and widespread poverty posed a serious threat to the existing social order. In her memoirs Secretary of Labor Frances Perkins tried to capture the severity of the situation for her readers.

It is hard today to reconstruct the atmosphere of 1933 and to evoke the terror caused by unrelieved poverty and prolonged unemployment. The funds of many states and localities were exhausted. The legal debt limit of many states had been reached, and they could borrow no more, even for so urgent a matter as relief. The situation was grim in city, county, and state. Public welfare officers had reached the end of their rope, and special committees, appointed by governors, mayors, and county officials, had exhausted their imagination as well as their funds. The Federal Government and its taxing power were all one could think of.

Whatever plans the Roosevelt government might make to revive the normal economic life of the country, the urgent need was for direct relief to the unemployed. During the Democratic campaign Roosevelt had placed considerable emphasis upon this need. It had been basic in the appeal for votes that suffering would be relieved immediately.

Unemployment had been increasing steadily since the autumn of 1929. When Roosevelt took office in March 1933, it had reached its peak. No one has ever known the exact number out of work and in need. The kind of statistical information now capable of giving us a fairly good answer to that question was not available, but the estimates of persons out of work ranged from 13,300,000 to 17,900,000. The true figure is probably somewhere between, and the number in actual distress approached seventy-five per cent. of the unemployed.

National income had declined from $81,000,000,000 a year to $39,000,000,000. Banks were collapsing throughout the nation. Relief stations were closing down for lack of funds. Hunger marchers were on parade. Food riots were becoming more common. Crime, born of the need for food, clothing, and other necessities of life, was on the upsurge.

There were insecurity and terror in the agricultural regions, where sober farm people forcibly prevented sheriffs' sales on fore-closed mortgages. The increase in petty larceny was alarming. An honourable man like Dan Willard, president of the Baltimore & Ohio Railroad, when asked at a public meeting what he thought about the situation, said, "If a man whose family is hungry steals, I cannot blame him. I think I would do the same."

Frances Perkins, *The Roosevelt I Knew* (London, Hammond & Co., 1947), pp. 148–9.

2.2 Emergency measures for reform of the banking system, 5 March 1933

Raymond Moley was one of Roosevelt's ideas men, part of the informal Brains Trust of advisors that the President asked to help guide his policies. Well-grounded in economic theory, Moley shared Roosevelt's belief that the economic system had to be reformed, and that the process had to start immediately if collapse was to be averted. In his memoirs Moley recounted the banking emergency that faced the administration in March 1933 and the speed with which steps were taken to reform and strengthen the banking system.

In essence, we were facing a problem of public psychology more acutely than we were facing a problem of finance – that every step taken must be tested less on the basis of its ultimate desirability from a financial point of view than on the basis of its immediate effect in restoring confidence. The corollaries of these propositions were obvious. They recognized the need for

(1) 'Swift and staccato action.'

(2) The stressing of conventional banking methods and the avoidance of any unusual or highly controversial measures.

(3) The opening of as many banks as could possibly be opened within the realm of safety, since the greater the number opened the greater the probability of confidence in banks generally.

(4) The blacking out of the reputedly left-wing presidential advisers during the crisis.

(5) A tremendous gesture by the President and Congress in the direction of economy.

(6) A man-to-man appeal for public confidence by the President himself.

At noon on Thursday, March 9th, the new Congress met. At three o'clock the President's message was read. An hour later the Emergency Banking Bill, which no one but the congressional leaders had read, was passed by the House. It went through the Senate at seven-thirty o'clock that evening. Before nine o'clock FDR had signed it.

Raymond Moley, *After Seven Years* (New York, Harper and Brothers, 1939), p. 148. Reproduced in C. P. Hill, *Franklin Roosevelt and the New Deal* (London, Edward Arnold, 1975), pp. 30–1.

2.3 The first meeting of the Executive Council, 18 July 1933

Roosevelt knew that his administration had to show considerable dynamism in combating the depression. That dynamism was necessary to get things done, but also to reassure the public. The first meeting of the Executive Council on 18 July 1933 showed just how dynamic the administration was going to be in trying to restore the economy and relieve distress.

MEMORANDUM:
TO: The President of the United States
FROM: The Executive Secretary of the Executive Council

The following is a resume of the various reports received by the Executive Council as of July 17, 1933, submitted in response to the order of the President at the meeting of the Executive Council July 11, 1933.

SECRETARY OF STATE (Submitted by the Under Secretary):
(1) Steps are being taken to eventually lead to negotiation of trade treaties between the United States, and Argentina, Brazil, Chile, Colombia, Sweden and Portugal. Departments of Commerce, Treasury, Agriculture and Labor, the Tariff Commission, and the National Recovery Administration are represented on the Board.

(2) On July 13, representatives of about 30 countries, including Great Britain and France, agreed in principle to the idea of not increasing sugar production for the next several years. The Cuban Government has sent a delegation here which is conferring with the Conference called by the Department of Agriculture to co-ordinate all branches of sugar cane and beet industries.

ATTORNEY GENERAL:
Drive is being made against racketeers. In the Delaware County, Pennsylvania, conspiracy 96 persons were indicted; 60 have indicated intention to plead guilty.

There is a constant decline in prohibition cases due to inroads made by the lawful sale of beer.

An investigation into the increased cost of bread has begun; also an investigation into the recent increases in gasoline prices.

SECRETARY OF COMMERCE:
Steps being taken to transfer functions of the Shipping Board and Emergency Fleet Corporation to the Department of Commerce not later than August 10, 1933.

During last two weeks 1900 people have been separated from the Commerce Department. The list of those removed from service has been submitted to the Civil Service Commission with a view to their being certified for employment when such services are required by divisions of the government.

SECRETARY OF AGRICULTURE:
The wheat exporting countries, Canada, Argentina and Australia are unwilling to accept our proposal for reduction. It is possible, however, that export quotas can be agreed upon for '33–34 and '34–35 seasons.

SECRETARY OF THE INTERIOR:
For the administration of the Public Works program the Country has been divided into 10 Regions; a Regional Adviser to be appointed for each Region; and, an Advisory Committee of 3 to be appointed in each State.

State projects are to be submitted to the State Advisory Committees and will be forwarded by these State Committees direct to the Public Works Board in Washington.

With the advice of the President there has been approved, exclusive of Public roads, projects calling for an expenditure of $65,500,00.

ADMINISTRATOR OF THE INDUSTRIAL RECOVERY ACT:
Four additional deputy administrators appointed this past week.

THE TENNESSEE VALLEY AUTHORITY:
Muscle Shoals inventory being made. Geological study is being made of caves in Cove Creek Reservoir site. Roads, railroad and town site are being located near Cove Creek Dam site. Engineers studying problem of transmitting and distributing power. General financial and administrative system being developed. About 500 persons are now employed.

FEDERAL EMERGENCY RELIEF ADMINISTRATOR:
Developed co-operative plan whereby State and local relief units function in the organisation and maintenance of the re-employment bureau to be established in many local communities throughout the United States;

Established a method of checking relief rolls for the purpose of determining the number of persons who have been or will be returned to gainful occupation as a result of operation of emergency measures;

Adopted plan for care of transient unemployed; for vocational education of persons on relief rolls and adult education for all persons unemployed.

These plans have been worked out with the appropriate governmental agencies.

Reached agreement with Labor Department to pay transportation, to Countries of origin, of destitute families of aliens deported under Immigrant law.

Local Relief Administrators report rise in cost of relief due to increase in market prices.

The number of families in 29 large cities, dependent on relief, declined 3% in June as against May. In these cities, representing a total population of 25,000,000, one out of every six families was receiving relief.

Inaugurated plan to remove from relief rolls those not actually in need; estimate 10% reduction thereby.

Conducting investigation to ascertain possibility of removing families now on rolls in industrial centres to small districts or tracts of land where opportunities for permanent employment may be more favourable.

GOVERNOR OF FARM CREDIT ADMINISTRATION:
Established uniform rate of 5% interest on First Mortgage Loans to be made by Federal Land Banks through National Farm Loan Associations.

After canvass of Farm Mortgages held by closed and restricted banks in States of Illinois, Iowa and South Carolina, acceptable mortgages will be purchased within appraisal limits by the Land Banks of the Three Districts in which these States are situated.

Land Bank Commissioner reports the total number of appraisers on duty now 600 as compared with 210 on April 10.

CHAIRMAN OF THE BOARD OF THE HOME OWNERS LOAN CORPORATION:
At the close of March 4, the date the old Board ceased to exist, loans made by Regional Banks amounted to $12,710,366. Loans outstanding to date amount to $47,642,579.59. The weekly average amount of loans at the present time approximate $2,400,000 and it is estimated that loans made by January 1, 1934 will approximate $100,000,000.

General Managers have been appointed in 36 States and the District of Columbia; managers for the remaining states will be appointed during the coming week.

FEDERAL CO-ORDINATOR OF TRANSPORTATION:
Reports progress. Has selected key men for working out economies and research.

At request of the President, considered and reported on Kansas City Southern labor controversy.

DIRECTOR OF EMERGENCY CONSERVATIVE WORK:
Enrolment of men for Reforestation Work completed July 15, 1933 – work now under way in 47 states:

Approximately 300,000 men enrolled;

240,000 between 18 and 25;
35,000 experienced wooden;
25,000 Veterans;
14,400 Indians
1,360 Forest Camps established;
1,438 estimated will be functioning within week;

It is estimated 300,000 families are receiving monthly $20 or more in way of allotment from enrolled men.

ADMINISTRATOR OF AGRICULTURAL ADJUSTMENT:
Four Major Divisions:

(a) Production;
(b) Processing & Marketing;
(c) Finance;
(d) Publicity.

A

1 Production Division announced wheat program '33–'34–'35 and wheat processing tax for '33.

2 Cotton Plan acreage reduction and option plans for '33 and accompanying processing tax;

3 Tobacco plans for '33 reducing production of cigar leaf tobacco;

4 Plans covering other commodities are nearing completion.

B

Processing Division has held conference with 30 industrial groups – conducted 10 formal public hearings on milk agreements. Milk licenses for dealers and distributors have been determined – Chicago will no doubt be the first city to be covered by licenses.

C

Finance Division has arranged Commitment from RFC for maximum loan of $70 million to purchase Cotton and Cotton Futures from Farm Credit Administration. Has negotiated favourable contract with American Cotton Co-operative Association for marketing actual cotton to be acquired by Secretary of Agriculture.

D

Publicity Division is organised to handle all relations with the Press, arrange radio appointments and supply information required.

Minutes of the Executive Council, Washington, 18 July 1933, Official Files OF 70/1, Roosevelt Library.

2.4 Report of the interpreting economist to the Executive Council, 31 October 1933

During the first months of the new administration the Cabinet scrutinised the economic statistics for signs that their emergency measures were beginning to have some impact on the economic problems of the United States.

Summary
Preliminary data indicate that final figures for October will show a somewhat further decline in factory operations, especially in the output of semi-finished goods. Factory operations as a whole, however, will remain well above the highest levels of last year. The causes of this decline were outlined in the summary prepared on September 2 where it was pointed out, first, that 2/3rds of the huge advance in factory output between March and July was concentrated in the textile industry, the leather industry, and the steel industry; second, that all three of these large industries were operating at higher rates than could be sustained in view of the level of market demand for their products, and third, that there was little prospect of immediate expansion in other industries sufficient to offset a more balanced rate of operations in these industries. The recession in output which has occurred since July, therefore, was to be expected. It does not in itself represent a fundamental downward trend so much as reaction from an over-rapid expansion in particular industries earlier in the year.

The fundamental trend of industry, as contrasted with these month-to-month movements, is determined much more by conditions in the heavy industries where the depression is now concentrated. In canvassing the current prospects in these industries, the break in steel operations from an average of 59% of capacity in July to about 31% of capacity during the fourth week of October should not be overemphasised, since there was no evidence that consuming outlets for steel were operating at a rate sufficient to justify steel making at anything like 59% of capacity in July. So far as we can judge, the trend of final consuming outlets for steel has increased rather than decreased in recent weeks. While construction contracts are still low, they have increased steadily on a daily average basis since March (reflecting largely an increased volume of contracts for public works), and in the first half of October exceeded contracts last year. Demand for machine tools has also continued to rise since the Spring reflecting revival in the automobile industry and a scattered demand for improved factory equipment. The recent decline in automobile output is partly seasonal in character and represents preparation for the introduction of new models for 1934 which is expected to show a continuation of the revival in automobile demand which began last Spring. Railroad buying has remained low but should improve when the current negotiations over the price of steel rails are concluded.

Foreign Trade
Secretary Roper reports that United States exports during September were valued at $160,000,000 and imports at $147,000,000, leaving a net balance of merchandise exports of $13,000,000. Exports increased 22% from August as compared with a customary increase of 14% while imports decreased 5% as compared with a customary decrease of 1%. Taking the third quarter of the year as a whole, exports showed an expansion of 25% over last year as compared with an increase of 65% in imports. These large increases reflect higher prices for raw materials which enter heavily into our foreign trade as well as a larger physical movement of goods.

Labor
Secretary Perkins reports that the increase in average hourly wage rates and the decrease in average hours worked per week which was noted in August, continued in September. Taking the two months together, average hourly wages have increased from 42.7 cents to 51.4 cents, while average hours worked per week have declined concurrently from 42.3 to 36.1. These changes are clearly due to the YRA codes. Secretary Perkins states that the changes in wage rates do not necessarily represent an increase in total average weekly earnings, but they do represent shorter hours with no pay cut at the same time that employment was provided for thousands of additional workers.

Report of the Interpreting Economist to the Executive Council, 31 October 1933, Official Files OF 70/1, Roosevelt Library.

2.5 Gerald Johnson responds to those critics who argue that the entire New Deal is a series of emergency measures to meet the crisis of the moment, 1941

To some of Roosevelt's opponents the entire New Deal represented nothing more than a series of emergency measures thrown together in great haste. They accused Roosevelt of having no overall plan, or even set of guiding principles. Rather he simply responded to the crisis of the moment.

The crash of the banking system necessitated swift action in a dozen directions before the program could be considered; yet the program was always in mind, and the improvisations that were made were always of such a nature that they could be fitted into what had been planned. This accounts, partially at least, for two things, first, the astonishing certainty with which the President moved during that bewildering and frightening period, and, second, for the impression that much of the New Deal itself consisted of happy improvisations.

Gerald Johnson, *Roosevelt: Dictator or Democrat* (New York, Harper and Brothers, 1941), p. 189.

2.6 Harry Hopkins responds to criticism of New Deal planning

In responding to the crisis of early 1933 government planning was not entirely successful on a practical level as a blizzard of so-called alphabet agencies (CCC, PWA, FERA) were created to address particular aspects of the depression.

Contrary to general impression, the rise of emergency organizations is not coincident with the advent of the so-called New Deal ... The first emergency organization to be created was the Reconstruction Finance Corporation, which was set up on February 2, 1932, as a temporary financing organization to aid embarrassed banks, railroads and other business enterprises. Through amendment of the charter in July 1932 the Federal Government entered the field of relief, authorizing the Reconstruction Finance Corporation to lend $30,000,000 for relief purposes to States and municipalities ...

With the inauguration of President Roosevelt a conscious and elaborate emergency program was instituted, which developed in certain definite directions. A program for stimulating the recovery of agriculture and industry was launched with the passage of the Agricultural Adjustment Act (June 16, 1933) and the National Industrial Recovery Act (June 16, 1933) ...

Even before the recovery program was launched, Congress at the request of President Roosevelt crystallized a plan for employing unmarried young men on emergency conservation work in the national forests, national parks, and on State park projects under the supervision of national-parks officials. The corps of young men, known as the Civilian Conservation Corps, was organized under Army officers and was stationed in various camps, the men serving for board and wages of $30 a month. Most of the wages they were required to allot to dependants ...

In the meantime the Federal Government had entered actively into relief affairs, with the setting up by Congress of the Federal Emergency Relief Administration in May 1933. While continuing the policy previously followed of making grants to States, and letting State agencies dispense the relief themselves, the FERA set out at once to co-ordinate the miscellaneous relief structures then existing, and in a few States took over actual administration of relief ...

When in the meantime it became apparent that the public works construction program under the PWA provisions of the National Industrial Recovery Act was getting under way too slowly to bring about rapid recovery, President Roosevelt decided to apply the work relief idea on a national scale for the unemployed that were not being caught up by the heavy construction program. Diverting part of the public-works funds from the PWA he ordered the FERA in November 1933 to set up a Civil Works Administration (CWA) with a program of useful works projects, putting strong emphasis, for the first time, on white-collar workers and other neglected classes of the unemployed for whom no private work was in prospect. The triple objective of the program was to maintain the morale of the unemployed by giving them useful work at prevailing wages, to increase the social capital of the Nation by productive labor, and to hasten business recovery by putting new purchasing power rapidly into circulation ...

In addition to the main emergency organizations whose development has been thus traced, the Government has found it necessary to create a number of corporations to perform specific tasks. Thus the Federal Surplus Commodities Corporation (previously known as the Federal Surplus Relief Corporation) was set up in 1933 to aid both the AAA and federal relief programs by removing surplus farm products and utilizing them for relief purposes. The Commodity Credit Corporation was set up the same year to grant commodity loans on cotton, corn, and other agricultural commodities by means of which the price stabilization objective of the AAA could be realized. Two export-import banks were established as part of the National Recovery Administration program to promote foreign trade by Government-supported export credits; one was dissolved in 1936. Three coordinating and planning organizations, which were set up under the National Recovery Administration, have been continued by Executive order after the Supreme Court decision invalidating the main sections of the NIRA. These boards are the National Emergency Council, the National Resources Committee, and the Central Statistical Board. The last named was made a statutory board by act of Congress on July 25, 1936, with a duration of 5 years. A Prison Industries Reorganization Administration was created by Executive Order in September 1935 and its activities, predominantly of a research and advisory character, are financed by appropriations from the emergency budget.

Federal Writers Project, *Washington: City and Capital* (Washington DC, United States Government Printing Office, 1937), pp. 1038–42.

UNEMPLOYMENT

2.7 The growth and decline of unemployment, 1929–41

During 1930 and 1931 the number of unemployed grew alarmingly as the depression caused business failures and mass lay-offs of workers. The number of unemployed threatened the social fabric of the United States and civil disorder was an ever present threat. Thanks to the New Deal the unemployment figures improved steadily after 1933, but the mini-recession of 1938 showed the extent to which the American economy remained in poor health.

(a) Unemployment in thousands of persons 14 years old and over

Year	No. of Unemployed	Percentage of Labor Force
1929	1,550	3.2
1930	4,340	8.7
1931	8,020	15.9
1932	12,060	23.6
1933	12,830	24.9
1934	11,340	21.7
1935	10,610	20.1
1936	9,030	16.9
1937	7,700	14.3
1938	10,390	19.0
1939	9,480	17.2
1940	8,120	14.6
1941	5,560	9.9

Historical Statistics of the United States, Colonial Times to 1957 (Washington DC, United States Government, 1957), p. 73. Reproduced in C. P. Hill, *Franklin Roosevelt and the New Deal* (London, Edward Arnold, 1975), pp. 6, 48.

2.8 Three essentials for unemployment relief, 21 March 1933

In March 1933 Roosevelt tried to define the way in which unemployment would be attacked. Most importantly of all he needed to define the relationship between government at the federal and state level.

To the Congress:

It is essential to our recovery program that measures immediately be enacted aimed at unemployment relief. A direct attack in this problem suggests three types of legislation.

The first is the enrolment of workers now by the Federal Government for such public employment as can be quickly started and will not interfere with the demand for or the proper standards of normal employment.

The second is grants to States for relief work.

The third extends to a broad public works labor-creating program.

With reference to the latter I am now studying the many projects suggested and the financial questions involved. I shall make recommendations to the Congress presently.

For full text see *The Public Papers and Addresses of Franklin D. Roosevelt*, Vol. 2 (New York, Random House, 1938), pp. 80–4.

2.9 Informal remarks at a CCC camp, 12 August 1933

The Civilian Conservation Corps was set up in 1933 to provide work for men between the ages of 18 and 25 on projects involving reafforestation, road construction and soil conservation. Over 2 million young men were involved in CCC projects between 1933 and 1941.

I wish I could spend a couple of months here myself. The only difference between us is that I am told you men have put on an average of twelve pounds each. I am trying to lose twelve pounds.

It is very good to be able to visit these Virginia Civilian Conservation Corps camps. I hope that they are as inspiring all over the country as these I have seen today.

More important, I have seen the boys themselves, and all you have to do is to look at the boys themselves to see that the camps themselves are a success.

For full address see *The Public Papers and Addresses of Franklin D. Roosevelt*, Vol. 2 (New York, Random House, 1938), p. 322.

2.10 The need for discipline in the CCC, 19 December 1935

Despite Roosevelt's comments in document 2.9, life in the Civilian Conservation Corps was less than easy. Run by the military, disciplinary standards had to be met, as the following extract from a camp newsletter illustrates.

When asked to write a little something for our newspaper, I pondered over several thoughts but decided on something serious so if you fellows are looking for humour you had better not read any further.

Most of you fellows are a lot younger than myself, consequently I have learned several things in the past that you will have to learn for yourself in the future. But there is one universal rule you should all know – One cannot derive benefit from anything to a larger extent than the effort he puts into it. A large portion of daily camp routine cold [*sic*] be eliminated through each man understanding that this is his home for the time being and is to be treated as such. You wouldn't have to police up daily if everyone was thoughtful enough to throw ciggarttes [*sic*] papers and such where they belong. But since a few are not thinking, the whole company will have to police just as long and just as often as needs be until those few do learn.

The civilian conservation corps was created for a temporary reason only, and one of these days sooner or later, everyone of us will have to go into the world seeking employment. How much easier it will be if we have learned to give eight hours honest effort every day, because almost all of us will be employed for at least this length of time. Modern business has no room for "coldbrickers" and the ones who elect to shirk their duties will always find themselves out of a job. To the men who day after day do the task assigned to them I have this to say, that you will always have some satisfaction of a job well done, and that in itself will lead to happiness.

Perhaps some of you read the letter from a former enrollee that was on the bullitin [*sic*] board a few days ago. That is typical of the countless letters that have been received by the commanding officer during the past thirty one months. The answers we send, no matter how worded, result in the same thought. You choose to be absent without official leave; to receive a discharge for desertion; and now no one can help you even though you are most sincere in your desire to come back, and even though your family is depending on you for the bread they eat. At the time when your parents, your brothers and sisters needed you most you let them down and chose to go AWOL and receive a discharge for desertion. It's pitiful fellows!

Bob Lear in Newsletter of Waddington Log Camp, Oglebay Park, Wheeling, West Virginia, 19 December 1935, Vol. 1, No. 3, p. 1, Roosevelt Official Files OF 268/9, Roosevelt Library.

2.11 Education in CCC camps, May 1936

The Civilian Conservation Corps fulfilled a variety of roles: work relief, environmental improvement and also education and training. The importance of the latter in developing skills within the unemployed to make them more employable has sometimes been overlooked by New Deal historians.

The educational program in the Civilian Conservation Corps camps has made significant and steady progress during the past year. The objectives of the program have become clearer and more practical, and experience in camp work has developed many new and successful practices. Seventy-four percent of the enrollees are now voluntarily participating in some form of educational activity.

More than 500,000 American youths enrolled in the CCC during the past year. They came from all walks of life – farms, small towns, and cities. They came from homes surrounded by poverty; homes surrounded by luxury before the depression stripped them of all but the barest necessities; homes where educational opportunities were unknown; and homes where living conditions were unwholesome and insanitary. In the camps every enrollee, regardless of the home conditions from which he came, was given an equal chance to prove himself.

The Civilian Conservation Corps provides each enrollee with a ladder of achievement up which he may climb to a position of greater employability and citizenship. If his unemployment and loss of courage were due to his failure to fortify himself against these conditions earlier in life, the CCC gives him an opportunity to work, learn a trade, and make up some of his educational deficiencies. Learning to do by doing is the foundation of the CCC program.

The Civilian Conservation Corps program was initiated by President Roosevelt on March 21, 1933, when he sent a message to Congress asking for passage of legislation which would permit him to take a vast army of young men from city streets and rural homes and give them healthful work in the forests. A bill carrying out the President's recommendations was made law on March 31, 1933. Five days later an executive order was issued creating the office of Emergency Conservation Work and naming Robert Fechner, of Boston, Director. In this same order the Secretaries of War, Interior, Agriculture and Labor were instructed to assist the Director in selecting the men, establishing and operating a nation-wide chain of forest camps and in supervising the work program. Director Fechner's task was to execute the program and coordinate the activities of all departments. Under his direction the Labor Department selects the men and the War Department enrolls them, sets up and operates the camps and feeds, clothes and looks after the men from the time they enter the Corps until they are discharged. The Departments of Interior and Agriculture recommend work programs to the Director and supervise all work except a few projects which are under the supervision of the War Department. The Office of Education acts in an advisory capacity to the War Department in all educational matters. The director of CCC camp education, appointed by the U.S. Commissioner of Education, supervises the work of camp and corps area educational advisers, recommends programs and textbooks and in other ways unifies the educational program.

The major objectives of the Emergency Conservation Work program are:

1. To give employment to hundreds of thousands of young men who were unable to find jobs through ordinary industrial channels.

2. To start the nation on a sound conservation program which would conserve and expand the country's timbered resources.

3. To provide assistance to thousands of families dependent upon public relief for support.

4. To stimulate industry through purchase of supplies, equipment, etc.

5. To build up the morale and physical well-being of the young men

enrolled in the corps, to develop better citizenship, and to prepare them, through educational work, training on the job and other means, to find and maintain a place in the industrial world.

All phases of camp life contribute to the young men's education and development. From the officers commanding the camp he learns the value of regular habits, orderliness, sanitation and personal hygiene. The officer personnel also teaches him something of self-discipline and good citizenship. The work in the forests, parks and fields, under the supervision of the technical services provides training for the men in many practical skills, such as truck driving, operating of tractor and bulldozer, carpentering, stone masonry, and so forth. The educational program through its vocational training, its counseling of enrollees, its general academic instruction, and its coordination of all phases of education in the camps improves the enrollee's chances for finding and holding permanent employment and for making a place for himself in society. Leisure time activities which include publication of camp newspapers, production of plays and minstrel shows, glee clubs and orchestras, while primarily recreational also have educational and vocational possibilities.

Howard W. Oxley (Director of CCC Camp Education), Education in the Civilian Conservation Corps, May 1936, Official Files OF 268, Roosevelt Library.

2.12 White House statement and executive order creating Civil Works Administration to put 4 million unemployed to work, 8 November 1933

The Civil Works Administration, which was created by the executive order reproduced below, had a comparatively short existence from 1933 to 1934. In that time, however, some 4 million men were put to work on such things as road repair.

Four million men now out of employment will be put to work today under a plan announced by the President.

Two million of these will become self-sustaining employees on Federal, State and local public projects on November 16th, and will be taken completely off the relief rolls. An additional two million will be put back to work as soon thereafter as possible.

This plan will be administered by the newly created Civil Works Administration. The President today appointed Harry L. Hopkins as Administrator.

The Civil Works Administration will be financed jointly by funds from the Public Works Administration and the Federal Emergency Relief Administration, but States, cities, counties and towns will be required to provide the funds to meet their share of the Civil Works program.

Secretary Harold L. Ickes, Public Works Administrator, was prepared to make available an amount up to $400,000,000 to the Civil Works Administration.

The two million men comprise those now on work relief provided by local relief administrations operating under the State and Federal Emergency Relief Administrations. These will immediately be placed on regular pay at the hourly rates prevailing for similar work in the community. The program contemplates a thirty-hour week for the workers.

For full text see *The Public Papers and Addresses of Franklin D. Roosevelt*, Vol. 2 (New York, Random House, 1938), pp. 454–5.

2.13 Statement on the National Youth Administration, 26 June 1935

Established in 1935, the National Youth Administration provided part-time jobs for students, aged 16 to 25, in high schools, colleges and universities. The aim was to allow students to support themselves during their studies, and thereby to minimise the pool of potential unemployed. One further future repercussion would be a more highly educated workforce.

Satisfactory progress in setting up the work program for the unemployed is being made. This program calls for the removal of unemployed from direct relief to jobs and should be well under way during July.

I have determined that we shall do something for the Nation's unemployed youth because we can ill afford to lose the skill and energy of these young men and women. They must have their chance in school, their turn as apprentices and their opportunity for jobs – a chance to work and earn for themselves.

In recognition of this great national need, I have established a National Youth Administration, to be under the Works Progress Administration.

This undertaking will need the vigorous cooperation of the citizens of the several States, and to insure that they shall have an important part in this work, a representative group will be appointed to act as a National Advisory Board with similar Boards of citizens in the States and municipalities throughout the country. On these Boards there shall be representatives of industry, labor, education and youth because I want the youth of America to have something to say about what is being done for them.

Organizations along State and municipal lines will be developed. The work of these organizations will be to mobilize industrial, commercial, agricultural and educational forces of the States so as to provide employment and to render other practical assistance to unemployed youth.

It is recognized that the final solution of this whole problem of unemployed youth will not be attained until there is a resumption of normal business activities and opportunities for private employment on a wide scale. I believe that the National Youth Program will serve the most pressing and immediate needs of that portion of unemployed youth most seriously affected at the present time.

It is my sincere hope that all public and private agencies, groups and organizations, as well as educators, recreational leaders, employers, and labor leaders will cooperate whole-heartedly with the National and State Youth Administrations in the furtherance of this National Youth Program.

The yield on this investment should be high.

For full address see *The Public Papers and Addresses of Franklin D. Roosevelt*, Vol. 4 (New York, Random House, 1938), pp. 381–2.

2.14 Works Progress Administration Handbook, 1936

The Works Progress Administration was set up in April 1935 and incorporated some of the lessons learned with the Civil Works Administration. In 1939 it changed its name to the Works Projects Administration. Harry Hopkins was the senior administrator of the WPA, which employed millions of the unemployed on diverse projects ranging from the Federal Theater Project to road construction. One of the fundamental ideas behind the WPA was to make use of the skills of the individual unemployed. There was little sense, it seemed, in employing white-collar workers as manual labourers. Over 8 million people were employed by the WPA between 1935 and 1943.

Question. What is WPA?

Answer. The WPA is one of several Federal agencies established by the President and Congress to bring about recovery by giving work to the unemployed.

Q. Are there other agencies of the Government that have been set up to provide work for the unemployed?

A. Yes. Among these are the Public Works Administration (PWA), Civilian Conservation Corps (CCC), Resettlement Administration (RA).

Q. What is the largest number of workers these agencies ever employed?

A. During February 1936 the total number of men and women working was 3,853,000. As a result of an increase in private industry and seasonal agricultural employment more than 500,000 fewer are employed on work projects now (July 1936).

Q. Does the WPA give relief without work?

A. No. Direct relief is generally taken care of by the local people.

Q. Can any unemployed person get a job on WPA?

A. No, only those able-bodied unemployed persons who are in greatest need and who have been so certified by a local agency.

Q. Will all those certified by such local agency be given work?

A. Not necessarily. WPA is limited by the amount of money appropriated by Congress.

Q. How many people in one family are allowed to work on WPA?

A. Generally only one. If the family has a boy in the CCC camps or one of the family is getting work with the National Youth Administration (NYA), that does not necessarily keep the head of the family from working on WPA. Of course, no one under 18 years of age can be hired, except in NYA.

Q. Can old people or sick people work on WPA?

A. Certainly not if they are sick or so old that it is not safe for them or for others who work around them.

Q. Do race or color or beliefs keep a man from getting work on WPA?

A. No.

From http://newdeal.feri.org/texts/393.htm.

2.15 Works Progress Administration Guides, 1937

Reducing the number of the unemployed required considerable ingenuity. Planting new forests might be suitable work for physically fit young men, but there were thousands of others unsuited to manual labour. In finding work for such people, the Works Progress Administration recognised that not only was there a need to reduce the number of unemployed, but that their skills could be utilised for the long-term betterment of America. Unemployed writers, artists, photographers, actors, researchers and others could make a contribution to the nation that would sharpen their skills and put them back into work. For example, under the Federal Art Project 1,566 murals and 108,099 paintings were painted. Under the Federal Theatre Project 77 new plays were commissioned and over a thousand were performed. The Federal Writers Project was a further example of how the skills of white-collar workers might be utilised while reducing the number of unemployed. Under the Federal Writers Project teams of researchers and writers were set to work to compile a guide to each of the American states, involving people as well as places. The folklore of a state was considered as important as its geography. As a snapshot of the American states the Works Progress Administration Guides formed a valuable historical resource. Here, in the introduction to the Guide for Massachusetts, Harry Hopkins explains the purpose of the project.

Massachusetts: A Guide to Its Places and People is one of the volumes in the American Guide Series, written by members of the Federal Writers' Project of the Works Progress Administration. Designed primarily to give useful employment to needy unemployed writers and research workers, this project has gradually developed the ambitious objective of presenting to the American people a portrait of America, – its history, folklore, scenery, cultural backgrounds, social and economic trends, and racial factors. In one respect, at any rate, this undertaking is unique; it represents a far-flung effort at cooperative research and writing, drawing from all the varied abilities of its personnel. All the workers contribute according to their talents; the field worker collects data in the field, the research worker burrows in libraries, the art and literary critics cover material relevant to their own specialities, architects describe notable historical buildings and monuments; and the final editing of copy as it flows in from all corners of a state is done by the more experienced authors in the central offices. The ultimate product, whatever its faults or merits, represents a blend of the work of the entire personnel, aided by consultants, members of university faculties, specialists, officers of learned societies, oldest residents, who have volunteered their services everywhere most generously.

A great many books and brochures are being written for this series. As they appear in increasing numbers we hope the American public will come to appreciate more fully not only the unusual scope of this undertaking, but also the devotion shown by the workers, from the humblest field worker to the most accomplished editors engaged in the final rewrite. The Federal Writers' Project, directed by Henry G. Alsberg, is in the Division of Women's and Professional Projects under Ellen S. Woodward, Assistant Administrator.

From *Massachusetts: A Guide to its Places and People* (New York, Houghton Mifflin, 1937), p. vii.

2.16 Reform of the Public Works Administration, 1936

The Public Works Administration was set up in 1933 under the provisions of the National Industrial Recovery Act to provide work for the unemployed on developing the national infrastructure of roads, schools, dams and bridges. Between 1933 and 1939, under the control of the Secretary of the Interior, Harold Ickes, some 500,000 men were employed on over 34,000 projects. Although Ickes was comparatively conservative in his approach towards relief, the PWA was much criticised over the sums which it was spending. Public criticism led in 1936 to a major disagreement between Ickes and the President. It took all the skill of the latter to calm the former.

My dear Mr President:

I find myself differing fundamentally with your work-relief program as extended and modified under the bill now pending before the Senate. As I see it, the passage of this bill as written will destroy the Public Works Administration, a purpose which was indicated in statements made by you at a recent press conferences by which, in effect, you repudiated PWA and indicated a lack of confidence in me as Administrator. Little doubt of your attitude in this matter remains in my mind in view of your statement at the Cabinet meeting today when your orders made it impossible for me to respond to the request of the Senate Appropriations Committee to present a statement of what PWA has accomplished to date.

In the circumstances I have no option but to tender my resignation, both as Secretary of the Interior and as Administrator of Public Works …

Sincerely yours,
Harold L. Ickes
Secretary of the Interior

Dear Harold

1. PWA is not "repudiated."
2. PWA is not "ended."
3. I did not "make it impossible for you to go before the committee."
4. I have not indicated lack of confidence.
5. I have full confidence in you.
6. You and I have the same big objectives.
7. You are needed, to carry on a big common task.
8. Resignation not accepted!

Your affectionate friend,
Franklin D. Roosevelt

Harold L. Ickes, *The Secret Diary of Harold L. Ickes, 1933–36* (New York, Simon and Schuster, 1954), pp. 592–4.

AGRICULTURE

2.17 Remarks on signing the Farm Relief Bill, 12 May 1933

After his inauguration Roosevelt moved swiftly to address the problem of agriculture. The 1933 Agricultural Adjustment Act tried to limit agricultural over-production in order to raise farm incomes. The Act was coupled with the signing of a Farm Relief Bill which tried to stem the tide of foreclosures on farm mortgages. While the Agricultural Adjustment Act was a long-term measure designed to address the issue of farm income, the Farm Relief Bill was a shorter-term measure to address the mounting debts of farmers.

I have just signed the Farm Relief Bill, which includes the refinancing of farm debts.

The Act extends relief not only to farmer borrowers, but to mortgage creditors as well.

Holders of farm mortgages will have the privilege of exchanging them for Federal Land Bank bonds, the interest payments upon which are to be guaranteed by the Treasury of the United States.

Farmers whose mortgages are to be exchanged for these bonds will reap the benefit of lower interest rates and more liberal terms of payment.

It is to the interest of all the people of the United States that the benefits of this Act should be extended to all who are in need of them and that none should be deprived of them through ignorance or precipitate action.

For full address see *The Public Papers and Addresses of Franklin D. Roosevelt*, Vol. 2 (New York, Random House, 1938), pp. 175–83.

2.18 Roosevelt to Edward O'Neil, President of the American Farm Bureau Federation, on the improvement of agriculture, 8 December 1933

In a letter read to members of the American Farm Bureau Federation on 11 December 1933, Roosevelt voiced his continuing support for the principles of the Agricultural Adjustment Act.

The members of the Farm Bureau know, as I do, that the maladjustment between supply and demand has been years in the making, and that it cannot be corrected overnight. Nevertheless, in a few short months the whole complexion of the agricultural outlook has been changed. Money is getting into the hands of the people who need it; it is coming from higher prices for the things farmers have to sell; it is coming in the form of Government checks for those cooperating producers who are willing to swap a hazardous present for immediate improvement and a stable future. This money is paying bills; it is putting men back to work in the cities producing the things that farmers buy, and enabling those men in turn to buy things that farmers produce. The process has already gone a long way in the South among the cotton and tobacco growers; wheat growers are beginning to experience it now, and the farmers of the corn belt will soon be in a position to experience it from the corn-hog adjustment campaign.

For full address see *The Public Papers and Addresses of Franklin D. Roosevelt*, Vol. 2 (New York, Random House, 1938), pp. 520–1.

2.19 Article by William Amberson on the New Deal for sharecroppers, 13 February 1934

The sharecropper system, whereby tenant farmers would farm the land in exchange for a share of the crops grown, was widely blamed for rural poverty in the South.

Ultimately the plantation system must be liquidated. Dr. J. H. Dillard is quite justified when he writes: "Damn the whole tenant system.

There can be no decent civilization until it is abolished." We must do away with the whole antiquated scheme of landlord–tenant arrangements, to which there must always cling many of the worst features of chattel slavery without its benefits.

Forces are already working to accomplish this liquidation. Universal bankruptcy has threatened and will threaten again, as cotton prices fluctuate and interest and taxes pyramid. Official Washington is by no means entirely oblivious to the present situation; the basic difficulty is the lack of a unified program. The rural rehabilitation program of the FERA is establishing thousands of destitute families on a new and more independent basis, which may represent the entering wedge of a force that will ultimately transform the present system. The urgent need for a change has now been recognized by the PWA Mississippi Valley Committee, which in its report to Secretary Ickes advocates a federal program which will enable all tenants to acquire ownership of land. The alternative method of large-scale cooperative farms must also be tested. If tenure is absolutely guaranteed, without power to sell or mortgage, possibly on long-term leases from the government under a Federal Loan Authority, it will free a whole people from their present shackles and make possible the education of a more responsible and effective generation than the South has ever known.

The Nation, 13 February 1934, Vol. 140, No. 3632, p. 385.

2.20 Address on the Agricultural Adjustment Act, 14 May 1935

As the holder of a major estate Roosevelt was deeply interested in agriculture and its problems. With the 1933 Agricultural Adjustment Act under challenge in early 1935, he felt it important to lend his public support.

When we came down here to Washington that spring we were faced with three possible ways of meeting the situation. The first method that was suggested involved price fixing by Federal decree. We discarded that because the problem of overproduction was not solved thereby.

The second plan was to let farmers grow as much as they wanted of everything, and to have the Federal Government then step in, take from them that portion of their crop which represented what we called the exportable surplus and, in their name and on their behalf, dump this surplus on the other Nations of the world. We discarded that plan for a good many reasons and one was because the other Nations of the world had already taken steps to stop dumping. From that time on, with increasing frequency they were raising their tariffs, establishing quotas and clamping on embargoes against just that kind of proposition. And that is why we discarded that.

Therefore, we came to the third plan – a plan for the adjustment of totals in our major crops, so that from year to year production and consumption would be kept in reasonable balance with each other, to the end that reasonable prices would be paid to farmers for their crops and unwieldy surpluses would not depress our markets and upset the balance.

We are now at the beginning of the third year of carrying out this policy. You know the results thus far attained. You know the present price of cotton, of wheat, of tobacco, of corn, of hogs and of other ham products today. Further comment on the successful partial attainment of our objective up to this time is unnecessary on my part. You know.

For full address see *The Public Papers and Addresses of Franklin D. Roosevelt*, Vol. 4 (New York, Random House, 1938), pp. 175–80.

2.21 Address on agriculture, Fremont, Nebraska, 28 September 1935

In September 1935 Roosevelt could be found addressing farmers directly on the subject of agriculture. His choice of audience was symbolic of his identification with his fellow farmers.

It is almost exactly three years ago that I visited farms in this State; at that time I saw farmers threshing thirty-cent wheat and shelling twenty-cent corn. Much has happened during the three years that followed. At that time the prices of farm products were falling lower and even lower as markets vanished and surpluses accumulated; farm buildings and farm equipment were deteriorating month by month; soil fertility was being sapped as farmers struggled to raise enough bushels to meet their debts and their taxes. Country schools were closing and, most disheartening of all, thousands of farmers were losing their homes by foreclosure. That was true not only in this part of the great West, but it was true also in practically every State of the Union – North, South, East and West. That man-made depression – because it was that – was, as we know, followed in many parts of the country by the most severe drought in our recorded history ...

Three years ago I did not promise the millennium for agriculture. But I did promise that I should attempt to meet an intolerable situation – to battle that situation in every way that human effort and human ingenuity could devise. I said that I should do my best, and that if my efforts proved unsuccessful, I should tell the country frankly and try something else. But that was not necessary ...

The burden of agricultural debt, it is true, has not been eliminated, but it has been decisively and definitely lessened. Loans have been made through the Farm Credit Administration to nearly half a million farmers in this country since May, 1933 ...

My second effort in the immediate improvement of the farmer's position was to get him not only a relatively, but an absolutely, better return for his products ... From the summer of 1929, to the time when I took office in 1933, the prices of farm products, that is to say, the things that the farmer had to sell, had declined by 62 percent, while the prices of the things the farmer had to buy had fallen only 35 percent. Thus, the farmer of the Nation, on the average, had to use twice as many bushels of wheat, twice as many bushels of corn, twice as many tons of hay, twice as many hogs, twice as many bales of cotton, twice as much of all of his products, in order to buy the same amount of things that he needed. The closing of that gap was an important objective of this Administration. It still is, and we shall bend our efforts to hold the gains that we have made. The gap that was the measure of the farmer's despair and distress, after two and a half years of effort, in large part has been closed.

For full address see *The Public Papers and Addresses of Franklin D. Roosevelt*, Vol. 4 (New York, Random House, 1938), pp. 379–86.

2.22 Executive order 7027 establishing the Resettlement Administration, 1 May 1935

The Resettlement Administration was established in May 1935. It provided support to help farmers move from marginal land to more fertile areas. Low interest loans provided by the Resettlement Administration helped over 750,000 farming families to move to what they hoped would be a better life. Although the issue of resettlement was a comparatively small part of the New Deal, the issue was given a high profile by the publication of John Steinbeck's novel *The Grapes of Wrath* in 1939. It was turned into a major motion picture starring Henry Fonda the following year.

By virtue of and pursuant to the authority vested in me under the Emergency Relief Appropriation Act of 1935, approved April 8, 1935 (Public Resolution No. 11, 74th Congress), I hereby establish an agency within the Government to be known as the "Resettlement Administration," and appoint Rexford G. Tugwell, Undersecretary of Agriculture, as Administrator thereof, to serve without additional compensation.

I hereby prescribe the following functions and duties of the said Resettlement Administration to be exercised and performed by the Administrator thereof:

(a) To administer approved projects involving resettlement of destitute or low-income families from rural and urban areas, including the establishment, maintenance, and operation, in such connection, of communities in rural and suburban areas.

(b) To initiate and administer a program of approved projects with respect to soil erosion, stream pollution, seacoast erosion, reforestation, forestation, and flood control.

(c) To make loans as authorized under the said Emergency Relief Appropriation Act of 1935, to finance, in whole or in part, the purchase of farm lands and necessary equipment by farmers, farm tenants, croppers or farm laborers.

In the performance of such duties and functions the Administrator is hereby authorized to employ the services and means mentioned in subdivision (a) of Section 3 of the said Emergency Relief Appropriation Act of 1935, to the extent therein provided, and, within the limitations prescribed by said Section, to exercise the authority with respect to personnel conferred by subdivision (b) thereof.

To the extent necessary to carry out the provisions of this Executive Order the Administrator is authorized to acquire, by purchase or by the power of eminent domain, any real property or any interest therein and improve, develop, grant, sell, lease (with or without the privilege of purchasing), or otherwise dispose of any such property or interest therein.

The acquisition of articles, materials, and supplies for use in carrying out any project authorized by this Executive Order shall be subject to the provisions of Title III of the Treasury and Post Office Appropriation Act, fiscal year 1934 (47 Stat. 1489, 1520).

For the administrative expenses of the Resettlement Administration there is hereby allocated to the Administration from the appropriation made by the Emergency Relief Appropriation Act of 1935, the sum of $250,000. Separate allocations will be made hereafter for each of the authorized activities as may be needed.

For full address see *The Public Papers and Addresses of Franklin D. Roosevelt*, Vol. 4 (New York, Random House, 1938), pp. 143–55.

2.23 What is resettlement?

The roles and responsibilities of the Resettlement Administration were explained in the *Democratic Digest* in late 1935.

There's a big job ahead for the Resettlement Administration. It's to help some three-quarter of a million rural and urban families to get a new start in life. It's not merely to remove them from the rolls of present or potential relief clients, but to plan so that they may become and remain independent and self-supporting for a long time to come.

Many families are now living in localities where there was every opportunity to make an excellent living when their grandfathers or great grandfathers settled there. Advances in transportation, mechanization, science, growth of large industrial centers and the wastage of natural resources have all contributed to change this prospect. As a result, the population which moved in to do certain jobs, or to exploit certain natural resources is now left stranded without any means of sustaining themselves because the resources or industries are gone.

What's to be done? Bound as they are by lack of finances, in some instances even the physical requirements of decent living, they are incapable of extricating themselves from their present non-economic situation. Outside help is required.

It was to create new opportunities for such families that the Resettlement Administration was established under the authority of the Emergency Relief Appropriation Act of 1935.

Farm families living on sub-marginal land will be helped to relocate on more productive land and to establish themselves under more favourable conditions.

Low-income families employed in industry will have a chance to obtain suitable low-cost housing and wholesome living conditions.

Another most important job of this administration is to buy worn out land and devote it to the best possible uses. This briefly is the program of the Resettlement Administration which will be carried out by its four development divisions.

The main concern of the Rural Rehabilitation Division of the Resettlement Administration is aid for farm families. This work has two phases, Rehabilitation supplies funds for the purchase of land, livestock, seed, equipment and supplies, plus guidance in home and farm management. This is the first phase. With such aid, many a family is enabled to put its present farm back on a paying basis. Sometimes, however, this formula doesn't work. The present holdings may be so poor that even by diligent application of the old adage of hard work and lots of it the family cannot get a living from the soil.

> "We have made costly mistakes in the past. We expected too much from the land. We used it as an inexhaustible source of wealth which could be abused without penalty. We thought in terms of a single tenancy, a single lifetime, rather than in terms of a permanently rooted culture, developing through the generations toward something richer and more secure. All of these mistakes have now to be repaired; but it is a characteristic of our breed, or so I like to think, that once these mistakes have been clearly demonstrated, we have gone to work, without too much recrimination, to repair the damage and to found a new policy."
> R G Tugwell, Resettlement Administrator

In such cases, the only permanent solution is to assist the families to move to more productive land. This is resettlement, or the second phase.

Home economists play an important part in the development of the Rural Resettlement Division's program. It's the budgeting and guidance that go with the actual cash advances that in ninety-nine cases out of a hundred insures the family eventually achieving a healthful and adequate livelihood. A home supervisor is in personal contact with every family participating in the rural resettlement programme. These supervisors visit the families and obtain information as to the amount and condition of the food, clothing, fuel and equipment which they have on hand, what they are now producing, what they plan to produce at home, and what must be purchased. In other words, each homemaker is helped to make up a budget for the family for the coming year and to carry out the plans outlined....

Closely allied with the work of the Rural Resettlement Division is that of the Land Utilization Division. Although poverty in rural areas is not due to any one cause alone, we do know that it is invariably closely related to an unwise use of the land. Families are attempting to secure their livelihood by cultivating land too poor in fertility, too rocky, too hilly, too isolated, or too dry, to make successful farming possible. In some instances destructive farming practices for a generation or more have robbed the soil of its fertility while other lands have been settled that had better never been put to the plough. Wind and water erosion have done their part in destroying other once productive acres.

Dorothy McKinnon, 'What's Resettlement', *Democratic Digest*, December 1935, pp. 13–14, Official Files OF 15682, Roosevelt Library.

2.24 The signing of the Soil Conservation and Domestic Allotment Act, 1 March 1936

In response to the Supreme Court's decision in early 1936 that the 1933 Agricultural Adjustment Act was unconstitutional, the Soil Conservation and Domestic Allotment Act of 1936 tried to limit agricultural over-production by soil conservation measures. This marked a shift away from the Agricultural

Adjustment Act that had tried to control production by crop control. In 1938 Congress passed a further Agricultural Adjustment Act giving the Secretary of Agriculture the power to pay farmers to grow crops to improve soil fertility, and limiting the acreage of staple crops and farm products.

This legislation represents an attempt to develop, out of the far-reaching and partly emergency efforts under the Agricultural Adjustment Act, a long-time program for American agriculture.

The new law has three major objectives which are inseparably and of necessity linked with the national welfare. The first of these aims is conservation of the soil itself through wise and proper land use. The second purpose is the reestablishment and maintenance of farm income at fair levels so that the great gains made by agriculture in the past three years can be preserved and national recovery can continue. The third major objective is the protection of consumers by assuring adequate supplies of food and fibre now and in the future ...

In general, the new farm act follows the outlines of a longtime policy for agriculture which I recommended in my statement of October 25, 1935. The wise use of land which it seeks to encourage involves sound farm practice and crop rotation as well as soil conservation ...

Sound farming is of direct interest not only to farmers, but to consumers. To the extent that the new plan succeeds in its aim of preserving and improving farm lands, consumers will share substantially in the benefits. In years of surplus, consumers may lightly take for granted the continuance of adequate supplies of food and fibre; but the recurring dust storms and rivers yellow with silt are a warning that Nature's resources will not indefinitely withstand exploitation or negligence ...

For a long time, I have felt that there was need for concerted action to promote good land use. Years ago, as Governor of the State of New York, I took such steps as I could in that direction, and I described them in detail in a speech at French Lick, Indiana, June 2, 1931, on the subject "Acres Fit and Unfit." I said that, having reached a determination as to the best use of land, "we arrive at once at the larger problem of getting men, women and children – in other words, population – to go along with a program and carry it out." I said, "Government itself must take steps, with approval of the governed, to see that plans become realities."

As I made that speech, I was thinking in terms of my State, of other States and of the Nation. Now this new Act incorporates a system of Federal aid to function when State cooperation with the Federal Government can be arranged.

For full text see *The Public Papers and Addresses of Franklin D. Roosevelt*, Vol. 4 (New York, Random House, 1938), pp. 150–2.

THE TENNESSEE VALLEY AUTHORITY

2.25 Revolution by electricity

The Tennessee Valley Authority Act of May 1933 introduced an integrated approach to the economic problems of a particular area, the Tennessee Valley that stretched across seven states in the South. The Tennessee River would be controlled through the introduction of dams that would in turn produce cheap hydro-electric power. Schools would be built, and industry would be encouraged to relocate to an area where land and power were cheap and an educated workforce was available. Farming would be improved in the valley with the introduction of new crops and practices.

It is possible that history's verdict on the Roosevelt administration is being formed, not in Washington, but in the valley of the Tennessee River. Washington today is a city of desperate expedients, of brilliant (or not so brilliant) improvisations, of a frantic battle to hold things together until familiar processes can be induced to resume their working. But the Tennessee Valley is a vast proving-ground on which immediate construction is fitted to the framework of long-range planning in a deliberate effort to produce a new social order. Washington is trying to save the present from disintegration. The Tennessee Valley project is trying to fashion the future of a new America. Washington seeks recovery today. The Tennessee Valley contemplates revolution tomorrow. If Roosevelt loses at Washington he will, of course, lose everywhere. But if Roosevelt wins in the Tennessee Valley he will enter the pantheon of immortal Americans.

By now our wise men are fairly well agreed that the basic requirement to insure the American future is the substitution of some sort of economic planning for the get-rich-quick exploitation of our pioneer period ... Can this be attained under capitalism? The Tennessee Valley is the region in which the administration is trying to find out; the Tennessee Valley Authority is its attempt to prove that economic planning and capitalism are not incompatibles – at least, not when Capitalism is State Capitalism. On other fronts the administration is forced to proceed by rule of thumb, letting today's events control tomorrow's projects. But in the Tennessee Valley the blueprint rules. On this terrain Mr. Roosevelt is making his great gamble to find out whether the sort of future America that must be, can be sustained under the sort of American Government that now is ...

To those Americans who instinctively draw back from experimentation, may I offer this single suggestion ... Before damning what is going on as socialism or communism or anything else, why not give it a little time to see what will happen? It is just possible that the result may turn out to be no *ism* at all, but a richer American life.

Paul Hutchinson, 'Revolution by Electricity', *Scribners Magazine*, Vol. 96, No. 4, October 1934, pp. 193–200.

INDUSTRY

2.26 Roosevelt recommends the National Industrial Recovery Act to Congress, 17 May 1933

The National Industrial Recovery Act, creating the National Recovery Administration, brought in measures to self-regulate industry. The NRA supervised the drawing-up of codes covering such things as prices and labour conditions to control business behaviour. Once approved by the President the codes were backed by force of the law. By 1935, when the Supreme Court ruled that the NIRA was unconstitutional, around 500 trades were covered by the codes.

To the Congress:
Before the Special Session of Congress adjourns, I recommend two further steps in our national campaign to put people to work.

I

My first request is that the Congress provide for the machinery necessary for a great cooperative movement throughout all industry in order to obtain wide reemployment, to shorten the working week, to pay a decent wage for the shorter week and to prevent unfair competition and disastrous overproduction.

Employers cannot do this singly or even in organized groups, because such action increases costs and thus permits cut-throat underselling by selfish competitors unwilling to join in such a public-spirited endeavor.

One of the great restrictions upon such cooperative efforts up to this time has been our anti-trust laws. They were properly designed as the means to cure the great evils of monopolistic price fixing. They should certainly be retained as a permanent assurance that the old evils of unfair competition shall never return. But the public interest will be served if, with the authority and under the guidance of Government, private industries are permitted to make agreements and codes insuring fair competition. However, it is necessary, if we thus limit the operation of anti-trust laws to their original purpose, to provide a rigorous licensing power in order to meet rare cases of non-cooperation and abuse. Such a safeguard is indispensable.

For full text see *The Public Papers and Addresses of Franklin D. Roosevelt*, Vol. 2 (New York, Random House, 1938), pp. 202–6.

2.27 Presidential statement on the NIRA, 16 June 1933

The NIRA, setting up the NRA, with its system of codes of practice for business, represented the cornerstone of the administration's approach towards the problem of the depression in industry.

The law I have just signed was passed *to put people back to work*, to let them buy more of the products of farms and factories and start our business at a living rate again. This task is in two stages; first, to get many hundreds of thousands of the unemployed back on the payroll by snowfall and, second, to plan for a better future for the longer pull. While we shall not neglect the second, the first stage is an emergency job. It has the right of way.

The second part of the Act gives employment through a vast program of public works. Our studies show that we should be able to hire many men at once and to step up to about a million new jobs by October 1st and a much greater number later. We must put at the head of our list those works which are fully ready to start now. Our first purpose is to create employment as fast as we can, but we should not pour money into unproved projects ...

In my Inaugural I laid down the simple proposition that nobody is going to starve in this country. It seems to me to be equally plain that no business which depends for existence on paying less than living wages to its workers has any right to continue in this country. By "business" I mean the whole of commerce as well as the whole of industry; by workers I mean all workers, the white collar class as well as the men in overalls; and by living wages I mean more than a bare subsistence level – I mean the wages of decent living.

Throughout industry, the change from starvation wages and starvation employment to living wages and sustained employment can, in large part, be made by an industrial covenant to which all employers shall subscribe. It is greatly to their interest to do this because decent living, widely spread among our 125,000,000 people, eventually means the opening up to industry of the richest market which the world has known. It is the only way to utilize the so-called excess capacity of our industrial plants. This is the principle that makes this one of the most important laws that ever has come from Congress because, before the passage of this Act, no such industrial covenant was possible.

For full text see *The Public Papers and Addresses of Franklin D. Roosevelt*, Vol. 2 (New York, Random House, 1938), pp. 251–6.

2.28 The President enumerates the gains under the NRA and recommends its extension for two years, 20 February 1935

By 1935 the administration was well satisfied with the progress of the NRA. The fair labour codes, established under the NIRA, had proved surprisingly successful in many industries.

Industry as a whole has also made gains. It has been freed, in part at least, from dishonorable competition brought about not only by overworking and underpaying labor, but by destructive business practices. We have begun to develop new safeguards for small enterprises; and most important of all, business itself recognizes more clearly than at any previous time in our history the advantages and the obligations of cooperation and self-discipline, and the patriotic need of ending unsound financing and unfair practices of all kinds.

Hand in hand with the improving of labor conditions and of industrial practices we have given representation and consideration to the problems of the consuming public. And it is reasonable to state that with certain inevitable exceptions in the case of individual products there has been less gouging in retail sales and prices than in any similar period of increasing demand and rising markets.

The first codes went into effect in July, 1933. Since then approximately 600 have been added. The average age of these codes of fair competition which have been approved – 90 percent of the coverable employments are under code – is less than eleven months – a brief time indeed for the definite achievements already made. Only carping critics and those who seek either political advantage or the right again to indulge in unfair practices or exploitation of labor or consumers deliberately seek to quarrel over the obvious fact that a great code of law, of order and of decent business cannot be created in a day or a year.

For full text see *The Public Papers and Addresses of Franklin D. Roosevelt*, Vol. 4 (New York, Random House, 1938), pp. 80–4.

2.29 Executive order 7075 reorganising the NRA, 15 June 1935

The Supreme Court's ruling that some provisions of the NIRA were unconstitutional forced a dramatic retrenching of the New Deal in June 1935. The administration was forced to try to safeguard key parts of the work of the NRA and the NIRA.

By virtue of and pursuant to the authority vested in me by Title I of the National Industrial Recovery Act (48 Stat. 195), as amended by Senate Joint Resolution No. 113, approved June 14, 1935, it is hereby ordered as follows:

1. The National Industrial Recovery Board created by Executive Order No. 6859 of September 27, 1934, is hereby terminated, and to provide for the continuing administration of the provisions of Title I of the National Industrial Recovery Act there is hereby created the office of Administrator of the National Recovery Administration.

2. The Administrator of the National Recovery Administration shall administer the provisions of Title I of the National Industrial Recovery Act as amended by Senate Joint Resolution No. 113, approved June 14, 1935, and may exercise all of those powers heretofore conferred by Executive Order upon the National Industrial Recovery Board, subject to the limitations upon such powers contained in the said Senate Joint Resolution No. 113, and subject also to the further provisions of this Executive Order ... I hereby appoint James L. O'Neill as Acting Administrator of the National Recovery Administration.

3. For the further administration of Title I of the National Industrial Recovery Act as amended, there is hereby established the Division of Review. The Division of Review shall assemble, analyze, and report upon the statistical information and records of experience of the operations of the various trades and industries heretofore subject to codes of fair competition, shall study the effects of such codes upon trade, industrial and labor conditions in general, and other related matters, shall make available for the protection and promotion of the public interest an adequate review of the effects of the administration of Title I of the National Industrial Recovery Act, and the principles and policies put into effect thereunder, and shall otherwise aid the

President in carrying out his functions under the said Title. I hereby appoint Leon C. Marshall Director of the Division of Review.

4. There is hereby established the Division of Business Cooperation, the function and purpose of which shall be to aid in the voluntary maintenance by trade and industrial groups of standards of fair competition, in the elimination of unfair competition in the employment of labor or in trade practices, and in maintaining sources of information and records of experience useful in the work of the Division of Review, and to otherwise assist in effectuating, so far as possible, the policies of the National Industrial Recovery Act as amended. I hereby appoint Prentiss L. Coonley Director of the Division of Business Cooperation.

5. The Administrator ... shall proceed forthwith to reduce as rapidly as possible the number of persons now employed in the administration of Title I of the National Industrial Recovery Act to the number necessary to perform the duties of such Administration as herein, or hereafter, prescribed ... I hereby appoint George L. Berry Assistant to the Administrator of the National Recovery Administration to represent labor ...

7. All orders and regulations heretofore issued concerning the administration of Title I of the National Industrial Recovery Act are hereby modified to the extent necessary to make this order fully effective.

For full text see *The Public Papers and Addresses of Franklin D. Roosevelt*, Vol. 4 (New York, Random House, 1938), pp. 256–8.

2.30 National labour relations, April 1939

Trying to bring order and calm to America's industrial relations was one of the chief goals of the Roosevelt administration. With the striking down of the NIRA in 1935 the President brought in a new National Labor Relations Act which some were to criticise for being biased in favour of labour. Under it the right to bargain collectively was safeguarded, and a National Labor Relations Board was created to oversee the process. It could investigate labour practices and use the courts to prohibit activity which it deemed to be unfair. The passing

> of the Fair Labor Standards Act in 1938, safeguarding fair practices and standards in labour, further helped the cause of industrial relations. By 1939 the National Labor Relations Board was ready to proclaim itself a success.

The National Labor Relations Act grew out of conditions which produced for labor the maximum of frustration, resentment and incitation to the use of economic or physical force to achieve its ends. With the development of a modern industry the workman had become helpless in dealing with his employer on an individual basis. As Chief Justice Taft had pointed out, "Union was essential to give laborers opportunity to deal on equality with their employer." In theory, the right of employees to organize into unions and to bargain with their employer on a collective basis was acknowledged and accepted ... But in practice the right was a fraud and a delusion. For the employer had complete freedom to retaliate against any employee who sought a solution in collective action by discharging him or refusing to employ him, and thus effectively depriving him of a living ...

The situation cried for reform. Both a method of eliminating needless industrial warfare, and a means for assuring the worker protection in the exercise of elementary human rights, had to be found. The solution adopted by Congress was neither novel nor untried. On the contrary it was based upon half a century of legislation dealing with identical problems in the railroad industry, upon the work of the National War Labor Board in handling Labor relations in war industries during the war, and finally upon two years of intensive experience under Section 7(a) of the National Industrial Recovery Act. The National Labor Relations Act was passed after prolonged consideration ... Finally on July 5, 1935, the Act became effective.

The Act embodies three simple, yet fundamental, principles:

First, the employer must keep hands off the self-organization of his employees and must accept in good faith the practice and procedure of collective bargaining ...

Second, the obligations imposed by the Act must be enforced through a procedure that ... permits the swift and effective protection of the rights guaranteed ...

Thirdly, as implementing the rights of self-organization and collective bargaining, there must be a certain and rapid procedure for determining issues of representation among employees. Specifically, the Act establishes machinery for the investigation of questions concerning representation, with the holding of a secret election where necessary, and for certification of the designated representative.

Today these general principles are not openly challenged.

Report of the National Labor Relations Board to the Senate Committee on Education and Labor, April 1939, Official Files OF 716/4, Roosevelt Library.

2.31 A British commentator is disturbed at the antagonism in labour relations that exists under the New Deal, 19 September 1941

In September 1941 W. J. Brown, General Secretary of the British Civil Service Association, was invited to the United States and Canada to explain the British war effort. His diary records his shock at the extent of industrial unrest which existed under the New Deal, especially with a war looming.

This country terrifies me. Sixteen ships with stuff for Europe and China are tied up in the river, because of a dispute about a war bonus. A general strike in the coal industry threatens. And six times today I have seen pickets outside different establishments bearing placards saying that the establishment is "unfair" to this, that, or the other Union ... And hardly anywhere do I find any sense of the dreadful urgency of the situation in the world.

W. J. Brown, *I Meet America* (London, Routledge, 1942), p. 18.

SOCIAL SECURITY AND THE HOME

2.32 The centrality of social security to Roosevelt's thinking

In 1935 Congress passed an Act which provided unemployment benefits, retirement benefits for retired workers at age 65, death benefits to the families of workers dying before the age of 65, and federal aid for projects at the state level aimed at the disabled and the very young. The benefits were to be paid from a new tax on workers and their employers. The activities and policies of some of Roosevelt's radical opponents meant that to some extent he was forced to address social security. Frances Perkins, however, argued that it was always his intention to address the issue; it was just a question of political timing.

Before his inauguration in 1933 Roosevelt had agreed that we should explore at once methods for setting up unemployment and old-age insurance in the United States ... He always regarded the Social Security Act as the cornerstone of his administration and, I think, took greater satisfaction from it than anything else he achieved on the domestic front.

Frances Perkins, *The Roosevelt I Knew* (London, Hammond & Co., 1947), pp. 225–43.

2.33 The Home Owners Loan Act is signed – the President urges delay in foreclosures, 13 June 1933

While the creation of a social security system seemed a rather distant hope in the crisis of 1933, Roosevelt did take immediate action to stem the tide of foreclosures on mortgages on people's homes. Although the Home Owners Loan Corporation lasted only three years, in that time it helped almost a million home owners to retain their homes by refinancing their mortgages.

In signing the "Home Owners Act of 1933," I feel that we have taken another important step toward the ending of deflation which was rapidly depriving many millions of farm and home owners from the title and equity to their property.

The Act extends the same principle of relief to home owners as we have already extended to farm owners. Furthermore, the Act extends this relief not only to people who have borrowed money on their homes but also to their mortgage creditors.

It will, of course, take a little while to set up the machinery necessary to carry the principles of the Act into effect. In the meantime, I appeal to mortgage creditors and all others who have claims against home owners and ask them, until full opportunity has been given to make effective the refinancing provision of the Home Mortgage Act, that they abstain from bringing foreclosure proceedings and that they abstain from seeking to dispossess the home owners who are in debt to them.

Cooperation between the officials of the Home Owners Loan Corporation, the mortgagor and the mortgagees during the next few months will make many foreclosures unnecessary and will do substantial justice to all parties concerned.

For full text see *The Public Papers and Addresses of Franklin D. Roosevelt*, Vol. 2 (New York, Random House, 1938), pp. 233–7.

2.34 The achievement of a programme of national social and economic security, 19 June 1934

In 1934 Roosevelt set up a committee to investigate the question of social security.

By virtue of and pursuant to the authority vested in me by the National Industrial Recovery Act (ch. 90, 48 Stat. 195), I hereby establish (1) the Committee on Economic Security (hereinafter referred to as the Committee) consisting of the Secretary of Labor, Chairman, the Secretary of the Treasury, the Attorney General, the Secretary of Agriculture, and the Federal Emergency Relief Administrator, and (2) the Advisory Council on Economic Security (hereinafter referred to as the Advisory Council), the original members of which shall be appointed by the President and additional members of which may be appointed from time to time by the Committee.

The Committee shall study problems relating to the economic security of individuals and shall report to the President not later than December 1, 1934, its recommendations concerning proposals which in its judgment will promote greater economic security.

The Advisory Council shall assist the Committee in the consideration of all matters coming within the scope of its investigations.

The Committee shall appoint (1) a Technical Board on Economic Security consisting of qualified representatives selected from various departments and agencies of the Federal Government, and (2) an executive director who shall have immediate charge of studies and investigations to be carried out under the general direction of the Technical Board, and who shall, with the approval of the Technical Board, appoint such additional staff as may be necessary to carry out the provisions of this order.

For full text see *The Public Papers and Addresses of Franklin D. Roosevelt*, Vol. 2 (New York, Random House, 1938), pp. 220–5.

2.35 Message to Congress on social security, 17 January 1935

In January 1935 Roosevelt put his weight behind the report of the Committee on Social Security.

It is my best judgment that this legislation should be brought forward with a minimum of delay. Federal action is necessary to, and conditioned upon, the action of States. Forty-four legislatures are meeting or will meet soon. In order that the necessary State action may be taken promptly it is important that the Federal Government proceed speedily.

The detailed report of the Committee sets forth a series of proposals that will appeal to the sound sense of the American people ...

It is overwhelmingly important to avoid any danger of permanently discrediting the sound and necessary policy of Federal legislation for economic security by attempting to apply it on too ambitious a scale before actual experience has provided guidance for the permanently safe direction of such efforts. The place of such a fundamental in our future civilization is too precious to be jeopardized now by extravagant action. It is a sound idea – a sound ideal. Most of the other advanced countries of the world have already adopted it and their experience affords the knowledge that social insurance can be made a sound and workable project.

Three principles should be observed in legislation on this subject. First, the system adopted, except for the money necessary to initiate it, should be self-sustaining in the sense that funds for the payment of insurance benefits should not come from the proceeds of general taxation. Second, excepting in old-age insurance, actual management should be left to the States subject to standards established by the Federal Government. Third, sound financial management of the funds and the reserves, and protection of the credit structure of the Nation should be assured by retaining Federal control over all funds through trustees in the Treasury of the United States.

At this time, I recommend the following types of legislation looking to economic security:

1. Unemployment compensation.
2. Old-age benefits, including compulsory and voluntary annuities.
3. Federal aid to dependent children through grants to States for the support of existing mothers' pension systems and for services for the protection and care of homeless, neglected, dependent, and crippled children.
4. Additional Federal aid to State and local public health agencies and the strengthening of the Federal Public Health Service. I am not at this time recommending the adoption of so called "health insurance," although groups representing the medical profession are cooperating with the Federal Government in the further study of the subject and definite progress is being made.

For full text see *The Public Papers and Addresses of Franklin D. Roosevelt*, Vol. 4 (New York, Random House, 1938), pp. 43–6.

2.36 Social insurance: radio address by Frances Perkins, 25 February 1935

As the Roosevelt administration pushed its proposals through the legislative system Secretary of Labor Frances Perkins went on the radio to inform the American people about social security.

It has taken the rapid industrialization of the last few decades, with its mass-production methods, to teach us that a man might become a victim of circumstances far beyond his control, and finally it 'took a depression to dramatize for us the appalling insecurity of the great mass of the population, and to stimulate interest in social insurance in the United States.' We have come to learn that the large majority of our citizens must have protection against the loss of income due to unemployment, old age, death of the breadwinners and disabling accident and illness, not only on humanitarian grounds, but in the interest of our National welfare. If we are to maintain a healthy economy and thriving production, we need to maintain the standard of living of the lower income groups in our population who constitute 90 per cent of our purchasing power.

England, with its earlier industrialization, learned this lesson earlier, as well. The world depression caught up with Great Britain sooner than it did with us. She has known the haunting fear of insecurity as well as we. The foresight of nearly three decades has, however, found her somewhat better prepared with the basic framework of a social insurance system. Social insurance in Great Britain has proceeded progressively since the first decade of the century. Championed by the liberal Lloyd George and beginning with the old age pension act of 1908, it has known many revisions and extensions. Since its inception, however, it has gradually overcome the opposition of its critics, and there has never been any thought of abandoning the system. It is today in a healthy state of growth.

Practically all the other industrial countries of Europe have had similar experiences. In the trial and error procedure of Europe's quarter century of social legislation – in that concrete experience – is contained sound truths as well as mistakes from which we can learn much.

But we cannot build solely on European experience. We, with our particular kind of State-Federal Government, our wide, expansive country, with its varying economic and social standards, have many needs different from those of the more closely knit, homogeneous European countries.

The American program for economic security now before our Congress follows no single pattern. It is broader than social insurance, and does not attempt merely to copy a European model. Where other measures seemed more appropriate to our background or present situation, we have not hesitated to deviate from strict social insurance principles. In doing so we feel that we have recommended the measures which at this time seemed best calculated under our American conditions to protect individuals in the years immediately ahead from the hazards which might otherwise plunge them into destitution and dependency.

Our program deals with safeguards against unemployment, with old-age security, with maternal aid and aid to crippled and dependent children and public health services. Another major subject – health insurance – is dealt with briefly in the report of the Committee on Economic Security, but without any definite recommendations. Fortunate in having secured the cooperation of the medical and other professions directly concerned, the committee is working on a plan for health insurance which will be reported later in the year. Our present program calls for the extension of existing public health services to meet conditions accentuated by the depression. Similarly, the provisions for maternal aid and aid to dependent and crippled children are not new departures, but rather the extension and amplification of safeguards which for a number of years have been a recognized part of public responsibility.

Let me briefly describe the other measures now under consideration which do represent something of a departure from our usual course.

Recognizing unemployment as the greatest of all hazards, the committee gave primary emphasis to provisions for unemployment – employment assurance. This measure is embodied in the $4,800,000,000 public works resolution, which is separate from, but complementary to, the economic security bill itself. Employment assurance, the stimulation of private employment and the provision of public employment for those able-bodied workers whom private industry cannot yet absorb is to be solely a responsibility of the Federal Government and its major contribution in providing safeguards against unemployment. It should be noted that this is the largest employment program ever considered in any country. As outlined by the President, it will furnish employment for able-bodied men now on relief, and enable them to earn their support in a decent and socially useful way. It will uphold morale, as well as purchasing power, and directly provide jobs for many in private industry who would otherwise have none.

For the 80 per cent of our industrial workers who are employed, we propose a system of unemployment compensation, or insurance, as it is usually called. In our concern for the unemployed, we must not overlook this much larger group who also need protection.

No one who is now employed can feel secure while so many of his fellows anxiously seek work. Unemployment compensation, while it has distinct limitations which are not always clearly understood, is particularly valuable for the ordinarily regularly employed industrial worker who is laid off for short periods because of seasonal demands or other minor industrial disturbances. He can, during this period when he has a reasonable expectation of returning to work within a short time, receive compensation for his loss of income for a limited period as a definite, contractual right. His standard of living need not be undermined, he is not forced on relief nor must he accept other work unsuited to his skill and training.

Unemployment insurance, wherever it has been tried, has demonstrated its value in maintaining purchasing power and stabilizing business conditions. It is very valuable at the onset of a depression, and even in the later stages will serve to carry a part of the burden of providing for the unemployed. For those who have exhausted their rights to unemployment benefits and for those who, in any case, must be excluded from its provisions, we suggest that they be given employment opportunities on public work projects. In these two measures, employment assurance and unemployment compensation, we have a first and second line of defense which together should form a better safeguard than either standing alone.

The unemployment compensation system has been designed to remove an obstacle which has long prevented progressive industrial States from enacting unemployment insurance laws – fear of interstate competition with States not having such laws. Having removed that obstacle, the law allows the States full latitude to develop the kind of unemployment compensation systems best suited to their individual needs.

Reproduced at www.ssa.gov/history/perkinsradio.html.

2.37 Letter to Federal Housing Administrator James Moffett on progress made under the National Housing Act, 6 March 1935

In June 1934 the Federal Housing Administration (FHA) was created under the provisions of the National Housing Act. The

> FHA provided insurance cover for mortgages advanced by private lenders against possible illness and unemployment on the part of the mortgage holder. By 1935 Roosevelt was satisfied that the FHA was doing an effective job in the campaign of his administration for greater social and home security.

I wish to express, through you, my gratification to the chairmen and members of the Community Better Housing Campaign Committees throughout the country because of the results they have accomplished in less than seven months of activity in calling to the attention of property owners the benefits to be derived under the National Housing Act in modernization and repair and also in construction of new homes.

I am particularly impressed with your statement that 6,174 communities have selected chairmen of their Better Housing Committees, and that between 250,000 and 300,000 volunteer workers are participating through these committees, in the work of acquainting property owners with the uses they can make of the Housing Act. It is good to know also that the Better Housing Committees now have a population coverage of approximately 70,000,000 and that 2,100 of these cities and towns are conducting house-to-house canvasses in which thousands of canvassers, in addition to the committee groups, are carrying on this work. I note that to date calls have been made on over 6,000,000 properties, and that the property owners have pledged 1,100,000 jobs for modernization and repair for a total value of $275,000,000, and that, in addition, you estimate there has already been spent since last August approximately $250,000,000 for modernization and repair.

As you point out, with the continued active cooperation of our civic-minded committees, house-to-house canvasses will be conducted by practically every community campaign committee, with many millions of home owners and business property owners yet to be contacted. This activity means that, with the advent of spring, an immense volume of business and employment will undoubtedly be generated. In other words, the American people will clearly see that the Housing Act provides for the Nation a way back to recovery and prosperity.

For full text see *The Public Papers and Addresses of Franklin D. Roosevelt*, Vol. 4 (New York, Random House, 1938), pp. 104–8.

2.38 Presidential statement upon signing the Social Security Act, 14 August 1935

There was an obvious note of pride when Roosevelt finally signed into law the Social Security Act in August 1935.

Today a hope of many years' standing is fulfilled. The civilization of the past hundred years, with its startling industrial changes, has tended more and more to make life insecure. Young people have come to wonder what would be their lot when they came to old age. The man with a job has wondered how long the job would last.

This social security measure gives at least some protection to thirty million of our citizens who will reap direct benefits through unemployment compensation, through old-age pensions and through increased services for the protection of children and the prevention of ill health.

We can never insure one hundred percent of the population against one hundred percent of the hazards and vicissitudes of life, but we have tried to frame a law which will give some measure of protection to the average citizen and his family against the loss of a job and against poverty-ridden old age.

This law, too, represents a cornerstone in a structure which is being built but is by no means complete. It is a structure intended to lessen the force of possible future depressions. It will act as a protection to future Administrations against the necessity of going deeply into debt to furnish relief to the needy. The law will flatten out the peaks and valleys of deflation and inflation. It is, in short, a law that will take care of human needs and at the same time provide for the United States an economic structure of vastly greater soundness.

I congratulate all of you ladies and gentlemen, all of you in the Congress, in the executive departments and all of you who come from private life, and I thank you for your splendid efforts on behalf of this sound, needed and patriotic legislation.

If the Senate and the House of Representatives in this long and arduous session had done nothing more than pass this Bill, the session would be regarded as historic for all time.

For full text see *The Public Papers and Addresses of Franklin D. Roosevelt*, Vol. 4 (New York, Random House, 1938), pp. 324–6.

2.39 The progress of social security: excerpts from a speech by John Winant, 16 September 1936

John Winant had been Chairman of the original Social Security Board. In September 1936 he reviewed progress over the previous few months.

The act became law on August 14, 1935, and appropriations implementing the Act were made available six months ago. We have gone forward in accordance with the schedule laid down in the law. As you know, the provisions of the act which the Social Security Board administers fall into three categories; first, public assistance; second, unemployment compensation; and, third, Federal Old-Age Retirement Benefits. Under the act, it was the intention of Congress that this wide-spread and coordinated program should first begin to function with respect to the public assistance provisions. These are the provisions which set up a system of Federal grants-in-aid to the States for aid to needy aged persons, to needy blind persons, and to dependent children. In addition, other aspects of the program not administered by the Social Security Board were scheduled to go into effect at once. These are the maternal and child welfare provisions administered by the Children's Bureau of the Department of Labor; the public health provisions administered by the Public Health Service in the Treasury Department, and the vocational rehabilitation provisions administered by the Office of Education in the Department of the Interior. Individual State action is necessary to receive Federal cooperation and aid under all provisions of the act excepting "Old Age Benefits," which is a Federal function.

Every State in the Union is now cooperating in three or more of the welfare programs set up by the act. Also, thirty-nine States and the District of Columbia are now participating in the public-assistance provisions of the act administered by the Social Security Board – which includes aid for needy aged persons, aid for the needy blind, and aid for dependent children. What is the record of acceptance with respect to unemployment compensation in this first year of the program? Briefly, this: Whereas one State only had an unemployment compensation law in operation prior to the passage of the Social Security Act, fifteen States and the District of Columbia now have such legislation. These sixteen laws cover more than 8,000,000 workers, or some 45 percent of the estimated total number of workers to be covered if all States had laws similar in coverage to those already passed.

www.ssa.gov/history/winants.html.

2.40 Progress and security under the Social Security Act

In this address to the National Conference of Social Work on 25 May 1937, Arthur J. Altmeyer, the Chairman of the Social Security Board, went into detail about some of the principles underlying the Social Security Act of 1935 and how those principles were playing out in practice.

Our first great task has been accomplished – the act is working. Through the recent action of the State legislatures which did not meet until 1937, State participation is going forward rapidly. But passing laws is only, as it were, the "curtain-raiser" in the evolution of such a program. It is already possible to distinguish at least three phases of this evolution, each with its distinctive emphasis – first, the double-barreled job of setting up administrative machinery and getting it into motion almost simultaneously; second, the development and integration of administration and of services within the present framework; and third, further expansion to liberalize existing provisions. These phases are not mutually exclusive; we do not complete one before we begin another. Though the initial phase of setting up State plans was the major task of the first year, it is still in process. Though the second phase of consolidating the gains – with the emphasis on quality rather than quantity – is now well under way, it will continue for months and even years. And though the third phase of further expansion is for the most part still in the future, some advances have already been made.

This overlapping process of evolution may seem slow and uneven, but more would almost certainly be lost than gained by attempting to short-cut it. Patience is a virtue which those who labor for social legislation can no more afford to neglect than foresight.

The policy of the Social Security Board has been conceived to facilitate, in so far as possible, these progressive phases in the development of the Social Security Act. In view of the fact that Federal cooperation was imperative if the States were to make these benefits and services available, the Board has been liberal in its interpretation of State conformity to the terms of the act, and has sought to give the States all possible aid in making a beginning. At the same time, it has organized competent field staffs under its Bureaus of Public Assistance and of Unemployment Compensation to work with the States, at their request. The Board is not interested in – nor does it believe the Social Security Act implies – the overhead imposition of rigid requirements; its objective is, rather, the development of comprehensive, well-rounded social security programs, both State and national.

The Board has, for example, consistently pointed out that public assistance cannot be divorced from the total welfare program in any State; that, indeed, there is a very real danger of promoting these services at the expense of other equally essential welfare measures. In most States – including 15 which have just recently passed the necessary legislation – a single State agency now administers all the State's non-institutional welfare activities, both those for which the State alone is responsible and also the Federal–State programs. So also, the same agency administers unemployment compensation and other labor legislation in 22 States, and in three others the agency administering unemployment compensation and that administering other labor laws have an interlocking membership. Although not even the soundest administrative plan can of itself solve all the problems of State coordination, these developments indicate a definite trend toward more effective integration in both public welfare and labor law administration.

www.ssa.gov/history/altm5.html.

2.41 Three year's of progress on social security

In 1938 Arthur J. Altmeyer reflected on the three years since the passing of the Social Security Act. He was convinced that there was much to celebrate.

From another angle, however, looking back to 1935 with our present perspectives, we are presented with a truly astonishing picture of growth and development. In 3 years – a negligible fraction of time in social and economic history – we have established and are operating Nation-wide old-age insurance, Nation-wide unemployment insurance, and Nation-wide public-assistance, public health, and welfare programs. The record of what has already been accomplished covers state and Territory in the Nation and probably affects directly or indirectly almost all the families of the American people.

In the less than 2 years since the old-age insurance provisions of the act were put into operation, we have established a smoothly working machine for the payment of benefits to nearly every man and woman in the country employed in commerce and industry. At the present time 40 million workers – a number approximately 80 percent of all the gainful workers in the country – have applied for old-age insurance accounts, and new accounts are being set up at the rate of about 450,000 a month. The earnings of workers reported by their employers, are being entered on these accounts and lump-sum payments have already been made to thousands of covered workers who have reached age 65 and to relatives or the estates of those who have died.

The job of establishing these millions of wage accounts for the Nation's wage earners and of organizing the details of a system for the payment of benefits when they become due presented an unprecedented administrative undertaking. The maintenance of wage accounts alone has repeatedly been called the biggest bookkeeping job in history. We were faced, furthermore, with the necessity of getting under way as rapidly as possible. Immediate establishment of administrative machinery was made imperative by the provision that claims for single cash payments could be filed even one day after the start of the program, although payment of regular monthly benefits – the major provision of this program – is not scheduled to begin until 1942. Experts in administrative organization and large-scale accounting procedures had begun planning for this enormous task as early as 1935, but the first actual steps were not taken until November of 1936, when the Social Security Board, with the help of the Post Office and the Treasury Departments, began the assignment of social security account numbers. Thanks to the efficiency of the preliminary work and the cooperation of these other Federal agencies, this initial task was well in hand by January 1, 1937, when the old-age insurance program went into effect.

Not even the war-time draft required so high a degree of active cooperation on the part of individual citizens as this Nation-wide initial assignment of account numbers. The rapidity with which it was accomplished is particularly gratifying to the Social Security Board. If evidence were needed, this was evidence in full measure that the American people regard old-age insurance as a great step forward in their march toward social security.

For sheer size and extent, the problem involved in establishing and administering old-age insurance has few parallels, if any. In unemployment insurance, however, the record of State legislative and administrative activity and the development of cooperative working relationships between the Federal Government and the several State authorities, particularly in a field so completely new to this country, is equally remarkable. Prior to consideration of the Social Security Act by Congress, only one State – Wisconsin – had passed an unemployment compensation law. While the act was being debated in Congress, several States enacted such laws; by August 14, 1937, 2 years after the passage of the Federal law, all 51 jurisdictions of the country had enacted unemployment insurance laws and these had been approved by the Social Security Board.

Social Security Bulletin, Vol. 1, No. 8, August 1938. Reproduced at www.ssa.gov/history/aja838.html.

3
New Deal people

Franklin D. Roosevelt was the inspiration and architect of the New Deal, but the New Deal was far from a solo effort. Thousands of individuals, from members of Roosevelt's Cabinet, to civil servants in Washington, to Harvard professors, were intimately involved with the implementation of the policies of the New Deal. The New Deal was a vast collective effort of government action, local and individual responses. In 1932 Roosevelt had a vision of how the problem of the depression might be tackled. It would be up to his lieutenants at the national and local levels to create the details of policy and to oversee their implementation and revision. Chief among his lieutenants were the members of the Cabinet who had particular departmental responsibilities. His first Cabinet appointed in 1933 included the following appointments: Secretary of State, Cordell Hull (replaced by Edward R. Stettinius Junior in 1944); Secretary of the Treasury, William Woodin (replaced by Henry Morgenthau Junior in 1934); Secretary of War, George H. Dern (replaced by Harry H. Woodring in 1937, replaced by Henry L. Stimson in 1940); Attorney General, Homer S. Cummings (replaced by Frank Murphy in 1939, replaced by Robert H. Jackson in 1940, replaced by Francis B. Biddle in 1941); Postmaster General, James A. Farley (replaced by Frank C. Walker in 1940); Secretary of the Navy, Claude A. Swanson (replaced by Charles Edison in 1940, replaced by Frank Knox in 1940, replaced by James Forrestal in 1944); Secretary of the Interior, Harold L. Ickes; Secretary of Commerce, Daniel C. Roper (replaced by Harry Hopkins in 1939, replaced by Jesse Jones in 1940, replaced by Henry Wallace in 1945); Secretary of Labor, Frances Perkins.

3.1 Roosevelt: the 'chief croupier' of the New Deal

In 1934 the American publishers Simon and Schuster published a book entitled *The New Dealers*. Published anonymously, the book represented an early interpretation of the origins, nature and personnel behind the New Deal. It argued that Roosevelt might be the front-man for the New Deal, but behind him lay a group of gifted individuals responsible for developing policies in particular fields. It represented a 'who's who and why in … [a] round up of American Democracy' (p. vii). The book was even-handed, both praising and criticising the Roosevelt administration.

Franklin Delano Roosevelt did not invent the New Deal; he does not own it; it is only by chance that he administers it; it would have come without him and it will go on even if he should cease to be its greatest advertisement.

His relation to the New Deal is not generally understood. He is its master of ceremonies, not the manager of the theater; its chief croupier, not the owner of the casino. He calls the numbers, guides the play and apportions the winnings and the losses. He is not responsible for the run of the luck or of the rules of the game. He is the agent rather than the director of events, the executor rather than the author of destiny.

So heretical will this view of the New Deal be to most people that probably only one man in America would agree unreservedly with these statements. That man is Franklin D. Roosevelt …

His greatest contribution to the New Deal has been moral energy.

His experiments have not been good ground-gainers, but his broken-field running has been phenomenal. Some of his measures have been flat failures, and his judgement both of men and methods leaves much to the imagination.

Partisan tub thumpers will deny this. They will say that Roosevelt is always right. They will point to the long series of new laws, to the bold experiments masquerading as conservatism, to the conservative measures dressed up as radical hussies, and of all the legislative pots and panaceas of the New Deal …

Roosevelt has accomplished … magnificent things, for which he deserves … his due of hero worship, long after his measures have been amended beyond recognition and the men of his choice slip back into the comfortable pygmy stature which is natural to most men.

He has given the people hope.

The country under Hoover was in utter despair, sunk in a moral apathy so profound that it was practically a coma ...

In a series of swift practical moves, Roosevelt restored us to our natural position as one of the world's great powers ...

This achievement is the result of no trickery. He has not done it with mirrors. It is based on his personality. That is to say, his methods are entirely natural to him, they have no element of insincerity, and oppose no barrier of trickery between himself and the public.

Unofficial Observer, *The New Dealers* (New York, Simon and Schuster, 1934), pp. 3–25.

3.2 Frances Perkins: the nature of the New Deal

Frances Perkins, aged 52, was sworn in as Roosevelt's Secretary of Labor on Inauguration Day. She was the first woman to be appointed to the Cabinet. As Governor of New York Roosevelt had appointed her Industrial Commissioner in 1930. She would remain in the Cabinet until 1945. In her memoirs she comments on the relationship of the members of the Roosevelt administration to the New Deal.

It is important to repeat, the New Deal was not a plan, not even an agreement, and it was certainly not a plot, as was later charged. Most of the programmes later called the New Deal arose out of the emergency which Roosevelt faced when he took office at the low point of the depression.

Undoubtedly he agreed with those chosen for the cabinet upon general policy and immediate steps. I had such an understanding with him, but it began with emergency rescue measures. Clearly he had a pattern of fiscal control in mind. I am pretty sure that there was some understanding with Henry Wallace about the Agricultural Adjustment programme, which was also a form of rescue work. But there was no central unified plan. There wasn't time or organization for that. The New Deal grew out of these emerging and necessary rescue actions.

The intellectual and spiritual climate was Roosevelt's general attitude that *the people mattered*. Government programmes designed to give reality to that attitude developed and fitted into one another out of the necessities of the times. The pattern emerged from the necessary action. The action was not projected from a central pattern, but the people mattered.

Frances Perkins, *The Roosevelt I Knew* (London, Hammond & Co., 1947), p. 141.

3.3 Harold Ickes: the social implications of the Roosevelt administration

On his appointment to the Cabinet in 1933 Harold Ickes, a 59-year-old Chicago lawyer, was a recent convert to the Democratic Party. He had been involved in progressive Republican politics before joining the Democrats in 1928. Roosevelt met him for the first time in February 1933 and formed such a high appreciation of him that he immediately asked him if he wanted to serve in the Cabinet. He duly became Secretary of the Interior.

There is now a chance such as there has never been before, not only to consolidate all the social gains to date but to make further substantial advances. In my opinion, there occupies the White House today the most humane, the most understanding and the most socially minded President that these United States have ever had. The slogan, "the forgotten man," was no mere campaign phrase flung trippingly from his tongue as a vote-catching device. It was the expression of a profound conviction, of a mature social purpose. If this was little understood during the campaign it is generally recognized now. President Roosevelt genuinely likes just human beings. This is no pose on his part. It is part of the warp and woof of his character. The people know that there is at the head of their government in Washington a man genuinely and unaffectedly devoted to their interests.

Reduced to its simplest terms, the social revolution of which I have spoken consisted in turning out from the seats of power the representatives of wealth and privilege and exploiting ruthlessness and substituting for them a man whose purpose it is to make this country of ours a better place to live in for the average man and woman. It is not the desire of President Roosevelt, as I understand him, to pull anyone down. It is a passion with him to build people up. But if it is necessary in his process of building up to ward off with his shield the mailed fist of the marauder he will do it ... Our government is no longer a laissez-faire government, exercising traditional and more or less impersonal powers. There exists in Washington a sense of responsibility for the health, safety and well-being of the people. One of President Roosevelt's first announcements was that the government would not permit its citizens to starve. And he has kept the faith. The federal government has not only poured out its treasures to provide food, clothing and shelter for the unemployed, it has sought in every way possible to restore the morale of the people and to reestablish our social order upon a sounder and more durable foundation.

Harold L. Ickes, address given at the 21st annual meeting of Survey Associates. Reproduced in *Survey Graphic*, Vol. 23, No. 3, March 1934, p. 111.

3.4 Harry Hopkins: the South and the work of the Works Progress Administration

Harry Hopkins was one of Roosevelt's closest aides during the New Deal era. From 1933 to 1934 he was director of the Civil Works Administration, and from 1935 to 1938 he was head of the Federal Surplus Relief Administration and the Works Progress Administration. A forceful personality who believed in getting the job done by whatever means were available, he endured frequent criticism of the agencies which he headed. Here Hopkins talks about his visit to Memphis, Tennessee, to meet with the administrators of eleven southern states to discuss how the Works Progress Administration could tackle the problems of the South. It was delivered in a nation-wide broadcast on the Columbia Broadcasting System on 5 August 1938 and a text of it was released to the newspapers for the following day.

The South, with one-fourth of the population, receives one-seventh of the national income. With one-fourth of the people, it has less than one-thirtieth of the life insurance ... If the combined bank deposits of the United States had been distributed in June 1933 on a per capita basis, every person in the North would have received $419, every person in the West $222, and every person in the South only $81 ...

It is certainly not that the other regions have superior resources or superior people. In 1860 the South was rich and prosperous. Crushed by the Civil War and the incredibly vicious period of Reconstruction, it beat its indomitable way back to a measure of prosperity in the next forty years. But the economic and industrial march of other sections had been going steadily ahead – and the South has never regained her relative position ...

There are many factors which have held it back. The after-effects of the Civil War itself, the whole trend of the development of our industrial economy, the tariff, the railroads and the effects of the one-crop system ...

What are some of the things that have been done up to now? The CCC has taken thousands of unemployed young men off the streets and used their energies to preserve the soil and forest assets of the Nation ...

The rural rehabilitation program was started when nearly 400,000 families were on relief in the cotton counties. It was realized that the mere handing out of relief did not rehabilitate a farmer, so in 1934 the Government started making loans to down-and-out farmers instead of giving a dole.

We can be proud of the magnificent work of the Soil Conservation Service in its cooperation with thousands of farmers to preserve the land. Here on the banks of the mighty but muddy Mississippi we need no statistics as to the thousands of tons of precious topsoil carried away daily by water ...

As for the WPA, I cannot help but feel satisfaction and pride in the contributions to better life and better living that it has made. I think about the fact that it has employed jobless teachers who made it possible for one million illiterate grown people in this country to read and write.

It has built, with the sinews of men who had no jobs, enough farm-to-market roads to reach about five times around the world.

The WPA has built sorely needed water and sewer systems, schools, parks and libraries for thousands of communities, large and small. It has provided school lunches for an army of undernourished children.

It has fought malaria all over the South and has advanced the battle against this disease by thirty years.

All those efforts of Federal agencies are good beginnings, but they are *only* beginnings. We must go on or we will go backward; there is no standing still.

National Archives Record Group 69, Series 737, Box 7, Washington.

3.5 Harry Hopkins and the telephone

The telephone was a highly effective weapon in the hands of Harry Hopkins. It allowed him to monitor WPA projects around the country and to respond to any problems. Those telephone calls were transcribed to ensure that a proper record was kept. On 12 April 1934 Hopkins called an official in Charleston, South Carolina, to discuss some problems with a WPA project in the state. The drive, determination and forcefulness of the WPA Administrator caught the official somewhat by surprise.

Mr Hopkins: I want to ask you about an airport you may have heard a lot about, at Laurens, S.C.

SC: Yes, we started some work there, but we've had to stop it because we had no money for materials.

Mr Hopkins: What materials – about how much would you need for materials?

SC: Between $600 and $700; about $600. A congressman called Mr. Miller about that airport. Mr Miller told him that money allotted for this month had been set aside for labor.

Mr Hopkins: Are you fellows on the spot on these airports?

SC: Several Congressmen have been worrying us lately.

Mr Hopkins: There has been a hell of a lot of argument about these airports. They never can see the explanation. How much would it cost to do all the airports in South Carolina that are started?

SC: Well that would be a guess on my part.

Mr Hopkins: $20,000 or $25,000?

SC: Oh, nothing like that. We can do that. We can furnish the labor. They get in a jam over $500 here and $500 there for materials ...

Mr Hopkins: When will you see Mr. Miller?

SC: Probably tonight or tomorrow morning. He has been in a court case for the last two or three days.

Mr Hopkins: Will you tell him about this and ask him to call me tomorrow morning. I am favorably disposed to getting this airport business closed up and I want to find out how much it would cost to do them. I am particularly interested in this one at Laurens.

Record of telephone conversation between Hopkins and an assistant of Mr Miller, Charleston, South Carolina, Hopkins Papers 24/77, Roosevelt Library.

3.6 Hopkins and Ickes compared

> The British Foreign Office was keenly interested in events in the United States and used a variety of informants to keep it abreast of changes in the American scene. Here one of them, Dr Gustav Stolper of Wall Street, New York, gives his impressions of two of the architects of the New Deal.

The right-hand man of the President for the execution of the Lend-Lease program is Harry Hopkins, his closest political friend, known to the world as the organizer of the WPA. Few members of the New Deal family have been more abused and disparaged than Harry Hopkins. Actually Harry Hopkins is probably one of the few ablest organizers whom the United States may muster today. The WPA itself, whatever one may think about its underlying philosophy, was a miracle of organization. Within a few weeks Harry Hopkins had taken off the streets and put to work three million men. He could not be too fastidious in his choice of methods. He was not allowed to be offended by political graft and corruption. He had to take America as it is with all its virtues and vices if he wanted the job done. A man like Ickes who was responsible for PWA would rather leave a job undone than permit graft to interfere. To Ickes honstey [*sic*] always stands above efficiency. Hopkins does not care to reform the world if this impedes his work. Mr Hopkins has no title and no office. He receives a modest salary, has a bedroom in the White House which serves at the same time as his office room. But everybody knows that a telephone call from him or any of his secretaries has the authority of an order from the White House although this informal procedure is not always expeditious and too often creates even greater confusion.

Report 155, 13 June 1941, for the British Foreign Office on Events in America, by Dr Gustav Stolper, Wall Street, New York, British National Archives (Public Record Office) TNA: PRO FO371/26244.

3.7 Henry Morgenthau Jr

Born in 1891 in New York to wealthy parents, in 1913 Henry Morgenthau Jr purchased a farm in Dutchess County, New York. The farm specialized in apple growing and dairy farming. In 1929, when Roosevelt was Governor of New York, Morgenthau was appointed Chairman of the New York State Agricultural Advisory Commission. In the following year he was appointed State Commissioner of Conservation. He played an important role in framing the agricultural policy of the incoming Roosevelt administration in 1932 and on 17 November 1933 he was appointed Acting and Under Secretary of the Treasury when Secretary of the Treasury William Woodin was forced to resign due to ill-health. For eleven years he served as Secretary of the Treasury, raising $450 billion for the federal government in the forms of taxes and loans, while favouring a balanced budget whenever possible. He resigned from the Treasury in July 1945 and died in Poughkeepsie, New York, on 6 February 1967.

Henry Morgenthau, Jr, his [Roosevelt's] Secretary of the Treasury, is an organizer and administrator par excellence. Whether he is anything more than that – except a country gentleman – is not revealed by his shy taciturnity. Certainly, no one has accused him of incubating economic ideas of any sort.

Henry the Morgue – as FDR has playfully called him for many years – has been a member of the Roosevelt gang since 1914. In the fall of 1913 Morgenthau bought some land in Dutchess County, about fifteen miles from the Roosevelt estate. The following spring he met

Roosevelt and thus began a social acquaintance which gradually ripened into close friendship and intimate political association.

Morgenthau is a young man as American politicians go, nine years younger than Roosevelt himself ...

During the 1932 campaign, Roosevelt used him to maintain contact with the farm organizations throughout the country. While Tugwell and M.L. Wilson worked out the crop reduction plan, Morgenthau lined up the farm leaders ...

It was ... on the basis of achievement that Roosevelt sent him to the Treasury, first as Acting Secretary, then as Secretary in his own name. It was a bigger job than he had dreamed of holding, traditionally the biggest job in the Government ...

Yet his actual administration of the job has been both efficient and constructive. In six weeks he gave the Treasury the most severe series of shocks it has had in a generation. He called the bureau heads into his office, ordered them to pay no attention to political influence from either party, and converted these "family conferences" into regular weekly affairs at which each bureau chief has to read a report of the week's work in his bureau ...

The secret of his ability at administration is revealed through the method by which he picks his assistants. He works with two "Brains Trusts." The monetary brains trust – that invisible team of Professors Warren and Rogers – was given to him ready-made. His job is to do what they tell him, through Roosevelt, must be done. For that purpose he has organised a first class administrative brains trust. Here are four of them: Herbert E. Gaston, Herman Oliphant, Roswell Magill and William H. McReynolds.

They were each of them selected as being the best man available for the job ... without reference to politics.

Unofficial Observer, *The New Dealers* (New York, Simon and Schuster, 1934), pp. 106–13.

3.8 Edward R. Stettinius Jr

Edward Reilly Stettinius, the son of a banker, was born in 1900. He worked with General Motors and US Steel before in

1939 becoming a member of the Defence Advisory Committee and chairman of the War Resources Board. In 1941 he became Administrator of the Lend Lease programme. That programme was to have a massive economic impact on the United States. The Lend Lease programme channelled further millions of dollars into the American economy, creating jobs and boosting demand. In this extract from his wartime book on Lead Lease, Stettinius highlights the significance of the war in boosting demand and the American economy.

Hundreds of millions in Lend-Lease funds were directly invested before Pearl Harbor in new factories, shipyards, processing plants, storage depots and other facilities in this country which, taken together, made an important addition to our industrial plant. These investments, now totaling nearly $900,000,000, have been made in thirty-four out of the forty-eight States in the Union. They range in size from more than $142,000,000 for war plants in Michigan to $14,000 for a dry skim-milk plant in North Dakota.

The Lend-Lease program has had an equally marked effect on our capacity to produce food. To meet the new Lend-Lease food needs, the Department of Agriculture announced on April 3rd, 1941, that its "ever-normal granary" program was to be greatly expanded. The Department told the farmers that the Government would support prices of pork, dairy products, eggs and poultry, and other such needed foods "at levels remunerative to producers."

In the following weeks, calls were made for increasing United States annual egg production by 300,000,000 dozen eggs, for increasing milk production by from 6 to 8 per cent, for a one-third increase in cheese production, for packing 15,000,000 additional cases of canned tomatoes, and for a 35 per cent expansion of acreage planted to the dried beans which are so important as a protein substitute for meat in Lend-Lease food deliveries.

Although the support buying program was announced very late in the year to affect 1941 farm production, nevertheless the output of food that year was the greatest we had ever had.

Edward Stettinius, *Lend Lease* (New York, Penguin, 1944), p. 75.

3.9 Henry A. Wallace: the New Farm Act

Henry Agard Wallace, appointed Secretary of Agriculture in 1933, was a key figure in the New Deal. Born in Iowa in 1888, from 1910 onwards he was an assistant editor, and after 1924 editor, of *Wallaces' Farmer*, an agricultural journal. He was recognised as an agrarian expert and his expertise in plant genetics saw him develop several new strains of corn. In politics he was a member of the Republican Party until 1928, but in 1932 he helped to win Iowa for the Democrats. His appointment in 1933 was widely welcomed – American agriculture was now in the hands of an expert. From 1941 to 1944 he was Vice-President of the United States. In 1946 he resigned from the Truman administration in a disagreement over policies towards the Soviet Union. In 1948 he launched his own Progressive Party and campaigned for the presidency. He received over a million popular votes but failed to win a single vote in the electoral college. He died in 1965. Here, in this speech given in March 1938 against the background of a new Agricultural Adjustment Act, he demonstrates his understanding of the importance of soil conservation.

First of all, the New Act continues and strengthens the work of the Triple A on soil conservation. Farmers everywhere in the United States may take part in the program regardless of what crop they grow. So we may think of one part of the Act as making soil conservation an important and enduring framework for the whole program. Then there is another part of the Act. This part makes available certain supplemental measures for the producers of five commodities listed in the Act. These commodities are corn, wheat, cotton, tobacco and rice. Let me enumerate three of the supplemental measures. First national acreages big enough to produce plenty for domestic and export markets and in addition for larger than average carry-overs. Second, storage loans, to put a plank under prices when threatened by a slump and also to finance farmers in holding surplus supplies until they are needed and will bring a good price. Third, marketing quotas which can be used when the Ever Normal Granary overflows, provided always the farmers are so unitedly in favor that at least two-thirds of those taking part in a referendum vote to put the quotas into effect. These new provisions are to be dove-tailed into the AAA soil conservation work. All payments are to be conditioned on soil conservation ... This new Act comes to grips with a big and practical question. That question is how to protect both food supplies and farm income against extreme swings due to tricky weather.

Radio address delivered 7 March 1938.

3.10 Rex Tugwell: 'friend of the reds', 21 March 1933

The opponents of the Roosevelt administration were not above resorting to smear tactics against its leading members. Rex Tugwell, Assistant Secretary of Agriculture in 1933 and later Chairman of the Resettlement Administration, was the target of some particularly vicious attacks.

A vigorous denunciation of the alleged communist sympathies of Prof. Rexford G. Tugwell, Assistant Secretary of Agriculture, marked the House Debate yesterday on the farm bill.

Representative Hart of Michigan, a Democrat, said Mr. Tugwell had been influential in framing the bill, in conference with farm leaders. He then read into the Record from a Communist magazine words of praise for the professor's earlier interest in communistic national planning ...

"Let us see who collaborated in the writing of this bill," Mr Hart said. "Prof. Tugwell of Columbia University, is the Assistant Secretary of Agriculture ... Let us see who Tugwell is. He is a member of the advisory committee of the American Civil Liberties Union. This is the organization which defends anarchists when they shoot somebody. He is one of the ten contributors to Socialistic Planning and Socialistic Progress. This is Mr. Tugwell's history. He spent two years, I am told, in Russia ..."

"This measure will be passed under the cry of 'Back the President,'" Representative Hart said. "I am one of those who started backing our President way back in 1930. I backed him on his banking legislation. I voted for it. I backed him again on the economy measure."

After denouncing the activities of the farm lobby he added: "I cannot go along with any program of this kind."

Earlier in the debate Representative Clarke, of New York, ranking Republican member of the Agriculture Committee, had told the House, "If you read that book by Tugwell, you will find where the Soviet ideas and Socialistic tendencies of this bill come from."

Mr Tugwell is author of a number of works on economics, including two on the Russian system of economic dictatorship.

Washington Post, 22 March 1933, in FBI investigation, subject Rexford Tugwell, FBI files box 2, Roosevelt Library.

3.11 Hugh Johnson: chief of the NRA and *Time* magazine's 1933 man of the year

Hugh Samuel Johnson (1882–1942) was a professional soldier who by 1918 had risen to the rank of brigadier general. Having demonstrated some considerable political and administrative skills during the First World War, in 1933 he was asked to head the National Recovery Administration. His talents were put to good effect settling labour disputes and drawing up codes of fair trading to regulate the activities of businesses across America. With the demise of the NRA in 1935 he was appointed administrator at the Works Progress Agency.

The year was more than one third gone before Man of the Year Johnson burst like a flaming meteorite on the country. On May 19 the *New York Times* first reported that he, "soldier, lawyer and manufacturer," had been offered "almost unlimited powers" under "the pending Industrial Regulation Bill." As administrator of the Wartime Draft General Johnson had enjoyed publicity aplenty, but since then he had been out of sight in the news. After June 16, when the Recovery Act was signed, Man of the Year Johnson's scowl, his broad mouth and furrowed brow, his pithy epithets, the daily state of his health and temper, made acres of newspictures, miles of news copy every 24 hours. He was not the Administrator of NRA. He was NRA. In plotting their common course through the last six months of 1933, future historians will mark well these dates:

July 9 – The cotton textile code is signed, providing a 40-hr. week, $12 minimum weekly wages, abolishing child labor – the first and still the most satisfactory trade agreement. It was arrived at, said General Johnson, "in a goldfish bowl."

July 27 – With heavy industry lagging behind in the codification march, the President sends 5,000,000 "re-employment agreements" to 5,000,000 employers of whom 3,000,000 sign. The Blue Eagle is born ...

Aug. 5 – National Labor Board is created to settle the wave of strikes created by the resurgence of organized Labor.

Aug. 19 – "The most memorable date in NRA history." ... Since early morning, Administrator Johnson has been toiling with three groups of stubborn industrialists. Just before midnight, when the President is leaving for Hyde Park, General Johnson dashes for the White House. "Three major codes signed!" he cries. "That's a day's work!" Estimated jobs created: lumber, 115,000; steel, 50,000; oil, 240,800 ...

Dec. 11 – Some 150 dry cleaners are hauled to Washington for price agreement violations. To the Federal Trade Commission were handed 100 of their cases, NRA's greatest "crackdown." ...

Of the 3,000,000 Blue Eagles NRA has issued, only 48 have been revoked. It has fought eight code violators in the courts, has won seven cases. Pending are twelve more. To date 168 codes have been approved. Seventy-five more will be approved by New Year. Man of the Year Johnson believes that he has put 4,000,000 people to work, [and] has upped the national payroll $2,500,000,000 in the past half-year.

www.time.com/time/special/moy/1933.html.

3.12 Eleanor Roosevelt: the danger of war

Eleanor Roosevelt's marriage to Franklin gave him a political ally just as much as a companion. From the cause of civil rights to the campaign for world peace she was not afraid to give the administration a lead. Over time her views changed, most notably in the way that she drifted away from the pacifist cause to a firm belief in the need to confront fascism. Here we see

Eleanor begin to question her principles in response to the sinking of the gunboat USS *Panay* at the hands of the Japanese air force on 12 December 1937.

At the present time Japan is under the domination of a small military group. I do not think we have pushed her into her actions by anything we have done. Even the wife of the Japanese Ambassador nearly weeps whenever she talks about the Panay incident, and if you will go through the events of the past few weeks, you will notice that Japan has tried deliberately to find out how much England, France, and America would stand without going to war. I think her militarists have decided that we would not stand much more so we may be spared further exhibitions ...

I have never believed that war settled anything satisfactorily, but I am not entirely sure that some times there are certain situations in the world such as we have in actuality when a country is worse off when it does not go to war for its principles than if it went to war.

Reproduced in J. P. Lash, *Eleanor and Franklin: The Story of their Relationship Based on Eleanor Roosevelt's Private Papers* (New York, Signet, 1971), p. 736.

3.13 The Brains Trust

The 'Brains Trust' of the Roosevelt administration attracted considerable public interest and comment. To some it appeared as little more than a novelty; to others it was yet another gimmick. Here James Farley, Roosevelt's campaign manager in 1932 and 1936, explains its origins.

[The Brains Trust] resulted simply from the fact that when Roosevelt was running for President he needed the assistance of people who could give him detailed information and technical assistance on specific problems. For example, while he knew far more about agriculture than most men in public life and knew that it was vitally important to raise the income of the farming class, he needed a lot of statistics on grain exports, the volume of various crops, the relief efforts made by other administrations, and a raft of similar information on which to base his talks. The same was true of banking, relief, and other issues.

The first man brought in was Raymond Moley, a professor at Columbia University, who helped Roosevelt in a study of judicial problems while the latter was still Governor of New York State. He knew his subject thoroughly and was called in time and again when information was needed on other subjects with which he was familiar. When the campaign got under way, a number of others were likewise employed for the same purpose and they met in a group in order to collaborate and to exchange information. The group included Rexford G. Tugwell, another Columbia University man, who was first brought in by Moley ..., Adolph Berle, an authority on banking and corporations, Judge Sam Rosenman, long a close friend and adviser to Roosevelt, and Hugh S. Johnson, who later attained nationwide fame as the dynamic head of the NRA. Basil O'Connor, Roosevelt's former law partner, sometimes acted as an intermediary between the group and Roosevelt, and a number of others, experts on individual subjects, were called in from time to time. The group was wholly informal, and perhaps no one would ever have noticed it except for the fact that an enterprising newspaperman, who, I believe, was James Kieran of the *New York Times*, tagged it with the name "Brains Trust," which stuck and immediately made the group front-page news. Later most of these men came to Washington to assist Roosevelt in the same capacity.

James A. Farley, *Behind the Ballots: The Personal History of a Politician* (New York, Harcourt Brace & Co., 1938), p. 214.

3.14 Foreign policy and the needs of the New Deal

Cordell Hull, who was Secretary of State from 1933 until 1944, was one of the key figures of the Roosevelt administration. Even though foreign policy was secondary to domestic policy for much of the 1930s, he was at pains to emphasise the link between the two.

The outstanding question before the world today is peace. The present Administration is dedicated to a program of constructive effort for peace. It has followed, in all its dealings with other peoples, the good neighbor policy ... The trade agreements program is an instrument for the furthering not only of prosperity but also of peace. The fourteen trade agreements that have been made are not only trade building achievements. They are in every true sense "treaties of commercial peace." These fourteen agreements and those that are to follow are designed not alone to reestablish the flow of mutually profitable trade between the United States and the rest of the world and to restore full and stable prosperity for our nation by reopening adequate foreign markets for our vital surplus-producing branches of agriculture, mining and manufacturing industry. They are also a means of exerting our influence for the reestablishment throughout the world of flourishing trade, based upon equal treatment for all, upon fair-dealing and friendly liberality in international commercial relations ...

They are a solvent for economic distress, which breeds war. Economic distress opens the way for the demagogue and the agitator, foments internal strife, and frequently leads to the supplanting of orderly democratic government. It creates international friction, fear, envy, and resentment, and destroys the foundation of world peace. Some nations are tempted to seek escape from distress at home in military adventures beyond their frontiers. Even peace-loving nations are forced to divert their national effort from the creation of wealth and from well-being to the construction of armaments.

In the past few months we have witnessed a swift increase in international political tension; a recrudescence of the military spirit, which sees no goal in life except triumph by force; an expansion of standing armies; a sharp increase in military budgets; and actual warfare in some parts of the globe. Human and material resources are being shifted, on a truly alarming scale, in a military direction rather than one of peace and peace pursuits.

Through the trade agreements program we have striven to divert the attention of the nations from preparation for armed conflict, born of economic misery and despair, to the preservation of durable peace, based upon economic contentment and prosperity.

Address of Cordell Hull, Secretary of State, in the Auditorium Minneapolis, Minnesota, 7 October 1936, broadcast on the blue network of the National Broadcasting Company, Official Files OF 20, Roosevelt Library.

3.15 New Dealers at the city level: Mayor Edward J. Kelly of Chicago

It was important that enthusiasm for the New Deal extended beyond the boundaries of the federal government to include governors, state officials and city mayors. The latter were particularly important politically. City bosses like Edward Kelly in Chicago, Jim Curley in Boston, Tom Pendergast in Kansas City and Frank Hague in Jersey City had played a major role in delivering the North-East to Roosevelt in 1932.

Second Inaugural Address, April 8 1935
The most important problem facing us is to provide jobs and wages for our men and women who want to work, but who have been denied the opportunity of honest labor.

We will find jobs for these honest citizens – jobs which will enable them to support themselves and their families and enable them to maintain their self-respect.

I have labored with my own hands and I know the joy that comes to a man from putting in an honest day's toil, knowing that as a result he is able to support himself and family.

Chicago always has been a city of workers, and we will keep it that way. Work and wages – not unemployment – that is our goal for every Chicagoan able to work.

We hope to give every earnest and willing man and woman in Chicago the opportunity to earn a decent living. Nothing is of greater importance.

We will restore courage, hope and ambition in the hearts of Chicagoans. We will never permit a generation to grow up discouraged, pessimistic and without hope. We older citizens have a responsibility to the boys and girls of Chicago, in our country and in our American institutions.

The surest way of getting that faith is by opening the doors of opportunity to these youngsters. It is our duty to prove to them that industry and honesty will be rewarded. That can be done by a program that means jobs and wages.

To aid in getting more work and more wages, the City has planned projects involving the expenditure of more than Seven Hundred

Million dollars. These have been submitted to the Federal government for examination, consideration and approval of such as they deem most advantageous.

I hope and confidently expect that a large part of this program will be approved by Washington. It provides for public improvements, constructions and betterments, which are useful, beneficial and necessary. This program does not invade the realm of private affairs.

It is a plan to improve living conditions in Chicago – a plan that will substantially contribute to the health, safety and convenience of the people.

It contemplates the building of sewers, the increase of water pressure, filtration plants, a maternity hospital for poor mothers, enlargement of the Municipal Tuberculosis Sanitarium, resurfacing of Four Hundred miles of macadam streets, rehabilitation of the Fire and Police Alarm systems, elimination of dangerous grade crossings, construction of adequate airport facilities, building of new bridges, enlargement of playgrounds and beaches, building of highways, construction of garbage incinerators, improvement of the street lighting.

These improvements contemplate an approach to Chicago's ultimate goal of being the cleanest, best paved, most brightly lighted, healthiest, safest and happiest city in the world.

To be sure, such a program involves the expenditure of an enormous amount of money, but none of it is for fads, artificial beauty, or other unnecessary extravagances. There will be no improvements which will increase the taxes on real estate or personal property, or impose any special assessments.

This program will provide tens of thousands of persons with employment, add to family incomes, provide for the necessities of life and stimulate business generally.

It is frankly acknowledged that this is an ambitious plan. Some may criticize it as being too extensive, but the outlook spells success.

When I assumed office, one of my well-wishers remarked that I had been handed the toughest job of any mayor in the country. Others made like comments; no one presented a rosy picture. But with the aid of this capable City Council and well-meaning citizens sincerely interested in the city's growth and welfare, substantial and encouraging results were obtained.

It was my greatest desire then – and still is – to decrease the number of unemployed. One of my first official acts was to appoint a Chicago Recovery Administration. It helped. Then came the Keep Chicago

Ahead committee. It assisted more. Still more beneficial was the prevailing upon the World's Fair officials to continue another year. These and other agencies brought millions of people to Chicago, who, in turn, brought more millions of money to spend and helped further employment here.

Second inaugural address of Chicago Mayor Edward J. Kelly, 8 April 1935, from Chicago Public Library, Inaugural Addresses of the Mayors of Chicago. www.chipublib.org/004chicago/mayors/speeches/intro.html.

3.16 New Dealers at the city level: Fiorello La Guardia of New York

Perhaps the most important exponent of the New Deal at the city level was Fiorello La Guardia of New York. He attended the Law School at New York University and was a dedicated social activist and a Republican. Elected to the House of Representatives in 1916, he would be swept out of office by the 1932 Democrat landslide that would bring Roosevelt to power. From 1934 until 1945 he served as Mayor of New York. During that time he played a key role in shaping the New Deal in New York. In this speech in Congress on 10 January 1933 he emphasises the point that the problems of urban and rural areas are interlinked and that the city takes a keen interest in the problems of the country.

What chance has the farmer to-day when we leave him to the mercy of what once was the law of supply and demand? When the farmer took his product to town to sell to the consumers waiting for it, and they had no other source of supply, then indeed, it might have been applicable. But what chance has the farmer when the demand is controlled by manicured-finger men in Chicago and New York dealing in agriculture by means of the ticker tape and controlling the prices of the farmer's commodities? What chance has the farmer got, under a system of supply and demand, with elevators, storage houses, and refrigerators where food can be garnered and held so as to control the market price? The farmer can not store his product. He has not the facility, and besides he needs immediate cash …

Personally, I should prefer to avoid all circumvention and provide for straight price fixing for all surplus agricultural commodities. Eventually we will come to that. The habit of thinking along certain constitutional lines makes many timid ...

It is my belief that in the face of the existing emergency, with the complete nation-wide bankruptcy of the farmers of the country, that we could do so. When a farmer sells his products at less than it cost him to produce, and that is what he is doing every day, and unable to exchange his products for the necessaries of life and for the commodities which he needs to raise his products, he is not selling at such prices of his own free will. He is selling under duress.

Congressional Record, 10 January 1933, pp. 1489–93.

3.17 New Dealers at the city level: the Conference of Mayors

Mayors in particular cities like New York played a major role in shaping and delivering the New Deal. Working together the mayors of even the smallest of American cities could provide a snapshot, and, if needs be, a critique of the progress of the New Deal. The 1937 Report of the Conference of Mayors focused on the question of relief and, in particular, on the operation of the administration. The report highlights the importance of the leader at the city level in making the New Deal function effectively, as well as the political significance of the Conference of Mayors.

Introduction

On January thirteenth last, we presented to the Congress of the United States what in our judgment was at that time a comprehensive survey of the relief needs of the country, together with an estimate of the amount of Federal appropriations which would be necessary to meet those needs during the fiscal year 1936–1937. On March twelfth last, we gave to the President what in our judgment was a fair and impartial appraisal of the WPA program of the National Government. This latter report was given consideration by the House Committee on Appropriations when hearings were held on the Deficiency Bill last

Spring. Today, on the basis of studies made within the past two weeks by the United States Conference of Mayors, we present the results of a nation-wide survey of the existing relief situation and probably future needs with special reference to the responsibilities facing the Government *for the balance* of the current fiscal year, namely, for the period up to June thirtieth next. We are deeply hopeful that this report may be helpful to the Administration in its preparation of recommendations to the Congress with regard to the continuation of the Works Progress Administration Program.

Unemployables A Local and State Responsibility
At the outset, we desire to reiterate that we are definitely opposed to any demands being made upon the National Government for additional Federal appropriations for *direct relief*. The problem of providing adequate aid to the so-called 'unemployable' relief group, is a responsibility which we believe rests solely with the localities and the states – and while the 'unemployable' load is a heavy one, it is up to our states and localities to provide the finances required to meet this need. In our judgment no *better or sounder formula* than Federal responsibility for the destitute able-bodied workers on the one hand and city and state responsibility for the unemployable group on the other, has yet been advanced. We have little faith with those who expect the National Government to do it all. In assuming this burden of direct relief, may we point out that cities are in addition contributing 18 per cent of the total cost of the present WPA program as well as paying out of local resources 55% of the cost of all municipal PWA projects approved by the Government. The facts show:

Costs of Relief to Localities

Year	Direct Relief Costs	Local Share of CWA and WPA	Totals
1933	199 million	21 million	220 million
1934	226 million	69 million	295 million
1935	243 million	46 million	289 million
1936	190 million	225 million	415 million

And this financial burden, under our existing tax laws, has been and is being met almost exclusively through the only source of revenue open to local governments, namely, the *general property tax*.

Work and not the Dole

We are charged also with the responsibility of again reporting to the Federal Government, in accordance with formal action taken at our last Annual Conference, that we believe *work and not the dole* is the American way of providing for the unemployed. By adopting this national policy not only have we maintained human life but we have received from our large expenditures something of value and benefit to every community in the nation.

The integrity, usefulness and public benefit of the WPA work which *can be undertaken or continued in operation* during the next six months is attested to by reports from practically every city in the country.

Typical examples, from among the detailed data found in Section II of this Survey, are as follows:

> "The WPA projects which the City has sponsored and which it is ready to undertake or continue during the next six months represent most useful and needy work of benefit to the people of Boston. These projects contemplate, among other things, the demolition of unsafe buildings, increase of airport and park and playground facilities, reconstruction of highways, extension of sewage and water lines, and improvements in public buildings such as the City's hospitals, fire stations, police stations, and schools." (City of BOSTON)

> "The City of Los Angeles has twenty-six projects in operation under the WPA for a total expenditure of $44,362,000. It is ready to undertake 132 projects, all of which have been approved by WPA officials, for a total expenditure of $20,386,000. Every item in these lists represents useful and needed improvements of a permanent nature for the benefit of the people of this city. They include such work as Sanitary Sewers, Storm Drains, Street Improvements, Airport construction, and Park and Playground development." (City of LOS ANGELES)

> "The projects sponsored by the City of Dayton and Montgomery County are needed improvements and of immeasurable benefit to the people of this community. These projects have done and are doing much to improve the condition and beauty of Dayton. Amongst these projects permit us to mention

the Dayton Municipal Airports, a close to seven hundred thousand dollar job; McCook Field improvement; Sewage Disposal improvements which run between eight and nine hundred thousand dollars; various swimming pools and school buildings. These works are not only public benefits but reflect favourably, I believe, upon the attitude of our citizens toward this program." (City of DAYTON)

"All of the projects sponsored by the City are useful and of benefit to the community. Our construction projects are all for needed improvements which would be done by the City if funds were available. We have a large amount of construction work to be done within the next few years, and will be able to employ relief labor on many of these projects." (City of MILWAUKEE)

"The construction program in San Francisco under WPA auspices represents every municipal activity, and is one we are proud of." (City of SAN FRANCISCO)

"All Works Projects submitted by the City of Detroit represent useful and needed improvements, and are of definite benefit to the people of our community." (City of DETROIT)

"The city projects now operating and planned for the next six months represent very useful and needed improvements in the city. These projects consist primarily of sewers, streets, and other similar projects which will be of lasting benefit." (City of LOUISVILLE)

"Every project that the city has undertaken has been beneficial and useful to the community." (City of OAKLAND)

"The projects which the city has sponsored are of a highly desirable nature such as: grading and gravelling of streets; removal of old street-car tracks and repaving; installation of sewers and water mains; construction of playgrounds; and airport improvements." (City of FLINT)

"It has been the policy of the city of Kalamazoo to sponsor only worthwhile projects." (City of KALAMAZOO)

"During the year 1936 every effort has been made by the City Administration to improve the character and quality of the WPA program in this County. This applies both to the preparation of plans and to the supervision of the work in the field. Many good, useful, and necessary improvements were made, such as repairing and reconstruction of streets, improvements to parks and recreational areas, improvements to public buildings, and public property generally, and the development of the Lake Front and the Municipal Airport. The latter two improvements are undoubtedly the outstanding WPA projects in the State of Ohio. Neither is completed at the present time. In the case of the Lake Front development additional work for WPA employment is available for a period of at least two years. The City is also expecting to employ private landscape architects for the purpose of conceiving and making complete development plans for all of the large parks owned by the City. This will provide additional work for WPA for a number of years hence. Also, the City expects to go forward with its program of improvements to streets, sewers, buildings, and other public property." (City of CLEVELAND)

"The projects we authorized application for all represent useful and needed benefits to the people of our community." (City of READING)

"The City of Akron takes considerable pride in the integrity and permanent usefulness of the projects which we have sponsored." (City of AKRON)

The Existing Situation

On March eighteenth last, in submitting his message dealing with the relief problem to the Congress, the President requested an appropriation of $1,500,000,000 in order that the WPA would be enabled to provide work for the destitute unemployed during the fiscal year 1936–1937. It was indicated that only $1,500,000 was being requested, instead of the two billion stated in the message as being the minimum amount necessary to carry the then WPA load for a twelve month period, on the basis that upon business was to be placed major responsibility for reducing the financial burden of the Government through absorption of WPA workers by private industry. This was stated in the following words:

"The ultimate cost of the Federal works program will thus be determined by private enterprise. Federal assistance which arose as a result of industrial disemployment can be terminated if industry itself removes the underlying conditions. Should industry co-operatively achieve the goal of reemployment, the appropriation of $1,500,000,000, together with the unexpended balances of previous appropriations, will suffice to carry the Federal works program through the fiscal year 1937. Only if industry fails to reduce substantially the number of those now out of work will another appropriation and further plans and policies be necessary."

While improvement in business in general and the reemployment of private industry since last March has been *substantial and encouraging*, and the trend is still undoubtedly upward, the fact remains that these economic advances have not obviated substantial need for direct relief and for the WPA work opportunities for the destitute employable persons. We understand that funds available to the Works Progress Administration are sufficient to carry the program only through the present month, and we assume, therefore, that within a very few days the President will submit to the Congress, in accordance with his message of last March, a statement of the requirements for WPA for the balance (five months) of the present fiscal year. It is to this specific problem that this report from the major cities of the country is directed.

Let us emphasise at this point that no group of public officials in the United States more deeply deplores the fact that the relief rolls still remain at a high level and that business has not been able to absorb the great majority of the unemployed than do the chief executives of the important urban areas throughout the nation. The welfare and progress of these great industrial communities, their very life, depend upon sound business conditions and regular employment in private industry of *all* of their citizens. Of course this is the goal toward which we all must work, and let it be said that each city has endeavoured to do its part in this effort. However, the efforts of all concerned have not as yet been adequate to eliminate unemployment and destitution.

The emergency problem facing the Federal Government is, therefore, that of determining the financial requirements for WPA for the next five months. To that end our survey has endeavoured to chart the *probable relief* picture, insofar as WPA is concerned, for this period. Based on reports submitted by 100 major cities to the United States Conference of Mayors, the details of such reports being attached herewith as supporting data, the following conclusions have been made and are herewith presented:

1. *It is apparent that the number of those eligible to and receiving WPA work during December cannot be expected to be decreased within the next five months.*

2. *As a matter of fact, reports from a number of cities show that a substantial number of employable relief persons have not at any time up to now been given WPA work. This number is conservatively estimated, on the basis of individual studies made, at approximately 500,000 cases.*

On December 31, after careful combing of WPA rolls resulting in the elimination of all non-relief workers, 2,200,000 persons were employed by the Works Progress Administration. If we add to this number those employable relief persons who are eligible to WPA work opportunities but have not yet been given work, we find that the probable number of persons who ought and should be employed this Winter and Spring numbers approximately 2,700,000 persons. This number represents the minimum number of *employable relief cases,* for which general group the Government has rightfully and courageously assumed responsibility.

In support of (1) above, the following are *typical reports from among the reports* submitted by 100 cities and which reports are attached herewith:

> "While industrial employment in 100 representative concerns in Cuyahoga County has nearly doubled since 1933, and is now within 10 per cent of the peak of employment in such industries in 1929, the number of relief cases has increased about 30 per cent during the same period ... It appears that the relief load has apparently reached a 'resistance level' and that henceforth the closing out of cases will become more difficult ... *No substantial reduction* in relief load can be expected with the next six months." (City of CLEVELAND)

> "We do not look for any increase in industrial employment, basing this on the industrial employment index which now stands at 117.7, the highest point of the industrial employment index since September, 1929." (City of DETROIT)

> "According to relief authorities, there is no indication of the relief load being lessened in the coming Winter and Spring." (City of ST LOUIS)

"Considering employables on direct relief and those now employed on WPA, there are approximately 16,000 persons depending on the Government for sustenance. *This condition exists in spite of the fact that industrial employment now tops the 1929 figure for the same month*." (City of TOLEDO)

"We are of the opinion that the figures as of November fifteenth are rock bottom and until industry takes up some of this load, the problem of providing work for these people will be with us." (City of SAN FRANCISCO)

"The load to be carried by WPA for the winter and early spring months *will be greater* than at present, due to dismissal of seasonal employees by industries and contractors, and due to completion of the Parklawn Housing Project." (City of MILWAUKEE)

"The need for WPA employment during this winter *will not be any less than at present.* Unless private employment picks up considerably this *non-relief, no substantial decrease* in need of WPA can be expected this spring." (City of LOUISVILLE)

"This chart shows *no indication* that the relief load for the coming winter will be less than a year ago; rather, it shows the opposite." (City of DES MOINES)

"There is *no indication* that the load for the coming winter and spring months should be less than is now carried by WPA ... Instead of a decrease, the number should be substantially increased for the months of January, February and March." (City of ST PAUL)

"From all information we have, the relief load can be expected *to be increased* during the winter and spring months ... Present industrial employment is as high as this district can possibly go." (City of YOUNGSTOWN)

"There is absolutely no indication that the relief load for the present winter months *should be less than now carried by the WPA*. Industrial activity, even near to normal in the Wheeling district, has failed by a large number to absorb available labor, and the winter months, bringing cessation of much outdoor work, has increased the number of persons seeking employment and relief. For the next three months the relief needs will be increased, rather than diminished, as can be realized from the growing number of applicants for relief and work, reported by the Ohio County Department of Public Assistance, and the Works Progress Administration. The former organization is now carrying a case load of 888 families, while the WPA is employing approximately 1,350 persons, all with dependent families. The only pending change in this situation will be the removal of some fifty indigent aged persons from the county relief rolls to the old-age pension list. Meanwhile, a steady and definite increase in relief needs is in progress, due to restricted opportunities for private employment in winter weather." (City of WHEELING)

"There are now approximately 23,000 persons engaged on WPA projects in Boston. Every indication is that the WPA load for the coming winter and spring months should be increased rather than lessened. At no time has the WPA program cared for more than 50% of the needy employables in this community. The City of Boston is now spending for relief between $11,000,000 and $12,000,000 a year, of which approximately one-half is raised by borrowing to prevent a further increase in our tax rate, now $38 a thousand. There appears *to be no prospect of the absorption into private employment* of any very substantial number of present WPA workers during the coming winter or spring months." (City of BOSTON)

In support of (2) above, namely, that many employable relief persons have not yet been given WPA work, the following are typical:

"Los Angeles County has approximately 15,000 cases of employable persons who are receiving direct relief because the Federal Work Program has not absorbed them." (City of LOS ANGELES)

"There are still about 4,000 workable people on the relief rolls in the City of St Louis, who have not been absorbed by the WPA program." (City of ST LOUIS)

"WPA has never absorbed all the needy employable cases in Cuyahoga County. At present, there are more than 10,000 needy employable cases on direct relief. In order to absorb all employables the WPA quota for this district should be fixed at approximately 45,000." (City of CLEVELAND)

"The number of persons actually assigned and working on WPA projects in the City of New Orleans as of December, 1936 is 20,407. The number of persons eligible and waiting assignment in New Orleans for this same period is 1,701." (City of NEW ORLEANS)

"There are approximately 8,000 persons in the City's relief rolls who are employable and who are not and never have been afforded WPA employment. In addition, there are about 4,000 cases being provided for by the City's Welfare Department where there are one or more employables in the family, who are not and never have been afforded WPA employment. Beside these, there are approximately 15,000 persons who are registered as qualified for WPA employment and who have not received the same, and who have not applied for and are not receiving relief from the City." (City of BOSTON)

"There are still many employable relief cases in the city who have never been on WPA." (City of CINCINNATI)

"The number of employable relief cases in this city who have not yet been given employment on WPA, is, as near as we can determine, about 2,500." (City of MILWAUKEE)

"It is readily seen that WPA has never assumed the full burden of taking care of the able-bodied unemployed." (City of SAN FRANCISCO)

"Never since the end of the CWA program has more than 2/3rds of the employable persons on relief been given jobs on work relief projects." (City of DES MOINES)

"On December first, there were about 520 certified persons awaiting assignment on WPA projects. Although we have been very careful in investigating everyone before certifying him for a WPA project, there has always been a very substantial number more on the certified list than the quota allowed the City of Louisville, and in many cases there has been a waiting period of several months before an assignment is given. Even assuming that the present WPA persons will be without work there will be no chance of their receiving work either private employment or on the Federal work program, as our quota is below what it should be." (City of LOUISVILLE)

"There are in Hillsborough County about 3,000 people now employed by WPA. An additional 3,000 people are registered and certified as relief cases who have been unable to get any employment with WPA. There are an additional 3,000 people registered for WPA employment but who have not yet been certified to WPA, but who are eligible to be certified for WPA employment." (City of TAMPA)

"A report from the local Emergency Relief Administration dated December 10th, shows a total of 1,011 cases on direct relief; 481 are listed as employables not employed on WPA. This has always been a disappointment to us since WPA was expected to take all employables off relief. At no time have all been taken off relief and this group has increased greatly in the last few weeks." (City of KALAMAZOO)

"There are about 6,000 certified WPA cases – quota is a present 3,007, others have not been absorbed. Business is on the upgrade, but not enough to take care of the balance of the employables." (City of LOWELL)

"In the city alone, there are practically as many employable relief people as the number now working under WPA, and these unemployed have not yet been absorbed by any Federal Work Program." (City of YOUNGSTOWN)

"The number of employable relief people in Akron who have not yet been given WPA work is 1,274." (City of AKRON)

Based on an average cost to the Federal Government of $65 per month per worker, if the WPA program is to meet the problem of providing work for the total employable relief population approximately $877,500,000 will be required for the 5 months period – February 1 to June 30. We sincerely trust and petition that this responsibility will be full accepted.

Conclusion

In conclusion, may we emphasize the cardinal principles which we believe should be maintained in our approach to the existing relief situation.

1. It should now be realized by the nation that the problem of unemployment relief is no longer of an "emergency" character.

2. That unemployment is a national problem requiring continuing national action.

3. That Federal responsibility for those who are involuntarily unemployed and destitute is both proper and required by present conditions.

4. That in meeting this responsibility work and jobs and not soup kitchens and breadlines is the American method.

5. That provision for the unemployable group is a truly local and state responsibility which should in all cases be assumed.

6. That the present WPA has done and is doing useful and needed public work of benefit to the people of the nation.

We again express, on behalf of the United States Conference of Mayors, our deep appreciation of the sympathetic consideration given by the Government to the problems facing the cities.

A Report on the Existing Relief Situation Covering 100 Major American Cities with Special Reference to the Continuation of the WPA Work Program through June 30, 1936, Washington DC, 2 January 1937, Official Files OF 1892/2, Roosevelt Library.

3.18 New Dealers in academe: Felix Frankfurter to President Roosevelt, 29 May 1935

Felix Frankfurter arrived in New York as a 12-year-old immigrant from Austria in 1894. At age 24 he graduated from the Law School at Harvard. After serving as Chief Assistant to the District Attorney for the Southern District of New York from 1906, he became special counsel to the Secretary of War in 1911. From 1914 until 1939 he was a member of Faculty at the Harvard Law School. In 1933 Roosevelt offered him the post of Solicitor General but he turned it down. However, he continued to act as a friend and advisor to Roosevelt and in 1939 he was appointed an Associate Justice of the Supreme Court. He resigned because of ill-health in 1962 and died in 1965. In this letter we see the quality of the advice which Roosevelt received from Frankfurter and other academics. The letter is a response to Roosevelt's frustration with the Supreme Court. Frankfurter counsels patience and that Roosevelt's response to the problem should be limited.

In the interest of clarity may I put in a few words on paper the gist of my thoughts on the issue of the Supreme Court vs. The President.

1. Postponement of fighting out that issue at the present time does not rule the issue out as one on which you may later go to the country. I assume that a strategist like you will select time and circumstances most favorable for victory. I suspect that events may give you better conditions for battle than you have even now.

Decisions in other cases may accumulate popular grievances against the Court on issues so universally popular that the Borah's, the Clarks, the Nyes and all the currents of opinion they represent will be with you in addition to the support you have today. That is why I think it is fortunate that the Administration has pending before Congress measures like the Social Security bill, the Holding Company bill, the Wagner bill, the Guffey bill. Go on with these. Put them up to the Supreme Court. Let the Court strike down any or all of them next winter or spring, especially by a divided Court. Then propose a Constitutional amendment giving the national Government adequate power to cope with national economic and industrial problems. That will give you an overwhelming issue of a positive character arising at the psychological time for the '36 campaign, instead of mere negative issue of being "agin" the Court which, rising now, may not be able to sustain its freshness and dramatic appeal until election time.

2. That approach has these advantages:

(a) It defines a sharp issue – of the increase of Congressional power on industrial and economic problems – instead of attacking the Supreme Court's vague general powers. A general attack on the Court, unlimited in the changes it may cause, would give opponents a chance to play on vague fears of a leap in the dark and upon the traditional loyalties the Court is still able to inspire.

(b) It cuts across all technicalities of law and presents an issue which the common man can understand and which he can feel means something personally important to him.

Reproduced in Max Freedman (ed.), *Roosevelt and Frankfurter: Their Correspondence 1928–1945* (London, Bodley Head, 1967), pp. 272–3.

3.19 New Dealers overseas: John Maynard Keynes's open letter to President Roosevelt, 31 December 1933

Some of Roosevelt's admirers were also cogent critics of the policy of the administration. English economist John Maynard Keynes was a world authority on economic matters and in December 1933 the *New York Times* asked him to offer his views on the New Deal. These were published in the form of an open letter to Roosevelt. Some scholars have argued that Roosevelt was heavily influenced by Keynesian economic theory, which postulated that the best response to an economic downturn was for the government to pump money into the economy, even if that increased government borrowing. Government expenditure would create jobs and lead ultimately to an economic upturn as consumers began spending again. Large elements of the New Deal can be interpreted as a Keynesian response to the depression, but other parts of it, like cutting payments by the federal government to some employees, seem like a traditional conservative response to an economic downturn. When Keynes and Roosevelt met in May 1934 both sides came away disillusioned. Keynes was surprised at Roosevelt's less than precise understanding of economic theory, and Roosevelt was perplexed by the inability of the English economist to talk to him in a language which he understood.

At the moment your sympathisers in England are nervous and sometimes despondent. We wonder whether the order of different agencies is rightly understood, whether there is a confusion of aim, and whether some of the advice you get is not crack-brained and queer …

You are engaged on a double task, Recovery and Reform; – recovery from the slump and the passage of those business and social reforms which are long overdue. For the first, speed and quick results are essential. The second may be urgent too; but haste will be injurious, and wisdom of long-range purpose is more necessary than immediate achievement. It will be through raising high the prestige of your administration by success in short-range Recovery, that you will have the driving force to accomplish long-range Reform. On the other hand, even wise and necessary Reform may, in some respects, impede and complicate Recovery. For it will upset the confidence of the business world and weaken their existing motives to action, before you have had time to put other motives in place. It may over-task your bureaucratic machine, which the traditional individualism of the United States and the old "spoils system" have left none too strong ...

Now I am not clear, looking back over the last nine months, that the order of urgency between measures of Recovery and measures of Reform has been duly observed ... In particular, I cannot detect any material aid to recovery in the National Industrial Recovery Act (NIRA), though its social gains have been large. The driving force which has been put behind the vast administrative task set by this Act has seemed to represent a wrong choice in the order of urgencies ... NIRA, which is essentially Reform and probably impedes Recovery, has been put across too hastily, in the false guise of being part of the technique of Recovery ...

You may be feeling by now, Mr President, that my criticism is more obvious than my sympathy. Yet truly that is not so. You remain for me the ruler whose general outlook and attitude to the tasks of government are the most sympathetic in the world. You are the only one who sees the necessity of a profound change of methods and is attempting it without intolerance, tyranny or destruction.

New York Times, 31 December 1933.

3.20 A Latin American comment on the New Deal

Unsurprisingly Latin America took a keen interest in how its large and powerful neighbour to the north was trying to deal with its economic problems.

I admire President Roosevelt more for what I see in him as a humanitarian thinker than for what circumstances have compelled him to say or do as a politician. He knows, I presume, that his country is not yet sufficiently indoctrinated with the theories implicit in the New Deal. The people have been led to accept whatever brings immediate relief, but not what implies a change in the economic or political pattern.

... Whatever the political destiny of the New Deal may be, its fundamental idea will remain; it will be a conception of the new function of the State, at least in time of emergency. But I do not think that the extent of this experiment in national thinking will stop here. I believe the idea will gain ground that State intervention should not wait for an emergency to force private interests to yield to public interests in the economic field.

Carlos Davila in B. P. Adams, *You, Americans* (New York, Funk and Wagnalls Co., 1939). Reproduced in Nicholas Halasz, *Roosevelt Through Foreign Eyes* (Princeton, D. Van Nostrand Co., 1961), pp. 45–6.

MEDIA SUPPORT FOR THE NEW DEAL

3.21 Uncle Zeke's column for Station WPG Atlantic City, 4 May 1933

Media support for the New Deal was a vital part of its success. Most of the American newspaper press, usually willing to put a favourable spin on stories about the President and his administration, was a willing partner in the New Deal. The rise of popular radio in the 1920s meant that radio stations and their presenters also constituted an important voice of political comment on the New Deal. On 4 May 1933 Station WPG Atlantic City carried an editorial strongly pro-Roosevelt. The President of the Atlantic City Publishing Company sent Roosevelt a copy of the editorial.

I say without fear of successful contraction [*sic*] ... that the election of Franklin D. Roosevelt saved this nation from revolution. This man Roosevelt has put a new hope in the hearts of our people and is without doubt the most effective antidote against the half-baked theories of rabid radicalism that the times have produced. To be sure, the President has taken many radical steps himself since assuming command ... and by that very action immediately and completely extracted the thunder from the prating demagogues whose only recipe for the present day ills, would be the tearing down of our government.

Yet the President, with all the great records of excellent work accomplished since March 4 ... to his credit ... will have to keep moving ahead with his program rapidly during the next six months if serious trouble is to be avoided, particularly in the middle west.

Uncle Zeke's column for Station WPG Atlantic City, contained in Lewis M. Herrman, President Atlantic City Publishing Company, to Roosevelt, 7 June 1933, President's Personal File PPF 200/137, Roosevelt Library.

4
New Deal foreign policy

Many traditional studies of the Roosevelt years tend to divorce the New Deal and the foreign policy of the Roosevelt administration. The traditional picture of American foreign relations after 1918 is of a country retreating into isolationism as a result of the First World War. America's combat losses in 1918 had an impact on the American public that led to the rejection of the kind of internationalism, and activist presidency, which President Woodrow Wilson had favoured from 1913 to 1919. The Republican presidents of the 1920s (Harding, Coolidge and Hoover) were content to play a minimum role in world affairs. After 1933 Franklin Roosevelt was less content to play this role, but mindful of the prejudices of the American public he went along with it anyway. Realizing the dangers of the Nazis in the late 1930s he slowly prepared public opinion, and the United States, to go to war, which the Japanese forced on America by their attack on Pearl Harbor on 7 December 1941. Under this narrative of events the New Deal and the approach of war can be neatly separated from each other for the benefit of historians interested in writing about one or other issue, but not both. However, such compartmentalisation leads to a somewhat distorted picture of the work of the Roosevelt administration.

In his day-to-day work Roosevelt experienced little sense of this compartmentalisation. The Supreme Court and Hitler could threaten trouble on the same day and there was a crossover from one area to another. War, the danger of it, and preparations for it, could, and did, have a massive impact on the economy. While the United States might have retreated into political semi-isolation after 1918 (the Kellogg-Briand Pact to outlaw war in 1928 being an obvious instance where the United States came out of political isolation), the same could not be said of her behaviour in the field of international finance and business. Here the United States remained very active. From 12 June to 27

July 1933 the United States would take part in the world economic conference to try to find a solution to the depression. That conference would founder because of Roosevelt's concerns about proposals for currency stabilisation and nations would be left to come up with their own solutions to the depression.

There was a further way in which foreign affairs and the New Deal were intimately connected. For rhetorical effect Roosevelt likened the depression to an emergency that was as serious as war itself. Undoubtedly the situation was critical, but Roosevelt was interested in more than simply scaring the American public. He wanted to ensure that those with power or privilege would not be content to maintain the status quo in which millions were suffering. He reasoned that a compliant Congress and Supreme Court were necessary for him to drive his reforms through, and that in order to maintain the pace of reform he needed to interpret liberally his powers as President. He needed the kind of authority and ability to act decisively on the home front as he could potentially enjoy abroad as commander-in-chief of the American armed forces. Rhetorically blurring the division between the domestic and foreign powers of the presidency was a deliberate ploy to allow Roosevelt to enhance his position as President.

By his very nature and past experience Roosevelt believed that the United States had to play a role in world affairs. He also recognised that after the horrors of 1914–18 most Americans wanted as few political ties as possible with Europe. The rejection of the Treaty of Versailles by Congress in 1919–20 had been a profound blow to the liberal interventionist section of opinion within the Democratic Party. Roosevelt knew that he had to respect the neo-isolationist views of the majority of Americans. In the 1930s American foreign policy was largely reactive as the administration responded to crises as they arose, while entering into largely unfruitful dialogue with other countries over war in South America and the world economic crisis. However, in the late 1940s as Italy attacked Abyssinia in 1935 and Germany reoccupied the Rhineland in 1936 Roosevelt became convinced of the evils of the European dictators. He was also increasingly alarmed at the expansionist tendencies of Imperial Japan, which launched full-scale hostilities on China in 1937. In 1940, as France fell to Germany, it became clear that the United States would have to increase its aid to Britain or see her fall. Similarly, Japanese demands on the French colonial administration in Indo-China indicated that the United States would have to take a lead in curbing Japanese expansionism. With the American public opposed to involvement in the war Roosevelt knew that safeguarding America's vital interests would be no easy task.

Too much has been made of the close relationship which developed between Churchill and Roosevelt, after the former assumed the British premiership in May 1940. Churchill, desirous of the unity of Empire and the English-speaking peoples, was apt to over-romanticise his relationship with the American President, and in the 1950s and beyond historians were a little too willing to accept Churchill's view at face value. Thus American entry into the war after 1940 became a matter of when rather than if. More recent analyses have sought to revise this view. As Brian McKercher notes:

> It is crucial to understand the nature of the Churchill–Roosevelt wartime relationship that began with that first exchange of letters and lasted until Roosevelt's death in April 1945. For a long while the personal ties that developed between these two men, ties that became genuinely friendly, were portrayed as the basis of an Anglo-American 'special relationship' ... Only after France surrendered to Germany on 22 June 1940 and Britain faced the Axis alone did Churchill begin serious communications with Roosevelt. The reason was simple: he needed to court friendly Powers to sustain Britain's war effort. For his part, after June 1940, Roosevelt appreciated that a German-dominated Europe presented grave strategic problems for the United States. (B. J. C. McKercher, *Transition of Power: Britain's Loss of Global Pre-Eminence to the United States 1930–1945*, Cambridge, Cambridge University Press, 1999, p. 280)

On both sides there was self-interest. As R. A. Divine has commented, in 1941 the United States found itself as a 'reluctant belligerent' in a war which would make America a superpower. While Churchill was content to represent Roosevelt as a President instinctively knowing what was right but limited in his internationalism by isolationist opinion in the United States, Divine's analysis of American foreign policy from 1933 to 1941 is savage:

> American foreign policy was sterile and bankrupt in a period of grave international crisis. Although it was the single most powerful nation on the globe, the United States abdicated its responsibilities and became a creature of history rather than its molder.

> By surrendering the initiative to Germany and Japan, the nation imperiled its security and very nearly permitted the Axis powers to win the war. In the last analysis the United States was saved only by the Japanese miscalculation in attacking Pearl Harbor. (R. A. Divine, *The Reluctant Belligerent*, New York, John Wiley & Sons, 1965, p. 158.)

While Churchill's overly romanticised picture of his relationship with a saintly and enlightened Roosevelt can be dismissed as wishful thinking rather than reality, and the American President can be condemned for his 'sterile' and 'bankrupt' foreign policy, one salient point is easily overlooked. Roosevelt was the President of the United States of America. The welfare of its people was his responsibility. As commander-in-chief, the lives of America's servicemen were his responsibility. The British Empire, Europe and Asia were not his responsibility, nor were their interactions, or the lives of non-Americans. Roosevelt was not a believer in the missionary element in American foreign policy: that because of her size, history and outlook America had a unique and exceptional role to play in world affairs. For him, and especially in the circumstances of the Great Depression, charity began at home, and if the war developed in certain ways which might materially or strategically benefit the United States then he was quite prepared to exploit America's good fortune.

Part of the cost of the process of America turning into a superpower between 1939 and 1941 would be borne by the American taxpayer, and part of it by the British Empire, which set about liquidating its transferable assets in a war of survival. The New Deal had been a fireworks display of government activity that had penetrated the gloom of the depression. The show was as impressive as it was costly, but it did not permanently change the night of the depression into the day of prosperity. That transformation would be left to the altogether bigger fireworks display of the Second World War. The sums pumped into the economy by the New Deal were dwarfed by those invested as a result of the Second World War. Tanks had to be built, ships repaired, airfields built and many other tasks achieved. By 1941 the New Deal had not secured full employment, or anything like it. As a result of the Japanese attack on Pearl Harbor the Japanese would succeed where the American President had toiled for so long and for so hard with only partial success. The result would be that America was put back to work, the economy boomed and standards of living rose.

4.1 The good neighbour policy, 12 April 1933

Since the Monroe Doctrine of 1823 the United States had maintained the role of guardian of Latin American affairs. Under Theodore Roosevelt and Woodrow Wilson that role of guardianship had extended to the right of military intervention in Latin America. In a speech to representatives of the Pan American Union in April 1933 Franklin Roosevelt maintained that the United States would continue to act as guardian of the affairs of the western hemisphere, but he sought to give that role a more attractive, less bellicose face.

In my Inaugural Address I stated that I would "dedicate this Nation to the policy of the good neighbor – the neighbor who resolutely respects himself and, because he does so, respects the rights of others – the neighbor who respects his obligations and respects the sanctity of agreements in and with a world of neighbors." Never before has the significance of the words "good neighbor" been so manifest in international relations. Never have the need and benefit of neighborly cooperation in every form of human activity been so evident as they are today.

Friendship among Nations, as among individuals, calls for constructive efforts to muster the forces of humanity in order that an atmosphere of close understanding and cooperation may be cultivated. It involves mutual obligations and responsibilities, for it is only by sympathetic respect for the rights of others and a scrupulous fulfillment of the corresponding obligations by each member of the community that a true fraternity can be maintained ...

The people of every Republic are coming to a deep understanding of the fact that the Monroe Doctrine ... was and is directed at the maintenance of independence by the peoples of the continent. It was aimed and is aimed against the acquisition in any manner of the control of additional territory in this hemisphere by any non-American power.

Reproduced in J. F. Watts and Fred Israel (eds), *Presidential Documents: The Speeches, Proclamations, and Policies That Have Shaped the Nation from Washington to Clinton* (London, Routledge, 2000), pp. 268–9.

4.2 Roosevelt to Jesse I. Straus, American Ambassador in Paris, 13 February 1936

Jesse Straus was the American Ambassador to Paris. He repeatedly warned Roosevelt about the decline of France as a Great Power. Public morale was low and the military unprepared for a war. Here Roosevelt responds to Straus's warnings and reveals his growing pessimism at the situation.

One cannot help feeling that the whole European panorama is fundamentally blacker than at any time in your life or mine. In 1848 revolutions in a dozen countries synchronized because of a general European demand for constitutional representative government: but at that time economics, budgets, foreign exchange and industrialism were not in the picture and the problem was ten times more simple than it is today. In 1914 the situation was eighty per cent military, and again vastly simpler than today.

As I have told you, I have been increasingly concerned about the world picture ever since May, 1933. There are those who come from England and France and Germany who point to the fact that every crisis of the past three years has been muddled through with a hope that each succeeding crisis will be met peacefully in one way or another in the next few years. I hope that point of view is right but it goes against one's common sense.

The armaments race means bankruptcy or war – there is no possible out from that statement.

You are in the best listening post in what may be the last days of the period of peace before a long chaos, and I am very happy, indeed, to have your careful judgement after these two and a half years of observation.

Those articles and the letter from England are correct proof of the British dilemma. Heaven only knows I do not want to spend more money on our Army and Navy. I am initiating nothing new unless and until increases by other nations make increases by us absolutely essential to national defense. I wish England could understand that – and, incidentally, I wish Japan could understand that also.

My warm regards to you and Mrs. Straus. Keep up the good work!

Elliot Roosevelt (ed.), *The Roosevelt Letters* (London, Harrap, 1952), pp. 168–9.

4.3 American reactions to the remilitarisation of the Rhineland, 9 March 1936

On 7 March German troops occupied the demilitarised zone in the Rhineland. Its status had been determined by the Treaty of Versailles in 1919, and accepted by Germany as part of the Locarno Pact of 1925. The breach of two international treaties was a serious challenge to the post-war settlement, coming a year after Germany had announced her intention of remilitarising, but the Western democracies preferred talk rather than action. Indeed, in Britain and the United States there was considerable sympathy for Germany's actions. The Treaty of Versailles was regarded as excessive and Germany the victim of a vengeful peace. Hitler took the inaction of the democracies as a sign that the Western democracies would not oppose his ambitions in Eastern Europe. Here the German Ambassador in Washington notes with considerable satisfaction American reactions to the remilitarisation of the Rhineland.

In today's press conference the Secretary of State [Cordell Hull] said that, although he was keeping himself informed of events in Europe, he had no cause at all to concern himself with the Rhineland affair. To an enquiry about this he replied in confidence that no foreign power had so far appealed to the American Government for support of any kind ... The State Department's attitude to the German action continues to be friendly. It is felt that the German step was to have been expected, that it is indeed understandable, since, after all, it is German territory which is involved, and that it promises a pacification of the European atmosphere which would have been unthinkable as long as Germany had not obtained full sovereignty. A high-ranking official remarked that if America were in the same position as Germany she would naturally take the same course at the first opportunity offered.

In Congress circles the reaction, with some exceptions, is in general also sympathetic. In all utterances by members of Congress the desire not to intervene in European affairs finds expression. They do not believe in a war either. A few senators are inclined to say that Germany is right and are speaking with some harshness of the Versailles Treaty, which, they say, should have been changed long ago. Elsewhere, too, the general attitude here has not altered, except that the remark that, from now on, Germany can no longer be trusted is more often heard. Those papers which are known to be basically hostile to us continue to attack us. They deplore London's clear intention of leaving Paris in the lurch, and welcome Italy's apparent intention of making use of the crisis to get out of the cul-de-sac in which she had landed as a result of the Abyssinian adventure.

German Ambassador in the United States to Foreign Ministry, 9 March 1936, *Documents on German Foreign Policy* (London, HMSO, 1966), pp. 66–7.

4.4 Neutrality Act, 1937

In 1935, 1936 and 1937 Congress passed Neutrality Acts that sought to prevent American involvement in another world war. Their passage was a reflection of the increasingly troubled state of world relations. In 1931 Japan had seized the Chinese province of Manchuria. Four years later Benito Mussolini's Fascist Italy invaded Abyssinia. During the Abyssinian crisis the League of Nations, whose creation had been championed by President Woodrow Wilson in 1918–19, was dealt a fatal blow by the desperate double-dealing of the British and the French. The world seemed set on a path to violence, a fact emphasised by Nazi Germany. Adolf Hitler had become Chancellor in January 1933 and was heavily implicated in an attempted *coup d'état* in Austria in 1934. In March 1935 he announced that Germany would no longer be bound by the military clauses of the Treaty of Versailles. An isolationist American public reacted fearfully against the growing tide of disorder. Roosevelt meanwhile fretted that the attitude of the American public, reflected in Congress, sharply limited his freedom of manoeuvre for American foreign policy. In an attempt to insulate the United States from a possible new world war, Congress passed three Neutrality Acts. Each one went further in limiting the discretionary powers of the President. Isolationists in the Senate such as Gerald Nye (Republican) of North Dakota, Robert Taft (Republican) of Ohio and Burton K. Wheeler (Democrat) of Montana sincerely hoped to avoid the tragedy of another generation of Americans being sent to die to settle the seemingly interminable squabbles of Europe. Roosevelt, however, by nature favoured intervention against what he saw as the forces of evil. From 1935 until 1941 he would first have to fight the forces of isolationism.

JOINT RESOLUTION
To amend the joint resolution, approved August 31, 1935, as amended.
Resolved ...

EXPORT OF ARMS, AMMUNITION, AND IMPLEMENTS OF WAR
Section 1. (a) Whenever the President shall find that there exists a state of war between, or among, two or more foreign states, the President shall proclaim such fact, and it shall thereafter be unlawful to export, or attempt to export, or cause to be exported, arms, ammunition, or implements of war from any place in the United States to any belligerent state named in such proclamation, or to any neutral state for transshipment to, or for the use of, any such belligerent state ...

FINANCIAL TRANSACTIONS
Section 3. (a) Whenever the President shall have issued a proclamation under the authority of section 1 of this Act, it shall thereafter be unlawful for any person within the United States to purchase, sell, or exchange bonds, securities, or other obligations of the government of any belligerent state or of any state wherein civil strife exists ...

TRAVEL ON VESSELS OF BELLIGERENT STATES
Section 9. Whenever the President shall have issued a proclamation under the authority of section 1 of this Act it shall thereafter be unlawful for any citizen of the United States to travel on any vessel of the state or states named in such proclamation, except in accordance with such rules and regulations as the President shall prescribe: ...

New York Times, 2 May 1937.

4.5 Roosevelt and appeasement, 16 April 1938

1938 was a bad year for the Western democracies as Hitler's Germany annexed Austria in March, and then threatened Czechoslovakia with war if she did not hand over to Germany her borderlands that contained significant numbers of ethnic Germans. This led, in September 1939, to the calling of an international conference at Munich which would lead to the division of Czechoslovakia in the name of appeasing Germany. On 6 April 1938 John Cudahy, the American Ambassador in Ireland since 1937, sent Roosevelt a long telegram expressing his disgust at British Prime Minister Neville Chamberlain's policy of appeasement, which he considered to be 'the most weak, vacillating, humiliating policy England has ever presented'. Roosevelt wrote back to express his sympathy with the Ambassador's view, and hinted at the domestic difficulties which he faced in framing the foreign policy of the United States.

Over here there is the same element that exists in London. Unfortunately, it is led by so many of your friends and mine. They would really like me to be a Neville Chamberlain – and if I would promise that, the market would go up and they would work positively and actively for the resumption of prosperity. But if that were done, we would only be breeding far more serious trouble four or eight years from now.

Roosevelt to Cudahy, 16 April 1938, Cudahy Papers, Roosevelt Library.

4.6 Roosevelt's notes for his meeting with the Italian Ambassador, 19 March 1939

On 15 March, in violation of the Munich Agreement, Germany occupied the remaining part of Czechoslovakia. Roosevelt raised the issue with Prince Colonna, the new Italian Ambassador.

Muss. holds key to peace
Hitler – bad shape – war as way out.
Has to have Italy. Then cast her aside.
1. Neutrality Act amended
2. World opinion mobilized
Eventual loss of war
3. Italy's int with west. democ.
4. Go slow – with France
5. Sit around table and work it out
6 Get nothing in *end* by wars
7. Save peace – save dom. of Europe by Germany.

Elliot Roosevelt (ed.), *The Roosevelt Letters* (London, Harrap, 1952), p. 259.

4.7 Reconsideration of the Neutrality Act, June 1939

In early 1939 there was an attempt to amend the Neutrality Act to allow America to continue selling arms and other goods to belligerents in the time of war. Although the Neutrality Laws were amended, the House of Representatives was not prepared to vote to allow the sale of arms. During the course of the congressional debates over the proposals in June 1939 the divisions within American politics over foreign policy were manifested.

Representative W. Burgin (Dem.) of North Carolina:
The United States wants peace. There can be no doubt about that. I believe that feeling exists in the heart of all our people, regardless of party, race, or creed. We want to keep war out of the United States, and we want war kept out of the world. I believe this will or desire for peace permeates the thinking of every man in public life, from President Roosevelt down to the least and last man. No one, I think, in this House will vote for any legislation except with this in mind. I believe the President's action in the past trying times has been a potent factor in discouraging the spread of the war spirit in other parts of the world.

Congressional Record (76th Congress), June 1939, p. 8178.

Representative E. Izac (Dem.) of California:
I want the Members to bear in mind as I go along with my remarks the fact that the American people are demanding some kind of neutrality legislation for the express purpose of keeping us out of war. I am convinced the only reason that the Committee on Foreign Affairs held hearings as early as 1935 and passed a neutrality bill was because of the demand of the American public that we have something more than international law on which to rely in case the world again catches fire as it did in 1914. The present act is an evolution of the act of 1935. We have placed in the act something which I opposed, and which I will always oppose, a partial embargo. Whenever you have a partial embargo it is bound to be unneutral because no two nations are situated alike.

Congressional Record (76th Congress), June 1939, pp. 8234–5.

Representative L. Geyer (Dem.) of California:
The passage of this bill will serve the interests of peace everywhere, by to some extent lessening the danger of war in Europe. To my mind the best proof that the Bloom bill will have this effect is to be found in the press of those nations which are today mobilizing and preparing for war. The American people and the devotees of peace in every land, will welcome the passage of this bill as a step towards peace. But Rome and Berlin are shrieking that it is a form of "war mongering," and Hitler and Mussolini, through their controlled press, tell us to vote down the Bloom bill. With whom are you going to vote? With the American people; or with the war lords of fascism?

Congressional Record (76th Congress), June 1939, p. 8172.

4.8 Fireside chat on war in Europe, 3 September 1939

The German invasion of Poland on 1 September 1939 led Britain and France to declare war on Germany two days later. Despite the arguments of the isolationists Roosevelt knew that America faced the prospect of being sucked into the war. Her interests were global and German hegemony in Europe threatened the economy and security of the United States. Within ten hours of the outbreak of war the 13,581-ton liner *Athenia*, of the Donaldson Atlantic Line, was torpedoed by the German submarine *U-30*. Americans were among her 1,102 passengers and over the next few days horror stories of their fight for survival would fill the American press.

Tonight my single duty is to speak to the whole of America.

Until four-thirty this morning I had hoped against hope that some miracle would prevent a devastating war in Europe and bring to an end the invasion of Poland by Germany.

For four long years a succession of actual wars and constant crises have shaken the entire world and have threatened in each case to bring on the gigantic conflict which is today unhappily a fact.

It is right that I should recall to your minds the consistent and at times successful efforts of your Government in these crises to throw the full weight of the United States into the cause of peace. In spite of spreading wars I think that we have every right and every reason to maintain as a national policy the fundamental moralities, the teachings of religion, the continuation of efforts to restore peace – because some day, though the time may be distant, we can be of even greater help to a crippled humanity.

It is right, too, to point out that the unfortunate events of these recent years have, without question, been based on the use of force and the threat of force. And it seems to me clear, even at the outbreak of this great war, that the influence of America should be consistent in seeking for humanity a final peace which will eliminate, as far as it is possible to do so, the continued use of force between nations.

It is, of course, impossible to predict the future. I have my constant stream of information from American representatives and other sources throughout the world. You, the people of this country, are receiving news through your radios and your newspapers at every hour of the day.

You are, I believe, the most enlightened and the best informed people in all the world at this moment. You are subjected to no censorship of news, and I want to add that your Government has no information which it withholds or which it has any thought of withholding from you.

At the same time, as I told my Press Conference on Friday, it is of the highest importance that the press and the radio use the utmost caution to discriminate between actual verified fact on the one hand, and mere rumor on the other.

I can add to that by saying that I hope the people of this country will also discriminate most carefully between news and rumor. Do not believe of necessity everything you hear or read. Check up on it first.

You must master at the outset a simple but unalterable fact in modern foreign relations between nations. When peace has been broken anywhere, the peace of all countries everywhere is in danger.

It is easy for you and for me to shrug our shoulders and to say that conflicts taking place thousands of miles from the continental United States, and, indeed, thousands of miles from the whole American Hemisphere, do not seriously affect the Americas – and that all the United States has to do is to ignore them and go about its own business. Passionately though we may desire detachment, we are forced to realize that every word that comes through the air, every ship that sails the sea, every battle that is fought does affect the American future.

Let no man or woman thoughtlessly or falsely talk of America sending its armies to European fields. At this moment there is being prepared a proclamation of American neutrality. This would have been done even if there had been no neutrality statute on the books, for this proclamation is in accordance with international law and in accordance with American policy.

This will be followed by a Proclamation required by the existing Neutrality Act. And I trust that in the days to come our neutrality can be made a true neutrality.

It is of the utmost importance that the people of this country, with the best information in the world, think things through. The most dangerous enemies of American peace are those who, without well-rounded information on the whole broad subject of the past, the present and the future, undertake to speak with assumed authority, to talk in terms of glittering generalities, to give to the nation assurances or prophecies which are of little present or future value.

I myself cannot and do not prophesy the course of events abroad – and the reason is that because I have of necessity such a complete picture of what is going on in every part of the world, that I do not dare to do so. And the other reason is that I think it is honest for me to be honest with the people of the United States.

I cannot prophesy the immediate economic effect of this new war on our nation but I do say that no American has the moral right to profiteer at the expense either of his fellow citizens or of the men, the women and the children who are living and dying in the midst of war in Europe.

Some things we do know. Most of us in the United States believe in spiritual values. Most of us, regardless of what church we belong to, believe in the spirit of the New Testament – a great teaching which opposes itself to the use of force, of armed force, of marching armies and falling bombs. The overwhelming masses of our people seek peace – peace at home, and the kind of peace in other lands which will not jeopardize our peace at home.

For full text see www.mhric.org/fdr/chat19.html and www.fdrlibrary.marist.edu/090339.html.

4.9 The *Baltimore Evening Sun* denounces Germany for the sinking of the liner *Athenia*, 14 September 1939

The American newspaper the *Baltimore Evening Sun* went to particular pains to interview and record the experiences of American women who had lived through the sinking of the liner *Athenia* on 3 September 1939. The Nazi regime was denounced in the strongest terms as the newspaper highlighted that American women and children were now the victims of Hitler's aggression. Such events, as interpreted by the American media, would play a key role in shifting American opinion away from isolationism, allowing the Roosevelt administration to pursue a course of action which it felt was in the nation's best interests.

Mrs Dexter ... hated to talk of her experience. "We felt just a jolt when the explosion came. Oh it was terrible. I can't describe it."

"We almost hit the submarine," said Mary Katherine Underwood of Athens, Texas. "We were in a boat with thirty-eight women and only three men." ...

Miss Caroline Stuart of Plainfield, N.J., said: "I rowed for eight continuous hours. Look at these hands." They were still covered with blisters ...

The passengers of the *Athenia* were non-combatants, trying to get away from the war ... A great many of the passengers were women and children, whom Herr Hitler said he did not want to fight. Americans will find the calm of their neutrality somewhat disrupted by three facts:

1. That a great many women and children were unnecessarily attacked.

2. That a considerable number of these were Americans.

3. That it took Herr Hitler less than three days to offer this latest example of his lack of respect for his own word.

Baltimore Evening Sun, 14 September 1939, pp. 5–20.

4.10 Revision of the Neutrality Act, 19 September 1939

Even in the midst of world war the administration's policy continued to revolve around the whirlpool of American politics. Here the President's press secretary, Steve Early, informs of an interesting conversation he had in relation to the attempt to revise the Neutrality Act which was renewed at the outbreak of war.

MEMORANDUM FOR THE PRESIDENT

Representative Taylor, Chairman of the House Committee on Appropriations, told me today:

"Immediately after the President holds his conference tomorrow and the House and Senate have convened on Thursday – and the President's message has been received – a neutrality bill, approved in advance by the Administration, should be introduced in the House by Sam Rayburn, the Majority Leader.

The House will pass it immediately by a huge majority.

It would be immediately sent to the Senate and the Senate would have something that the Administration wants to work on – not the half way thing now before the Senate Foreign Affairs Committee.

I know that Sam Rayburn should take charge of the house bill. I believe that Congressman Martin, the Minority Leader, might join with Sam. This would have a tremendously fine effect on the country – this non-partisan championship of an Administration bill.

It would put the Republican isolationist Senate bloc on the spot.

The House should do this first. The enthusiasm of the members will cool if the House has to sit for a long time for Senate action, recessing and recessing. It would be much better to have the House act and then wait for the Senate than if the House has to sit idly by, with nothing to do, until the Senate acts.

From talking to members of the House in the cloakroom and around the capital generally, and with members of the Appropriations Committee, I know what I say. I can tell you also that many members of the House who loved Sam McReynolds and who admire Sam Rayburn will feel personally offended if Sol Bloom is allowed to lead the fight. Germans in the United States and in their home land will not be able, if Rayburn leads the fight, to say that the neutrality bill is nothing but a Jewish measure of revenge and retaliation.

Again, let me say, I know what I am talking about – that if Bloom leads this fight – many of us, at the start, will have an awful bad taste in our mouths and less heart to go on.

This is my very sincere recommendation to the President. It is based on 31 years of experience in the House and I know it expresses the sentiment of the House and the members of my Committee. The members of my Committee are important. Undoubtedly we will be getting requests for emergency appropriations."

STEPHEN EARLY

Memoradum by Steve Early, 19 September 1939, President's Secretaries' Files PSF 132, Roosevelt Library.

4.11 Roper opinion poll, September 1939

At the outbreak of war Roosevelt knew that whatever his personal sentiments he had to take note of the state of public and congressional opinion. The opinion polls revealed the fractured state of American opinion.

Which of these comes closest to describing what you think America should do about the present European war?

	Total	Sex: Male	Female	Age: Under 40	Over 40
	%	%	%	%	%
Enter the war at once on the side of England, France and Poland.	2.5	3.6	1.3	2.1	2.8
Find some way of supporting Germany.	.2	.2	.1	.1	.3
Take no sides but stay out of the war entirely, but offer to sell to anyone on a cash-and-carry basis.	37.5	43.0	32.2	37.8	37.2
Do not enter the war, but supply England, France, and Poland with materials and food, and refuse to ship anything to Germany.	8.9	9.0	8.7	8.8	9.0
Stay out now and for as long as we can, but go into war on the side of England and France if they are in real danger of losing, and in the meantime help that side with food and materials.	14.7	16.1	13.3	15.4	14.0
Have nothing to do with any warring country – don't even trade with them on a cash-and-carry basis.	29.9	23.6	36.1	29.9	29.9

From Robert E. Sherwood, *The White House Papers of Harry L. Hopkins*, Vol. 1 (London, Eyre and Spottiswoode, 1948), p. 129.

4.12 Neutrality Act, 3 November 1939

In September 1939 Roosevelt, seeking a revision of the neutrality legislation that effectively severed all American aid to the democracies, recalled Congress. The result, after considerable politicking, was the 1939 Neutrality Act allowing Britain and France to continue trading with the United States on a cash-and-carry basis.

Joint Resolution
To preserve the neutrality and the peace of the United States and to secure the safety of its citizens and their interests.

Whereas the United States, desiring to preserve its neutrality in wars between foreign states and desiring also to avoid involvement therein, voluntarily imposes upon its nationals by domestic legislation the restrictions set out in this joint resolution; and

Whereas by so doing the United States waives none of its own rights or privileges to which it and its nationals are entitled under the law of nations; and

Whereas the United States hereby expressly reserves the right to repeal, change or modify this joint resolution or any other domestic legislation in the interests of the peace, security or welfare of the United States and its people. Therefore be it

Resolved by the Senate and the House of Representatives of the United States of America in Congress assembled,

Proclamation of a State of War Between Foreign States

Section 1. (a) That whenever the President, or the Congress by concurrent resolution, shall find that there exists a state of war between foreign states, and that it is necessary to promote the security or preserve the peace of the United States or to protect the lives of citizens of the United States, the President shall issue a proclamation naming the states involved; and he shall, from time to time, by proclamation, name other states as and when they may become involved in the war ...

Commerce with States engaged in Armed Conflict

Sec.2 (a) Whenever the President shall have issued a proclamation under the authority of section 1 (a) it shall thereafter be unlawful for any American vessel to carry any passengers or any articles of materials to any state named in such proclamation.

(b) Whoever shall violate any of the provisions of subsection (a) of this section or of any regulations issued thereunder shall, upon conviction thereof, be fined not more than $50,000 or imprisoned for not more than five years, or both ...

(c) Whenever the President shall have issued a proclamation under the authority of section 1 (a) it shall thereafter be unlawful to export or transport, or attempt to export or transport, or cause to be exported or transported, from the United States to any state named in such proclamation, any articles or materials ... until all right, title and interest therein shall have been transferred to some foreign government, agency, institution, association, partnership, corporation, or national.

Reproduced in Hans-Adolf Jacobsen and Arthur L. Smith (eds), *World War II: Policy and Strategy – Selected Documents with Commentary* (California, Clio Books, 1979), p. 37.

4.13 Roosevelt's fear for the Low Countries, 8 May 1940

On 8 May 1940 Roosevelt wrote to John Cudahy, the American Ambassador in Brussels since 1939. The letter revealed Roosevelt's growing concern that Germany was about to attack the Low Countries, from which his family had originated. Roosevelt was particularly proud of his Dutch roots and would regard any attack on the Netherlands as a personal as well as a national issue.

The news today is very bad and, of course, my hope, being of the Netherlands on my father's side and of Belgium on my Mother's side, is that both nations will resist the rumoured ultimatum to the bitter end.

I hope the King will not forget my suggestion that he send the children and his mother to this country, and, as you know there is a cruiser at Lisbon which is available for just this. This thought includes the grandchildren of the Queen of the Netherlands and the children of the Luxembourg family.

I am in extremely good health but, of course, much depressed and much occupied with world affairs. As you know things in the Far East are still in an extremely uncertain state – and if the whole of the Mediterranean becomes involved the good people in this country will wake up to the world situation. They are already beginning to but still have a long way to go.

Take care of yourself and don't take any unnecessary risks.

Roosevelt to Cudahy, 8 May 1940, Cudahy Papers, Roosevelt Library.

4.14 Roosevelt expresses his concerns to the royal family of the Netherlands

In December 1939 Roosevelt had drafted a letter to the Queen of the Netherlands inviting her to send her children to stay with the President at his home at Hyde Park, New York. The invitation included Princess Juliana and her family. On 8 May 1940 the attention of the royal family of the Netherlands returned to the President's offer. Later that month, as Holland was invaded by German forces, the Dutch royal family would be evacuated to Britain by the Royal Navy.

The President desires me to say that any request from the Princess Royal for the despatch of a cruiser will of course be regarded as equivalent to a request from the Queen herself. The President suggests that in the interests of safety of the Princess and of her family it would be wise for them to consider travelling by way of France to Lisbon where this government has based a cruiser which could transport the royal family to the United States.

Any ship in the channel is of course liable to air attack.

Please inform the Queen that the President in line with his previous message will do everything possible to assure the safety of the Princess's family in the event that an emergency arises.

Acting Secretary of State to the Minister in the Netherlands, 8 May 1940, *Foreign Relations of the United States*, 1940, Vol. 1 (Washington DC, United States Government Printing Office, 1959), p. 187.

4.15 Joseph Kennedy on the war situation, 14 May 1940

Joseph Kennedy, the American Ambassador to London from 1938 to 1940, was convinced, especially after the fall of France in 1940, that America's best interests would be served by remaining a non-belligerent in the war. With an Irish background, Kennedy was no friend of the British and he constantly downplayed Britain's chances in the war. After he returned to the United States in October 1940 he publicly advocated isolation from the current war.

I just left Churchill at one o'clock. He is sending you a message tomorrow morning saying he considers with the (likely) entrance of Italy, the chances of the Allies winning is slight. He said the German push is showing great power and although the French are holding tonight they are definitely worried. They are asking for more British troops at once, but Churchill is unwilling to send more from England at this time because he is convinced within a month England will be vigorously attacked. The reason for his message to you is that he needs help badly. I asked him what the United States could do to help that would not leave the United States holding the bag for a war in which the Allies expected to be beaten. It seems that if we had to fight to protect our lives we would do better fighting in our own backyard. I said you know our strength. What could we do if we wanted to help you all we can. You do not need money or credit now. The bulk of our Navy is in the Pacific and we have not enough airplanes for our own use and our Army is not up to requirements. So if this is going to be a quick war all over in a few months what could we do. He said it was his intention to ask for the loan of 30 or 40 of our old destroyers and also whatever airplanes we could spare right now.

He said regardless of what Germany does to England and France, England will never give up as long as he remains a power in public life even if England is burnt to the ground. Why, said he, the Government will move to Canada and take the fleet and fight on.

J. Kennedy to Roosevelt, 14 May 1940, *Foreign Relations of the United States*, 1940, Vol. 3 (Washington DC, United States Government Printing Office, 1959), pp. 29–30.

4.16 Preserving the New Deal in war: radio address by Roosevelt, 26 May 1940

In a radio address to the nation on 26 May Roosevelt spoke out about the need to preserve the New Deal in the midst of a new, foreign-generated crisis.

We must make sure, in all that we do, that there be no breakdown or cancellation of any of the great social gains which we have made in these past years. We have carried on an offensive on a broad front against social and economic inequalities and abuses which had made our society weak. That offensive should not now be broken down by the pincers movement of those who would use the present needs of physical military defense to destroy it.

There is nothing in our present emergency to justify making the workers of our nation toil for longer hours than now limited by statute. As more orders come in and as more work has to be done, tens of thousands of people, who are now unemployed, will, I believe, receive employment.

There is nothing in our present emergency to justify a lowering of the standards of employment. Minimum wages should not be reduced. It is my hope, indeed, that the new speed-up of production will cause many businesses which now pay below the minimum standards to bring their wages up.

There is nothing in our present emergency to justify a breaking down of old age pensions or of unemployment insurance. I would rather see the systems extended to other groups who do not now enjoy them.

There is nothing in our present emergency to justify a retreat from any of our social objectives – from conservation of natural resources, assistance to agriculture, housing, and help to the under-privileged.

Basil Rauch, *The Roosevelt Reader* (New York, Holt, Rinehart & Winston, 1964), pp. 235–6.

4.17 Roosevelt to Lewis W. Douglas, in New York, 7 June 1940

In the aftermath of the fall of France in June 1940, the Roosevelt administration faced a critical decision: should it step up aid to Britain in order to maintain her in the war, or should the administration concentrate all its efforts on building up the military capacity of the United States. In a letter to a former ally, with whom he had fallen out over domestic policy in 1934, Roosevelt reveals that he has decided to increase aid to the British, even at the expense of the security of the United States. Roosevelt considered that the British had to be kept in the fight. The Royal Navy controlling the Atlantic formed a defensive shield behind which the United States could shelter and build up its strength. Douglas was later appointed War Shipping Administrator.

Dear Lew:

I beat you to it! Very many planes are actually on the way to the Allies, deliveries to this Government being put off. Furthermore, the Attorney General has given an excellent ruling under which we are acting. We are turning in old Army and Navy materiel to the manufacturers who have been given orders for new and up-to-date materiel. I have a sneaking suspicion that the old materiel which we are turning in will be on its way to France in a few days.

Actually I am adopting the "thought" that the more effective immediately usable materiel we can get to the other side will mean the destruction of an equivalent amount of German materiel – thereby aiding American defense in the long run.

So you see I am doing everything possible – though I am not talking very much about it because a certain element of the Press, like the Scripps-Howard papers, would undoubtedly pervert it, attack it, and confuse the public mind. This is inadvisable even though I am personally well accustomed to it.

I am glad you found the sentiment right in Arizona. Very soon there will be the simple statement you speak of.

Elliot Roosevelt (ed.), *The Roosevelt Letters* (London, Harrap, 1952), p. 319.

4.18 Meeting between Secretary of State Cordell Hull and the British Ambassador, Lord Lothian, 27 June 1940

On 27 June 1940, in the aftermath of the defeat of France, the British Ambassador Lord Lothian called on American Secretary of State Cordell Hull to discuss the growing problem of Japan. Japan had been expanding at the expense of China since the 1890s, marked by incidents such as the Japanese seizure of the province of Manchuria in 1931 and the outbreak of full-scale Sino-Japanese hostilities in 1937. German victory in the west meant that Japan might be tempted to try to seize the East Asian imperial possessions of French Indo-China and the oil-rich Dutch East Indies. That in turn might lead to the outbreak of war between the Japanese and the British and Americans. Britain was ill-prepared to fight a war against Hitler in Europe, against Mussolini in the Mediterranean and against Japan in the Pacific. Thus the British looked to America to take the lead role in preventing an expanded war in East Asia. In his memoirs Cordell Hull records his scepticism at Britain's suggestions as to the direction of American foreign policy.

Britain believed there were only two courses open. One was for the United States to increase pressure on Japan either by imposing a full embargo on exports to Japan or by sending warships to [the British fleet base at] Singapore, fully realizing that these steps might result in war. The second was to negotiate a full settlement with Japan ...

The following day, after discussing Britain's proposals with the President and with my associates at the State Department, I called Lothian ... back to my office. "Sending the fleet to Singapore," I remarked "would leave the entire Atlantic seabord, north and south, exposed to possible European threats. Our main fleet is already well out in the Pacific, near Hawaii.

"As to the embargo proposal, we have been progressively bringing economic pressure on Japan since last summer, now a year ago." I enumerated the list of steps we had taken in this regard ... "We've been doing and are doing everything possible short of a serious risk of actual military hostilities," I continued, "to keep the Japanese situation stabilized ..."

As to Britain's second proposal – a joint effort to bring about peace between Japan and China – I outlined ... the conversations between Arita and Grew in Tokyo during the past several weeks.

"Until the French surrender," I said, "the developments from these conversations were increasingly encouraging. But since the surrender the military group is moving in the direction of Hitler and Hitlerism, with all that this means ...

"Japan's leaders feel that an extraordinary opportunity lies before them to impose their political will in the Far East. They intend to pursue that objective wherever they are not confronted with material opposition. I see little to warrant the hope that the Japanese can be weaned away from this objective by offers of intangible concessions or of future material assistance."

Cordell Hull, *The Memoirs of Cordell Hull*, Vol. 1 (London, Hodder and Stoughton, 1948), pp. 897–8.

4.19 Roosevelt to David I. Walsh, in Washington, 22 August 1940

Senator David Walsh was chairman of the Naval Affairs Committee. He opposed the sale of war materials to Great Britain, which he felt would weaken the defence of the western hemisphere and lead to a reaction amongst the American public.

Dear Dave:

Here is the real meat in the coconut as expressed to me by a Dutchess County farmer yesterday morning. I told him the gist of the proposal which is, in effect, to buy ninety-nine year leases from Great Britain for at least seven naval and air bases in British Colonial possessions – not including the Dominion of Canada, which is a separate study on my part. The farmer replied somewhat as follows:

"Say, ain't you the Commander-in-Chief? If you are and own fifty muzzle-loadin' rifles of the Civil War period you would be a chump if you declined to exchange them for seven modern machine guns – wouldn't you?"

Frankly, my difficulty is that as President and Commander-in-Chief I have no right to think of politics in the sense of being a candidate or desiring votes. You and I know that our weakness in the past has lain in the fact that from Newfoundland to Trinidad our sole protection OFFSHORE lies in the three contiguous Islands of Porto Rico, St. Thomas and St. Croix. That, in the nature of modern warfare, is a definite operating handicap. If for fifty ships, which are on their last legs anyway, we can get the right to put in naval and air bases in Newfoundland, Bermuda, the Bahamas, Jamaica, St. Lucia, Trinidad and British Guiana, then our operating deficiency is largely cured ...

By the way, the fifty destroyers are the same type of ship which we have been from time to time striking from the naval list and selling for scrap for, I think, $4,000 or $5,000 per destroyer. On that basis, the cost of the right to at least seven naval and air bases is an extremely low one from the point of view of the United States Government – i.e., about $250,000!

I do hope you will not oppose the deal which, from the point of view of the United States, I regard as being the finest thing for the nation that has been done in your lifetime and mine. I am absolutely certain that this particular deal will not get us into war and, incidentally, that we are not going into war anyway unless Germany wishes to attack us.

Elliot Roosevelt (ed.), *The Roosevelt Letters* (London, Harrap, 1952), p. 319.

4.20 War and the policy of the United States, 4 November 1940

In late 1940 there was an ongoing debate about the extent to which America should aid Great Britain. After the fall of France in June 1940, Roosevelt had determined that the survival of Britain was a vital American interest, and the destroyers for bases deal had been concluded as a short-term measure to ensure the continuation of Britain in the war. By November 1940, as it became increasingly apparent that Britain was safe from German invasion until at least the summer of 1941, the attention of the administration began to turn to the longer term. Admiral William Leahy, the Chief of Naval Operations, was one of the most powerful voices in the debate.

Referring to my very brief touch in a recent conference as to the desirability of obtaining at once some light upon the major decisions which the President may make for guiding our future naval effort in the event of war, and in further immediate preparation for war, you may recall my remarks the evening we discussed War Plans for the Navy. I stated then that if Britain wins decisively against Germany we could win everywhere; but that if she loses the problem confronting us would be very great; and, while we might not lose everywhere, we might, possibly, not win anywhere.

As I stated last winter on the Hill, in these circumstances we would be set back on our haunches. Our war effort, instead of being widespread, would then have to be confined to the Western Hemisphere.

I now wish to expand my remarks, and to present to you my views concerning steps we might take to meet the situation that will exist should the United States enter war either alone or with allies. In this presentation, I have endeavoured to keep in view the political realities in our own country.

The first thing to consider is how and where we might become involved.

The immediate war alternatives seem to be:

(a) War with Japan in which we have no allies. This might be precipitated by Japanese armed opposition should we strongly reinforce our Asiatic Fleet or the Philippines Garrison, should we start fortifying Guam, or should we impose additional important economic sanctions; or it might be precipitated by ourselves in case of overt Japanese action against us, or by further extension of Japanese hegemony.

(b) War with Japan in which we have the British Empire, or the British Empire and the Netherlands East Indies as allies. This might be precipitated by one of the causes mentioned in (a), by our movement of a naval reinforcement to Singapore, or by a Japanese attack on British or Netherlands territory.

(c) War with Japan in which she is aided by Germany and Italy, and in which we are or are not aided by allies. To the causes of such a war, previously listed, might be added augmented American material assistance to Great Britain, our active military intervention in Britain's favor, or our active resistance to German extension of military activities to the Western Hemisphere.

(d) War with Germany and Italy in which Japan would not be initially involved, and in which we would be allied with the British. Such a war would be initiated by American decision to intervene for the purpose of preventing the disruption of the British Empire, or German capture of the British Isles.

(e) We should also consider the alternative of now remaining out of the war, and devoting ourselves exclusively to building up our defense of the Western Hemisphere, plus the preservation by peaceful means of our Far Eastern interests, and plus also continued material assistance to Great Britain.

As I see it, our major national objectives in the immediate future might be stated as preservation of the territorial, economic and ideological integrity of the United States, plus that of the remainder of the Western Hemisphere; the prevention of the disruption of the British Empire, with all that such a consummation implies; and the diminution of the offensive military power of Japan, with a view to the retention of our economic and political interests in the Far East. It is doubtful, however, that it would be in our interest to reduce Japan to the status of an inferior military and economic power. A balance of power in the Far East is to our interest as much as is a balance of power in Europe.

The questions that confront me are concerned with the preparation and distribution of the naval forces of the United States, in cooperation with its military forces, for use in war in the accomplishment of all or part or these national objectives.

I can only surmise as to the military, political, and economic situation that would exist in the Atlantic should the British Empire collapse. Since Latin-America has rich natural resources, and is the only important area of the world not now under the practical control of strong military powers, we can not dismiss the possibility that, sooner or later, victorious Axis nations might move firmly in that direction. For some years they might remain too weak to attack directly across the sea; their effort more likely would first be devoted to developing Latin American economic dependence, combined with strongly reinforced internal political upheavals for the purpose of establishing friendly regimes in effective military control. The immediacy of danger to us may depend on the security of the Axis military position in Eastern Europe and the Mediterranean, the degree of our own military preoccupation in the Pacific, and the disturbing influence of unsatisfied needs of Latin-America.

The present situation of the British Empire is not encouraging. I believe it is easily possible, lacking active American military assistance, for that empire to lose this war and eventually be disrupted.

It is my opinion that the British are over-optimistic as to their chances of ultimate success. It is not at all sure that the British Isles can hold out, and it may be that they do not realize the danger that will exist should they lose in other regions.

Should Britain lose the war, the military consequences for the United States would be serious.

If we are to prevent the disruption of the British Empire, we must support its vital needs.

Obviously, the British Isles, the "Heart of the Empire," must remain intact.

But even if the British Isles are held, this does not mean that Britain can win the war. To win, she must finally be able to effect the complete, or, at least, the partial collapse of the German Reich.

This result might, conceivably, be accomplished by economic starvation through the agency of the blockade …

Alone, the British Empire lacks the man power and the material means to master Germany. Assistance by powerful allies is necessary both with respect to men and with respect to munitions and supplies. If such assistance is to function effectively, Britain must not only continue to maintain the blockade, but she must also retain intact geographical positions from which successful land action can later be launched.

Provided England continues to sustain its present successful resistance at home, the area of next concern to the British Empire ought to be the Egyptian Theater.

Should Egypt be lost, the Eastern Mediterranean would be opened to Germany and Italy, the effectiveness of the sea blockade would be largely nullified; Turkey's military position would be fully compromised; and all hope of Russian intervention would vanish.

Any anti-German offensive in the Near East would then become impossible.

The spot next in importance to Egypt might be Gibraltar, combined with West and Northwest Africa. From this area an ultimate offensive through Portugal and Spain might give results equal to those which many years ago were produced by Wellington. The western gate to the Mediterranean would still be kept closed, provided Britain holds this region.

This brief discussion naturally brings into question the value to Britain of the Mediterranean relative to that of Hong Kong, Singapore and India. Were the Mediterranean lost, Britain's strength in the Far East could be much augmented without weakening home territory.

Japan probably wants the British out of Hong Kong and Singapore; and wants economic control, and ultimately military control of Malaysia.

It is very questionable if Japan has territorial ambitions in Australia and New Zealand.

But does she now wish the British out of India, thus exposing that region and Western China to early Russian penetration or influence? I doubt it.

It would seem probable that Japan, devoted to the Axis alliance only so far as her own immediate interests are involved, would prefer not to move military forces against Britain, and possibly not against the Netherlands East Indies, because, if she can obtain a high degree of economic control over Malaysia, she will then be in a position to improve her financial structure by increased trade with Britain and America. Her economic offensive power will be increased. Her military dominance will follow rapidly or slowly, as seems best at the time.

The Netherlands East Indies has 60,000,000 people, under the rule of 80,000 Dutchmen, including women and children. This political situation can not be viewed as in permanent equilibrium. The rulers are unsupported by a home country or by an alliance. Native rebellions have occurred in the past, and may recur in the future. These Dutchmen will act in what they believe is their own selfish best interests.

Will they alone resist aggression, or will they accept an accommodation with the Japanese?

Will they resist, if supported only by the British Empire?

Will they firmly resist, if supported by the British Empire and the United States?

Will the British resist Japanese aggression directed only against the Netherlands East Indies?

Should both firmly resist, what local military assistance will they require from the United States to ensure success?

No light on these questions has been thrown by the report of the proceedings of the recent Singapore Conference.

The basic character of a war against Japan by the British and Dutch would be the fixed defense of the Malay Peninsula, Sumatra and Java. The allied army, naval, and air forces now in position are considerable, and some future reenforcement may be expected from Australia and New Zealand. Borneo and the islands of the East are vulnerable. There is little chance for an allied offensive. Without Dutch assistance, the external effectiveness of the British bases at Hong Kong and Singapore would soon disappear.

The Japanese deployment in Manchukuo and China requires much of their Army, large supplies and merchant tonnage, and some naval force. It is doubtful if Japan will feel secure in withdrawing much strength from in front of Russia, regardless of non-aggression agreements. The winter lull in China will probably permit a withdrawal of the forces they need for a campaign against Malaysia. The availability of ample supplies for such a campaign is problematical.

Provided the British and Dutch cooperate in a vigorous and efficient defense of Malaysia, Japan will need to make a major effort with all categories of military force to capture the entire area. The campaign might even last several months. Whether Japan would concurrently be able successfully to attack Hong Kong and the Philippines, and also strongly to support the fixed positions in the Mid-Pacific, seems doubtful.

During such a campaign, due to her wide dispersion of effort, Japan would, unquestionably, be more vulnerable to attack by the United States (or by Russia) than she would be once Malaysia is in her possession.

This brings us to a consideration of the strategy of an American war against Japan, that is, either the so-called "Orange Plan," or a modification.

You have heard enough of the Orange Plan to know that, in a nutshell, it envisages our Fleet's proceeding westward through the Marshalls and the Carolines, consolidating as it goes, and then on to the recapture of the Philippines. Once there, the plan contemplates the eventual economic starvation of Japan, and, finally, the complete destruction of her external military power. Its accomplishment would require several years, and the absorption of the full military, naval, and economic energy of the American people. It must be understood that the Orange Plan was drawn up to govern our operations when the United States and Japan are at war, and no other nations are involved ...

Should we adopt the present Orange Plan today, or any modification of that plan which involves the movement of very strong naval and army contingents to the Far East, we would have to accept considerable danger in the Atlantic, and would probably be unable to augment our material assistance to Great Britain.

We should, therefore, examine other plans which involve a war having a more limited objective than the complete defeat of Japan, and in which we would undertake hostilities only in cooperation with the British and Dutch, and in which they undertake to provide an effective and continued resistance in ... Malaysia.

Our involvement in war in the Pacific might well make us also an ally of Britain in the Atlantic, for helping our ally and for defending ourselves, would, by just so much, reduce the power which the United

States Fleet could put forth in the Pacific.

The objective in a limited war against Japan would be the reduction of Japanese offensive power chiefly through economic blockade. Under one concept, allied strategy would comprise holding the Malay Barrier, denying access to other sources of supply in Malaysia, severing her lines of communication with the Western Hemisphere, and raiding communications to the Mid-Pacific ... United States defensive strategy would also require Army reinforcement of Alaska and the Hawaiian Islands, the establishment of naval bases in Fiji–Samoan and Gilbert Islands areas, and denial to Japan of the use of the Marshalls as light force bases ...

It is out of the question to consider sending our entire Fleet at once to Singapore. Base facilities are far too limited, the supply problem would be very great, and Hawaii, Alaska, and our coasts would be greatly exposed to raids ...

Let us now look eastward, and examine our possible action in the Atlantic.

In the first place, if we avoid serious commitment in the Pacific, the purely American Atlantic problem, envisaging defense of our coasts, the Caribbean, Canada and South America, plus giving strong naval assistance to Britain, is not difficult so long as the British are able to maintain their present naval activity. Should the British Isles then fall we would find ourselves acting alone, and at war with the world ...

Should we enter the war as an ally of Great Britain, and not then be at war with Japan, we envisage the British asking us for widespread naval assistance. Roughly, they would want us, in the Western Atlantic Ocean from Cape Sable to Cape Horn, to protect shipping against raiders and submarine activities. They would also need strong reenforcements for their escort and minesweeping forces in their home waters; and strong flying boat reconnaissance ... To their home waters they would have us send submarines and small craft, and to the Mediterranean assistance of any character which we may be able to provide. They would expect us to take charge of allied interests in the Pacific, and to send a naval detachment to Singapore.

This purely naval assistance, would not, in my opinion, assure final victory for Great Britain ...

Were we to enter the war against Germany and Italy as an ally of Great Britain, I do not necessarily anticipate immediate hostile action by Japan, whatever may be her Axis obligation ...

The strong wish of the American government and people at present seems to be to remain at peace. In spite of this, we must face the possibility that we may at any moment become involved in war. With war in prospect, I believe our every effort should be directed towards the prosecution of a national policy with mutually supporting diplomatic and military aspects, and having as its guiding feature a determination that any intervention we may undertake shall be such as will ultimately best promote our own national interests ...

A very strong pillar of the defense structure of the Americas has, for many years, been the balance of power existing in Europe. The collapse of Great Britain or the destruction or surrender of the British Fleet will destroy this balance and will free European military power for possible encroachment in this hemisphere.

I believe that we should recognize as the foundation of adequate armed strength the possession of a profitable foreign trade, both in raw materials and in finished goods. Without such a trade, our economy can scarcely support heavy armaments. The restoration of foreign trade, particularly with Europe, may depend upon the continued integrity of the British Empire.

It may be possible for us to prevent a British collapse by military intervention.

Our interests in the Far East are very important. The economic effect of a complete Japanese hegemony in that region is conjectural. But regardless of economic considerations, we have heretofore strongly opposed the further expansion of Japan ...

As I see affairs today, answers to the following broad questions will be most useful to the Navy:

(A) Shall our principal military effort he directed towards hemisphere defense ... ? ...

(B) Shall we prepare for a full offensive against Japan, premised on assistance from the British and Dutch forces in the Far East, and remain on the strict defensive in the Atlantic? ...

(C) Shall we plan for sending the strongest possible military assistance to both the British in Europe, and to the British, Dutch and Chinese in the Far East? ...

(D) Shall we direct our efforts toward an eventual strong offensive in the Atlantic as an ally of the British, and a defensive in the Pacific? ...

I believe that the continued existence of the British Empire, combined with building up a strong protection in our home areas, will do more to ensure the status quo in the Western Hemisphere, and to promote our principal national interests. As I have previously stated, I also believe that Great Britain requires from us very great help in the Atlantic ... if she is to be enabled to survive ...

The odds seem against our being able under Plan (D) to check Japanese expansion unless we win the war in Europe. We might not long retain possession of the Philippines. Our political and military influence in the Far East might largely disappear, so long as we are fully engaged in the Atlantic. A preliminary to a war in this category would be a positive effort to avoid war with Japan, and to endeavour to prevent war between Japan and the British Empire and the Netherlands East Indies ...

Accordingly, I make the recommendation that, as preliminary to possible entry of the United States into the conflict, the United States Army and Navy at once undertake secret staff talks with the British military authorities in Washington ... with a view to reaching agreements and laying down plans for promoting unity of allied effort should the United States find it necessary to enter the war under any of the alternative eventualities considered in this memorandum.

Memorandum for the Secretary of the Navy by Chief of Naval Operations, 4 November 1940, President's Secretary's Files PSF 59, Roosevelt Library.

4.21 British Embassy, Washington DC, to British Foreign Office, 8 January 1941

By the start of 1941 Britain was seriously short of negotiable assets and cash to fund the continued shipment of war supplies from the United States. German submarines and surface raiders were sinking an alarming number of British merchant ships in the Atlantic. Meanwhile, Britain faced a difficult war in the Mediterranean and North Africa against the Italians, and in the Pacific Japanese ambitions gave great cause for concern. British officials scrutinised every word issued by the Roosevelt administration for signs that America might soon be joining Britain in the war.

Telegram 3322 from Mr. Butler in Washington.
President's radio address on December 29th was the principal event of the week. Delivered in his impressive manner, President's firm declaration that the ideals and policies of totalitarian states constitute a threat to the security of the United States and that while there was no question of sending any American expeditionary force to fight abroad it was in the interest of American national defence to send all possible aid to Britain, was received with widespread approval. Even isolationist criticism was half-hearted and made no attempt to claim that in advocating aid to Britain the President was not representative of public opinion in this country. Some regret was expressed that the President had not explained in greater detail the exact steps he proposed to take to provide the promised assistance to Britain. It was, however, generally expected that President would cover this point in his message to Congress on January 6th.

Spurred on by the President's address the isolationists have been gathering their forces in anticipation of discussing in Congress the President's plans for helping Britain. Senator Wheeler, who seems to be recognized as leader of the isolationist group in Congress, made a radio broadcast on December 30th declaring that the President's policy was calculated to lead United States straight into war. Instead, the Senator argued, the United States should urge belligerents to accept a "just peace" as a basis for which he suggested "restoration of Alsace-Lorraine to France, restoration of German colonies, protection of all racial and religious minorities in all countries, internationalization of Suez Canal, no indemnities and reparations, arms limitation".

Senator Wheeler has made other pronouncements on much the same lines throughout the week and has been ... [joined] by Senator Vandenberg who in a newspaper interview urged that an effort be made to induce the belligerents to enter into peace negotiations before any steps to send additional aid to Britain were taken. None of these statements has met with any material support in the press, but it is clear that the isolationists in both houses intend to do what they can to obstruct the administration's plans to help Britain. They are small in numbers and without much great support from the public, [and they] can hardly hope to do more than delay adoption of President's proposals; but they are all expert politicians and their capacity for obstruction is considerable. The isolationist cause has hardly been helped by Mr Verne Marshall and his "no foreign wars committee". Mr Marshall made a bad impression at a press conference he held in

Washington on December 30th, and he made matters worse by declaring that one of his backers was the notorious oil magnate W.R. Davis, who he said had brought from Germany in October 1939 certain peace proposals which State Department had refused to consider. This statement not only provoked a rebuttal from the State Department but a series of attacks in the press on Mr Davies. Latter has denied that he is in any way a German agent, but the result has generally been to discredit Mr Marshall and his committee. On the other hand, under stimulus of unlimited demands that are to be made on American assistance the questions of war aims are increasingly discussed. Our friends would be strengthened by some British declaration to the effect that a just peace will not be prejudiced by provision of secret treaties.

British National Archives (Public Record Office) TNA: PRO FO371/26145.

4.22 The Lend Lease Act, 11 March 1941

The 1941 Lend Lease Act reflected the fact that Britain was no longer in a position to pay for the war material it required from the United States. The Lend Lease Act gave the power to lend or lease 'defense articles' to Britain for the duration of the war. The repayment terms were left deliberately vague. Roosevelt did not want the issue of war debts to cloud international relations after the Second World War as it had after the First. The term 'defense article' was given as wide definition as possible to ensure that the administration could supply whatever it sought fit to the British.

Further to Promote the defense of the United States, and for other purposes.

Be it enacted by the Senate and House of Representatives of the United States of America in Congress assembled, That this Act may be cited as "An Act to Promote the Defense of the United States."

Sec.2. As used in the Act –

(a) The term "defense article" means –

(1) Any weapon, munition, aircraft, vessel, or boat;

(2) Any machinery, facility, tool, material, or supply necessary for the manufacture, production, processing, repair, servicing, or operation of any article described in this subsection;

(3) Any component material or part of or equipment for any article described in this subsection:

(4) Any agricultural, industrial or other commodity or article for defense.

Reproduced in Hans-Adolf Jacobsen and Arthur L. Smith (eds), *World War II: Policy and Strategy – Selected Documents with Commentary* (California, Clio Books, 1979), p. 138.

4.23 America first: speech by Charles Lindbergh to the America First Committee, 23 April 1941

Through the America First Organisation, the distinguished aviator Charles Lindbergh played a leading role in mobilising those forces which were opposed to American intervention in the world war. Lindbergh had a very high opinion of German military strength and considered that American interests were best served by building up the military strength of the western hemisphere. This was in direct opposition to Roosevelt's policy of maintaining Great Britain in the war. Roosevelt reasoned that as long as Britain was able to fight Nazi Germany the United States were safe.

There is a policy open to this nation that will lead to success – a policy that leaves us free to follow our own way of life, and to develop our own civilisation. It is not a new and untried idea. It was advocated by Washington. It was incorporated in the Monroe Doctrine. Under its guidance, the United States has become the greatest nation in the world.

It is based upon the belief that the security of a nation lies in the strength and character of its own people. It recommends the maintenance of armed forces sufficient to defend this hemisphere from attack by any combination of foreign powers. It demands faith in an independent American destiny. This is the policy of the America First Committee today. It is a policy not of isolation, but of independence;

not of defeat, but of courage. It is a policy that led this nation to success during the most trying years of our history, and it is a policy that will lead us to success again.

We have weakened ourselves for many months, and still worse, we have divided our own people by this dabbling in Europe's wars. While we should have been concentrating on American defence we have been forced to argue over foreign quarrels. We must turn our eyes and our faith back to our own country before it is too late. And when we do this, a different vista opens before us. Practically every difficulty we would face in invading Europe becomes an asset to us in defending America. Our enemy, and not we, would then have the problem of transporting millions of troops across the ocean and landing them on a hostile shore. They, and not we, would have to furnish the convoys to transport guns and trucks and munitions and fuel across three thousand miles of water. Our battleships and submarines would then be fighting close to their home bases. We would then do the bombing from the air and the torpedoing at sea. And if any part of an enemy convoy should ever pass our navy and our air force, they would still be faced with the guns of our coast artillery and behind them the divisions of our Army.

The United States is better situated from a military standpoint than any other nation in the world. Even in our present condition of unpreparedness no foreign power is in a position to invade us today. If we concentrate on our own defences and build the strength that this nation should maintain, no foreign army will ever attempt to land on American shores.

Vital Speeches of the Day, www.votd.com/lindberg.htm.

4.24 Atlantic Charter, 14 August 1941

In August 1941 Roosevelt and the British Prime Minister, Winston Churchill, met on warships off the coast of Newfoundland. Together they drew up the Atlantic Charter, which represented, in effect, a series of war aims for both countries. It was an extraordinary event for the Prime Minister of a belligerent nation and the President of a neutral nation to link their futures in so public a way.

The President of the United States of America and the Prime Minister, Mr. Churchill, representing His Majesty's Government in the United Kingdom, being met together, deem it right to make known certain common principles in the national policies of their respective countries on which they base their hopes for a better future for the world.

First, their countries seek no aggrandizement, territorial or other;

Second, they desire to see no territorial changes that do not accord with the freely expressed wishes of the peoples concerned;

Third, they respect the right of all peoples to choose the form of government under which they will live; and they wish to see sovereign rights and self government restored to those who have been forcibly deprived of them;

Fourth, they will endeavor, with due respect for their existing obligations, to further the enjoyment by all States, great or small, victor or vanquished, of access, on equal terms, to the trade and to the raw materials of the world which are needed for their economic prosperity;

Fifth, they desire to bring about the fullest collaboration between all nations in the economic field with the object of securing, for all, improved labor standards, economic advancement and social security;

Sixth, after the final destruction of the Nazi tyranny, they hope to see established a peace which will afford to all nations the means of dwelling in safety within their own boundaries, and which will afford assurance that all the men in all lands may live out their lives in freedom from fear and want;

Seventh, such a peace should enable all men to traverse the high seas and oceans without hindrance;

Eighth, they believe that all of the nations of the world, for realistic as well as spiritual reasons must come to the abandonment of the use of force. Since no future peace can be maintained if land, sea or air armaments continue to be employed by nations which threaten, or may threaten, aggression outside of their frontiers, they believe, pending the establishment of a wider and permanent system of general security, that the disarmament of such nations is essential. They will likewise aid and encourage all other practicable measures which will lighten for peace-loving peoples the crushing burden of armaments.

Winston S. Churchill, *The Second World War*, Vol. 3 (London, Reprint Society, 1950), pp. 352–4.

4.25 White House news release on the Atlantic Charter meeting, 21 August 1941

The Atlantic Charter meeting needed careful explanation to the American public. Roosevelt stressed the dangers to the world posed by Nazism and that principle would be his guiding light.

TO THE CONGRESS OF THE UNITED STATES:
Over a week ago I held several important conferences at sea with the British Prime Minister. Because of the factor of safety to British, Canadian and American ships and their personnel no prior announcement of these meetings could properly be made.

At the close, a public statement by the Prime Minister and the President was made. I quote it for the information of the Congress and for the record:

The Congress and the President having heretofore determined through the Lend Lease Act on the national policy of American aid to the democracies which East and West are waging war against dictatorships, the military and naval conversations at these meetings made clear gains in furthering the effectiveness of this aid.

Furthermore, the Prime Minister and I are arranging for conferences with the Soviet Union to aid it in its defense against the attack made by the principal aggressor of the modern world – Germany.

Finally, the declaration of principles at this time presents a goal which is worth while for our type of civilization to seek. It is so clear cut that it is difficult to oppose in any major particular without automatically admitting a willingness to accept compromise with Nazism; or to agree to a world peace which would give to Nazism domination over large numbers of conquered nations. Inevitably such a peace would be a gift to Nazism to take breath – armed breath – for a second war to extend the control over Europe and Asia to the American Hemisphere itself.

It is perhaps unnecessary for me to call attention once more to the utter lack of validity of the spoken or written word of the Nazi government.

It is also unnecessary for me to point out that the declaration of principles includes of necessity the world need for freedom of religion and freedom of information. No society of the world organized under the announced principles could survive without these freedoms which are a part of the whole freedom for which we strive.

From Avalon project at Yale Law school, www.yale.ed/lawweb/avalon/wwii/atcmess.htm.

4.26 American press reaction to the Atlantic Charter

As noted by the British newspaper the *Daily Telegraph*, the significance of the Atlantic Charter was not lost on the American press and public. It was widely regarded as a landmark in Anglo-American relations, and an indicator that American intervention in the war was a matter of weeks rather than years away.

The CHICAGO DAILY NEWS' comment is: "The eight points are in line with the best American tradition and will meet with little serious criticism here.

Neither we nor the British wish to impose on other people a form of government they do not want. Our hopes and endeavours will be directed towards peace and prosperity for all, with freedom of the seas and minimum restrictions on trade. The aggressor nations after their defeat will have to be disarmed, and no doubt the policing of the world during the period of transition from war to peace will have to be done by the American and British navies and air forces. Unless we are mistaken, however, the most important implications of the official text reporting the historic meeting are to be found in the reference to the whole problem of the supply of munitions. These words, we fondly believe, bode ill for the Axis aggressors. They mean, we think, that those who need the arms will get the arms. They are an added assurance of final victory."

The KANSAS CITY STAR stated: "The Roosevelt–Churchill statement shows the difficulties of formulating war aims in any details while fighting is in progress. The spirit of political and economic liberalism permeates them, but they necessarily fail to indicate how the ideals set forth will be implemented. Perhaps the undisclosed discussion of immediate problems, such as Vichy and Japan, may prove of more consequence than the eight-point programme."

The ATLANTA CONSTITUTION said: "It is probable that this meeting will rank in world significance with the signing of the Magna Carta at Runnymede and the adoption of the Constitution of the United States. For in its declaration of purpose it outlines a programme for the freedom of the people of the entire world comparable with those historic steps towards the freedom of the peoples of individual nations. Besides such a programme the mouthings of small-souled Isolationists and political opportunists shrink to nothing. It sounds as a clarion call to sacrifice to duty for all men and women with a spark of freedom in their souls."

The DES MOINES TRIBUNE declared: "There has been an absolute need of presenting to the world a charter of purposes that will stand as an alternative to the New Order proposed by Hitler. The presenting of it, even in this very general form, will be important both as a part of war strategy and as a guide to what must follow the war. That Nazism must be frustrated as a condition to anything tolerable at all is obvious in to-day's situation, and it was essential that this, too, should be said."

The MIAMI HERALD stated: "Regardless of what captious Isolationists may level at President Roosevelt for joining with Mr Churchill in a declaration of war aims, no one can reasonably find fault with the aims themselves. The joint declaration is, of course, an admission by the President that we are engaged in an undeclared war on the Axis partners in crime and that we are prepared to take our place at the conference table anew when the time comes to discuss the terms of peace. The eight points obviously are intended to avoid the possibility of another Versailles Treaty with its potentialities for fomenting another war within a generation. Taken separately, the points probably do not mean much. Taken as a whole, however, that statement should bring hope to the overrun small nations of Europe that eventually, when Hitler is crushed, they may live again on their own land as free peoples."

The London correspondent of the CHRISTIAN SCIENCE MONITOR stated: "Britain and the United States have concluded an alliance pledging themselves to win the peace after this war. That is the far-reaching significance of this secret meeting and of the declaration which it produced."

The BALTIMORE SUN commented: "It is the instant gains from this conference that will give it value in the ultimate policies of post-war reconstruction. Unless there are instant gains there will be less opportunity to establish the rules of a liberal and human world."

Other comments were:

The LOS ANGELES TIMES said: "It may be taken for granted that the real purpose and most important results are not set out in the declaration. Plainly there is big stuff in the background."

The ST. LOUIS GLOBE-DEMOCRAT declared: "Mr Roosevelt has been placed in the anomalous position of announcing general war aims at a time when we are, theoretically at least, not at war. He has made far-reaching and serious commitments. In joining Britain in a common determination to achieve the final destruction of Nazi tyranny he has virtually pledged the United States to 'go over the limit' and the limit may be war. Obviously we cannot take a leading role in peace without playing a leading role in war."

The DETROIT FREE PRESS declared boldly: "We are at war. The joint declaration leaves no alternative. May the fruits of victory be more wholesome than the bitter fruits of Versailles."

One of the most extraordinary aspects of this epoch-making colloquy at sea between the two leaders was the fact that, although the American newspapers had been speculating about it for a week, none of them succeeded in obtaining any concrete information on the subject.

It is pointed out today that, for the first time in their history, the American people were ignorant of the precise whereabouts of their President for four days.

Daily Telegraph, 14 August 1941.

4.27 British press reaction to the Atlantic Charter

As evidenced by the *Daily Telegraph* on 15 August 1941, the significance of the Atlantic Charter to Britain's potential to win the Second World War was just as apparent to the British press as it was to the American press.

History has no precedent or parallel for the declaration which was broadcast from London yesterday by Mr Attlee and later issued from the White House in Washington. It announced to the world that the non-belligerent United States is in agreement with the belligerent British Commonwealth upon the war aims which must be attained if the dangers threatening both democracies, and civilisation itself, from Nazism and the Axis are to be averted. President Roosevelt, though his country is still at peace, has conferred with Mr Churchill on the measures which the American and British peoples are taking for their security against the Nazi armaments. The achievement of this unison of policy and concord of action is momentous.

Every circumstance of the manner in which it was secured adds to its force. There is much more than picturesque drama behind the blunt statement that the President and the Prime Minister "met at sea". They met upon the battlefield of the Atlantic. It was a day presaging doom to Hitler when, traversing those ocean lanes kept by parallel patrols of American and British squadrons, the leaders of the two democracies came into counsel and the ensigns of their two countries saluted each other. The world can have no better illustration of the course of the Atlantic battle. The meeting proclaims the change which by united effort has transformed 3,000 miles of ocean from an abyss dividing us into a means and a bond of union, an endless belt of communication and supply.

The statement falls into two parts, the first of which concerns immediate problems of supply, strategy and security. As to supply, both the President and the Prime Minister were accompanied by expert advisors and thus had at hand the means for swift judgement on essentials. They have already shown that their appreciation of each other's character and genius is as complete as their knowledge of the nations which they lead. These conferences will get things done. Lord Beaverbrook, as Minister of Supply, took part in them and is already in Washington for more detailed discussions. The problems are complex, for they now include the needs of Russia. Whatever nations "hold the line of freedom across the tyrant's path" have the material support of the United States. Over all is the governing consideration that the expanding United States forces must be fully equipped for their tasks. To adapt British and American production plans so that each develops the highest potential for the common purpose is urgently necessary.

Daily Telegraph, 15 August 1941.

4.28 Hitler reacts to changes in American policy: Fuehrer Naval Conference, 17 September 1941

On 17 September 1941 five United States destroyers began escorting British convoy HX150. It was the first time that the United States Navy had conducted close escort operations in defence of convoys. Between 17 September and 7 December 1941 the United States Navy helped to escort 26 British convoys across the Atlantic. Inevitably, given the intensity of the German war on Britain's sea lines of communications, there were casualties. On 17 October the USS *Kearny* was torpedoed, resulting in the deaths of eleven sailors, although the ship was able to limp to Iceland. On 31 October the USS *Reuben James* was sunk with the loss of 115 lives. The United States Navy was incurring casualties in an operation which some of Roosevelt's opponents believed was designed to produce sufficient deaths to enable the President to ask an enraged Congress for a declaration of war on Germany. In effect the United States Navy went to war well before the attack on Pearl Harbor on 7 December. On 11 December Hitler would declare war on the United States in recognition of the *de facto* war in the Atlantic which had been under way for weeks.

The strategic and political situation created by the speech of the President of the USA can be evaluated as follows: Roosevelt stated that the "time for active defence" has come. The US patrol vessels and aircraft will protect all merchant ships, not only United States ones, within the "American defence waters", and in so doing they will "no longer wait" until the warships of the Axis attack. The mere fact of their presence in these waters "is equivalent to an attack". From now on they will sail in these waters only "at their own risk". Thus the situation has become considerably clearer. In the future American forces will no longer be employed merely for reconnaisance but also for convoy duty, including escort of British ships. German forces must expect offensive war measures by these US forces in every case of an encounter. There is no longer any difference between British and American ships.

Fuehrer Conferences on Naval Affairs 1939–1945 (London, Greenhill Books, 1990), pp. 231–2.

4.29 Roosevelt to the Emperor of Japan, 6 December 1941

By December 1941 the crisis in American–Japanese relations was coming to a head, a fact clearly recognised in the tone of this letter from Roosevelt to the Emperor of Japan.

The people of the United States ... have eagerly watched the conversations between our two Governments during these past months. We have hoped for a termination of the present conflict between Japan and China. We have hoped that a peace of the Pacific could be consummated in such a way that nationalities of many diverse people could exist side by side without fear of invasion; that unbearable burdens of armaments could be lifted for them all; and that all peoples would resume commerce without discrimination against or in favor of any nation ...

More than a year ago Your Majesty's Government concluded an agreement with the Vichy Government by which five or six thousand Japanese troops were permitted to enter into North French Indo-China for the protection of Japanese troops which were operating against China further north. And this Spring and Summer the Vichy Government permitted further Japanese military forces to enter into Southern French Indo-China for the common defense of French Indo-China ...

During the past few weeks it has become clear to the world that Japanese military, naval and air forces have been sent to Southern Indo-China in such large numbers as to create a reasonable doubt on the part of other nations that this continuing concentration in Indo-China is not defensive in its character ...

There is absolutely no thought on the part of the United States of invading Indo-China if every Japanese soldier or sailor were to be withdrawn therefrom.

I think that we can obtain the same assurance from the Governments of the East Indies, the Governments of Malaya and the Government of Thailand. I would even undertake to ask for the same assurance on the part of the Government of China. Thus a withdrawal of the Japanese forces from Indo-China would result in the assurance of peace throughout the whole of the South Pacific area.

I address myself to Your Majesty at this moment in the fervent hope that Your Majesty may, as I am doing, give thought in this definite emergency to ways of dispelling the dark clouds.

Reproduced in Hans-Adolf Jacobsen and Arthur L. Smith (eds), *World War II: Policy and Strategy – Selected Documents with Commentary* (California, Clio Books, 1979), pp. 175–7.

4.30 Public reactions to Pearl Harbor, 7 December 1941

W. J. Brown, the General Secretary of the British Civil Service Clerical Association who had been in the United States since September, woke up to find that during his afternoon nap the Japanese had attacked Pearl Harbor.

I go to the Brussels for dinner, and then to a newsreel to note popular reaction to the war situation. There is no excitement, no jubilation, no flag-wagging, no cheers – only the same sort of grim acceptance of inevitability as one saw in England in 1939 when war came to us ... Roosevelt, who appears on the screen, is warmly applauded. Overnight his warnings have come true. Tomorrow all America will be lined up behind him, and I shouldn't be surprised if "America First", whose members have done so much to hamper him and to delay the awakening of the American people, were in the van of the procession.

W. J. Brown, *I Meet America* (London, Routledge, 1942), pp. 123–4.

5
New Deal critics

The anti-New Dealers represented a broad cross-section of American opinion from Communist union agitators through to Republican Right libertarians, Supreme Court judges through to revolutionaries. Roosevelt's policies antagonised the political fringes while the majority of Democrats and many Republicans found common cause in the New Deal. However, with the nation's economic difficulties continuing, the political fringes remained dangerous. From their midst might arise someone who might galvanise the discontented into more radical political change either through the ballot box or by direct action.

The intervention of a radical third party candidate in the 1936 presidential election, potentially handing victory to the Republicans, was a particular concern, and the President was worried in 1936 that he enjoyed little press support. He wrote: 'About 85 percent of the press of the Nation supported the opposition. Many newspapers and magazines went to the length of coloring, distorting, or actually omitting important facts in the news columns as well as in the editorial pages' (Franklin Roosevelt in the introduction to *The Public Papers and Addresses of Franklin D. Roosevelt*, Vol. 5, New York, Random House, 1938, p. 3). In the event, Roosevelt's hold on power was not seriously challenged by the Republicans, or by any other political force in the country.

However, New Deal criticism remains an interesting area. In many cases, Roosevelt's opponents were perceptive critics. Some, like Dr Francis Townsend, forced the New Deal to incorporate their concerns. Other critics, like the Supreme Court, had an even more fundamental impact on the New Deal. The Supreme Court's rulings that key sections of the New Deal legislative programme were unconstitutional led to some dramatic changes of policy and produced a number of political crises for the administration.

With the approach and outbreak of European war in 1939 criticism of the Roosevelt administration increasingly focused on foreign affairs and whether the President's policies might lead to American involvement in the world war. Prominent in the attack on the administration were some figures like Father Charles Coughlin who had been prominent critics of the domestic legislation of the New Deal in the mid-1930s. They were joined by new critics such as Charles Lindbergh, who spoke on behalf of the isolationist lobby group America First. Roosevelt's decision to run for a third term in 1940 excited Roosevelt's opponents greatly. They alleged that his willingness to break the convention set down by George Washington, that a president would only serve two terms of office, was concrete evidence of Roosevelt's megalomania. They alleged that he was an American dictator who would only leave office when he died. With the attack on Pearl Harbor on 7 December 1941, and American entry into world war, criticism of Roosevelt and his administration became more muted.

In the event some of Roosevelt's critics were proved right. After winning election for a fourth term in 1944 he would die the following year on 12 April while still in office.

THE ROOTS OF FEAR

5.1 No reason to fear the New Deal

> The New Deal was attacked by some on the right of American politics as being something new, indeed alien to the United States. Here one observer tries to reassure his readers that the New Deal is well within the traditions of American politics, although his references to Nazi Germany and Stalinist Russia would have confirmed exactly what some of Roosevelt's opponents feared.

The ideas on which Roosevelt rode into office were not new. They were the ideas of Henry George and the tax reformers on the 1880's, the ideas of Edward Bellamy and his inspired dream of a mechanical Utopia, the ideas of the Populists and Free Silver Crusaders of the 1890's, who protested against pauperized farmers in the midst of abundant harvests. They were the ideas of Samuel Gompers and the organization of labor as something more than one of the raw materials of industry, the ideas of Phillips Brooks and the cult of Christian chivalry. In fact, the New Deal consisted largely of the ideas which encouraged our forefathers to survive the crude hurly burly of the 1880's and '90's and which sent generations of idealistic young men to Yale, Harvard and Princeton to prepare themselves to serve as the moral aristocracy of the then distant future.

The methods by which Roosevelt applied the ideas of the New Deal were also old stuff. They were the methods of Grover Cleveland and the Civil Service reformers, the methods of Theodore Roosevelt and the "Square Deal," the methods of Woodrow Wilson and "the New Freedom." Above all, they were the methods of the World War, with its truce on partisan politics, its enlistment of non-political experts in responsibility for national reconstruction, its spawning of emergency inter-Departmental Committees, Boards and Administrations, and its wholesale use of publicity and propaganda to win and hold popular support for a prolonged national effort.

In addition to these, Roosevelt had the benefit of several other great national experiments as useful points of reference for the American New Deal. He had before him the spectacle of the Soviet Union with its recent dramatization of economic reorganization through the Five-Year Plan. He had before him the example of Fascist Italy with its regimentation of business, labor and banking in the Corporative State. He had before him the instances of Kemal, Mussolini and Hitler in restoring national pride and self-confidence to beaten or dispirited peoples ... .

He invented nothing in the New Deal.

This is his greatest achievement. He combined these familiar elements so calmly and with so friendly a smile, that even after a year of the New Deal there are still people who do not realize that a revolution has taken place ... His art is the combination of the familiar in such a manner as to produce the new.

Unofficial Observer, *The New Dealers* (New York, Simon and Schuster, 1934), pp. 4–5.

5.2 Gerald Johnson responds to those who liken the New Deal to Fascism or Communism

Critics of the New Deal were only too happy to suggest that in many respects it was un-American, owing more to the practices of Nazi Germany, Fascist Italy or Stalin's Russia.

Yet in the month of March, 1933, the positions of the two men [Hitler and Roosevelt] were strangely similar. Both had risen to power on the crest of a wave of protest set in motion by the same sort of grievances. Both took over countries economically in a state of collapse and visibly disintegrating socially. Both faced the problem of putting millions of idle men back to work immediately, and the even more urgent problem of putting some spirit into an apathetic and despairing people.

There were other similarities. In Germany, as in America, the people were not so much aflame with enthusiasm for the new leader as inflamed with wrath against the old ones. In Germany, as in America, the gravamen of the old leaders' offense was not so much what they had done as what they had failed to do. In Germany, as in America, the indictment of the old leaders included a multitude of counts, but there as here they may all be summed up as failure to obey the injunction of the Constitution of the United States "to provide for the general welfare." Finally, in Germany as in America, the new leader, largely because he was new, was given *carte blanche* to do what he thought best.

If we came out with the New Deal and the Germans came out with Nazism, the main reason is because we had chosen the author of the Commonwealth Club speech and the Germans had chosen the author of *Mein Kampf*. There is at least this much in the "leadership principle."

Even if you are one of those who regard the New Deal as Americanism at its worst, it is still Americanism. However distorted you may think its ideas, they are still ideas whose origin is to be found in the Constitution and the *Federalist*, not in Wagnerian opera. Its traditional hero is Mr. Jefferson, not Wotan; and Mr. Jefferson, with all his faults, was recognizably a statesman, and not a baritone singer seven feet high with cow-horns on his hat. We may have come off badly, but at least we came off with something that looks more like a government than a lunatic stage-manager's setting of the Ride of the Valkyries.

Gerald Johnson, *Roosevelt: Dictator or Democrat* (New York, Harper and Brothers, 1941), pp. 271–2.

5.3 The bureaucracy of the New Deal

Part of the problem with the New Deal was that it created an enlarged bureaucracy which moved at too fast a rate for some of the public. 'Big government' was both costly and controversial, especially in a time of depression. The enemies of the New Deal were not about to depict the bureaucrats in a sympathetic way, and some had little understanding of the suspicion of the federal government. Here Gerald Johnson sets out part of the problem.

The New Deal had offended a good many honest men, as well as all the crooks. To explain how and why would require going into the history of the movement in detail ... The basic trouble, however, was simple enough – things just came too fast. An amazing number of people in the United States – not politicians, bur ordinary citizens – are not prepared to oppose a single one of the major Roosevelt policies and yet dislike Roosevelt. He has not driven them in a direction they would prefer not to take, but he has driven them too fast and too far. As far as their rational processes are concerned, they have accepted the main things for which he stands; but they have not assimilated them emotionally. Hence, while they can tolerate the New Deal, they loathe the New Dealer.

To speed that was difficult must be added plenty of technical errors on the part of the administration personnel. Every incoming administration fills Washington with new faces, but the New Deal did more than that – it filled the capital with new types. The old-fashioned politician was almost submerged in the tide, and even the genus vividly described in the vernacular as the Stuffed Shirt became appreciably less prominent. The newcomers were of all sorts, including many highly intelligent and able men, but also including some who would try the patience of Job; and when they were placed in positions, important or unimportant, where they came into contact with the public, they proceeded to spawn Roosevelt haters with a fecundity that makes that of the rabbit seem the next thing to sterility. Many an honest citizen has gone to Washington in recent years full of good intentions and amiability, only to encounter some supercilious young squirt, sporting a shiny new Ph.D., and stuffed with such arrogance as can be developed only by those whose minds have gone stale through over-training. Of course, in such a case, the honest citizen ought to realise that the squirt is probably a fool, not for the lack of knowledge, but for lack of sense ... So often the outcome has been that the citizen, without changing his views on the main issues at all, has gone home blazing with fury and shouting for Landon, or for Wilkie, or for Melchizedek for President – anybody but Roosevelt.

Gerald W. Johnson, *Roosevelt: An American Study* (London, Hamish Hamilton, 1942), pp. 201–2.

THE REPUBLICANS

5.4 Republican weakness: Roosevelt to Colonel E. M. House, 16 February 1935

As the 1936 presidential election loomed, Roosevelt and other Democrats looked closely at a divided Republican opposition.

Here are the schools of thought of our Opponents at the present time:

1. Regular Republicans who want to stand by the Old Guard organization and nominate Vandenberg or someone even more conservative, even though this might mean defeat.

2. More liberal Republicans who think in terms of Glenn Frank and think they could win with such a candidate.

3. Progressive Republicans like La Follette, Cutting, Nye, etc., who are flirting with the idea of a third ticket anyway with the knowledge that such a third ticket would be beaten but that it would defeat us, elect a conservative Republican and cause a complete swing far to the left before 1940.

All of these Republican elements are flirting with Huey Long and probably financing him. A third Progressive Republican ticket and a fourth "Share the Wealth" ticket they believe would crush us and that then a free for all would result in which case anything might happen.

There is no question that it is all a dangerous situation but when it comes to Show-down these fellows cannot all lie in the same bed and will fight among themselves with almost absolute certainty. They represent every shade.

There is also a question that the rest of this session will be more or less of a madhouse – every Senator a law unto himself and everyone seeking the spotlight. Out of it all I am inclined to think that there will be such disgust on the part of the average voter that some well-timed, common sense campaigning on my part this spring or summer will bring people to their senses. Incidentally, the general economic situation is getting distinctly better, as you know, and, as this goes on, there will be added cries of "don't rock the boat."

This "rumor factory" called Washington almost gets under my skin – but as long as it does not actually do so, we are all right.

Do let me know any new things you hear.

Elliot Roosevelt (ed.), *The Roosevelt Letters* (London, Harrap, 1952), pp. 140–1.

5.5 Republican problems at the local level

The problems of the Republican Party extended from the national to the local level. Here local newspaper the *Worcester Telegram* laments the continuing weakness of the Republicans.

What the Massachusetts Republicans need is a party. There are the Republicans who vote with the Democrats at the nod of the Democratic Governor; there are those who are for liberal expenditures; there are those who are for paying as the state goes; there are the young Republicans ... ; there are the embattled women who are militant and the most convincing; there is the patient and cautious State Committee which hopes for the best; but there is still no rallying around anyone or anything.

Worcester Telegram, 4 August 1935. Reproduced in Harold Gorvine, 'The New Deal in Massachusetts', in John Braeman, Robert H. Bremner and David Brody (eds), *The New Deal: The State and Local Levels*, Vol. 2 (Columbus, Ohio State University Press, 1975), p. 21.

5.6 Comments by the 28th Governor of California, Frank Merriam, 8 January 1935

Frank Merriam was the Republican Governor of California from 1934 to 1939. Here in his 1935 inaugural address before the members of the California Senate and Assembly he shows some of the difficulties facing those who opposed the New Deal. While he states that he is prepared to work with the federal government for recovery, and that Republicans and Democrats needed to pursue a bi-partisan approach towards the economy, he stresses the Republican themes of individual responsibility, private enterprise and the necessity of keeping down the cost and size of federal government.

We must not come here as Republicans or as Democrats, or as the representatives of any political party, but as Californians – charged with the responsibility and inspired by the opportunity to serve our people and our State ... Public necessity, the security of our people, the employment of our citizens, the protection of our homes, the relief of destitution and suffering, the restoration of our constructive economic processes, and the wider and greater enjoyment of the full range of social justice and basic human rights should have, and must have, our undivided, unremitting, and unselfish care ...

With respect to all the methods to be employed or all the steps to be taken in attempting a solution of our many perplexing problems, we may not always see alike, but in the main we are in accord as to the ends to be attained; we have a common goal – service to the people ...

Now, hope is revived that the normal activities of industry, agriculture, business, and commerce will steadily improve to a point where the initiative and enterprise of our citizens will once again afford full opportunity for the employment of all our able-bodied citizens and for the proper and useful expansion of our productive enterprises.

But as fondly as some may believe, and as earnestly as others may hope, government itself cannot indefinitely assume the responsibility for meeting all the demands of this depression and this emergency.

Government, if it be intelligent, efficient, and devoted, can aid in the solution of these problems. Government can be the medium through which an enlightened people can express their ideals and their aspirations, but government cannot permanently assume responsibilities which the private citizen and private business must eventually discharge if our people are to remain free and independent ...

I have been deeply impressed with the general feeling upon the part of citizens everywhere in the State that taxes must be temporarily increased and that the so-called tax base must be broadened to gain revenues from new sources, but I have been equally struck by the fact that both individuals and groups are disposed to feel that "the other fellow" should be called upon to bear the added burden ...

Ours is the difficult and perhaps thankless task to see to it that no one unnecessary dollar be sought from the taxpayers; that no injustice be worked; that the individual or the corporation, or the business institution, pay all that equity and necessity demand ...

www.governor.ca.gov/govsite/govsgallery/h/index.html.

5.7 Alf Landon, Republican presidential candidate in 1936

Alfred Mossman Landon (1887–1987) was Governor of Kansas from 1933 to 1937. He broadly supported the New Deal, and in Kansas worked actively with the Roosevelt administration to relieve poverty. His criticisms of the New Deal were limited and the Republicans recognised him as a pragmatic and cautious progressive who could unite a divided party. In 1936 he contested the presidential elections for the Republicans, only to lose heavily. In this document he spells out his view and his concerns about the Republican platform for the forthcoming election. In defeat after 1936 he would play a vital role in revitalising the fortunes of the Republican Party, leading to its rather better performance in the 1940 presidential election.

To the delegates of the Republican National Convention: My name is to be presented for your consideration as a candidate for the nomination for President of the United States.

The platform recommended by your committee on resolutions and adopted by the convention has been communicated to me.

I note that according to the terms of that platform "the acceptance of the nomination tendered by this convention carries with it, as a matter of private honor and public faith, an undertaking by each candidate to be true to the principles and program herein set forth."

If nominated I unqualifiedly accept the word and spirit of that undertaking.

However, with that candor which you and the country are entitled to expect of me, I feel compelled before you proceed with the consideration of my name to submit my interpretations of certain planks in the platform so that you may be advised as to my views. I could not in conscience do otherwise.

Under the title of labor the platform commits the Republican party as follows: "Support the adoption of state laws and interstate compacts to abolish sweatshops and child labor, and to protect women and children with respect to maximum hours, minimum wages, and working conditions. We believe that this can be done within the Constitution as it now stands."

I hope the opinion of the convention is correct that the aims which you have in my mind may be attained within the Constitution as it now stands. But, if that opinion should prove to be erroneous, I want you to know that, if nominated and elected, I shall favor a constitutional amendment permitting the states to adopt such legislation as may be necessary adequately to protect women and children in the matter of maximum hours, minimum wages and working conditions. This obligation we cannot escape.

The convention advocates "a sound currency to be preserved at all hazards." I agree that "the first requisite to a sound and stable currency is a balanced budget." The second requisite, as I view it, is a currency expressed in terms of gold and convertible into gold.

I recognize, however, that the second requisite must not be made effective until and unless it can be done without penalizing our domestic economy and without injury to our producers of agricultural products and other raw materials.

The convention pledges the party to the merit system and to its restoration, improvement and extension.

In carrying out this pledge I believe that there should be included within the merit system every position in the administrative service below the rank of assistant secretaries of major departments and agencies, and that this inclusion should cover the entire Post Office Department.

Alfred M. Landon

Landon to the Republican Convention at Cleveland, Ohio, 9–12 June 1936, Office Files OF 2167A, Roosevelt Library.

5.8 The 1936 election

For the Republican Party 1936 was a very bad year. Alf Landon, their candidate in the presidential election, was decisively beaten by Roosevelt in a tense contest, and in congressional elections they encountered further failure. The *Greenwood Index-Journal*, one of South Carolina's most respected newspapers, captured the process by which Republican hopes turned to dust. The 1936 elections showed that, whatever their doubts about the New Deal, they fully trusted Roosevelt and his party.

'Nation Prepares To Select Chief'

Early Returns From East And South According To Forecasts

(By The Associated Press)

With the first sparks from the election anvil showing little of how the resulting fire will spread, millions of voters today pounded out at an increasing tempo their choice of national and state leaders.

First returns from New England, some of them cast shortly after midnight and others before the sun was well risen, gave a few votes edge to Republican Landon. Hardly had these ballots been recorded when a handful of Texan precincts came in with a majority for Democrat Roosevelt, swinging the tiny margin the other way.

But with statisticians figuring that an all-time record of 45,000,000 voters may record their choice before 11pm tonight, the first few hundred ballots of course told little.

Greenwood Index-Journal, 3 November 1936.

'Only Two States Cling to Landon'
Powerful Democratic Majorities Returned To Both Houses of Congress; All-Time High Of 523 Electoral Votes Collected By Roosevelt
(By The Associated Press)
The nation stepped out in a Roosevelt quickstep yesterday with a singular approach to electoral unanimity.

Only two states, Maine and Vermont, clung today to the torn and battered standard of Alfred M. Landon as New Hampshire went Democratic with only one precinct missing.

In the surge toward President Roosevelt, party alignments that had stood since the birth of the Republican party were uprooted and powerful Democratic majorities were returned by both houses of congress.

On the basis of the mounting totals, the Republican presidential nominee had just eight electoral votes. For Roosevelt and Garner there were 523, for an all time high in electoral majorities. The New Deal popular plurality seemed likely to approach 9,000,000 ...

Overnight returns showed 25 Democratic candidates for governor elected or leading and only five Republicans.

Greenwood Index-Journal, 4 November 1936.

5.9 The Republican duty to oppose: radio address by Wendell Willkie, 11 November 1940

The 1940 presidential election threatened to revolve around foreign policy. However, on this issue there was little to choose between the two candidates, the incumbent President and Wendell Willkie, the Republican nominee. Both favoured a strong national defence and expressed the hope that America could stay out of the war. Instead, the election turned on the New Deal and traditional Republican fears of big government, bureaucracy and the stifling of private enterprise. A lawyer and a businessman, as president of an Indiana utilities company in the 1930s Willkie had fought the encroachments of the New Deal on the business world. Selected by the Republicans as a dark horse candidate for the 1940 presidential election, he received almost 45 per cent of the popular vote. However, in the electoral college he only gained 82 votes to Roosevelt's 449. In a radio address after his defeat in 1940 he reminded the Republican Party that it still had a vital role to play in the public life of the United States. He died in 1944.

We have elected Franklin Roosevelt President. He is your President. He is my President. We all of us owe him the respect due to his high office. We give him that respect. We will support him with our best efforts for our country. And we pray that God may guide his hand during the next four years in the supreme task of administering the affairs of the people.

It is a fundamental principle of the democratic system that the majority rules. The function of the minority, however, is equally fundamental. It is about the function of that minority – 22,000,000 people, nearly half of our electorate – that I wish to talk to you tonight.

A vital element in the balanced operation of democracy is a strong, alert and watchful opposition. That is our task for the next four years. We must constitute ourselves a vigorous, loyal and public-spirited opposition party.

It has been suggested that in order to present a united front to a threatening world the minority should now surrender its convictions and join the majority ... – it must be rejected utterly ...

Our American unity cannot be made with words or with gestures. It must be forged between the ideas of the opposition and the practices and policies of the Administration. Ours is a government of principles, and not one merely of men. Any member of the minority party, though willing to die for his country, still retains the right to criticize the policies of the government. This right is imbedded in our constitutional system ...

It is your Constitutional duty to debate the policies of this or any other administration and to express yourselves freely and openly to those who represent you in your State and national government.

Let me raise a single warning. Ours is a very powerful opposition. On November 5 we were a minority by only a few million votes. Let us not, therefore, fall into the partisan error of opposing things just for the sake of opposition. Ours must not be an opposition against – it must be an opposition for – an opposition for a strong America, a productive America. For only the productive can be strong and only the strong can be free.

Now let me however remind you of some of the principles for which we fought and which we hold as sincerely today as we did yesterday:

• We do not believe in unlimited spending of borrowed money by the Federal government

• the piling up of bureaucracy

• the control of our electorate by political machines, however successful

• the usurpation of powers reserved to Congress

• the subjugation of the courts

• the concentration of enormous authority in the hands of the Executive

• the discouragement of enterprise

• and the continuance of economic dependence for millions of our citizens upon government

• Nor do we believe in verbal provocation to war.

Vital Speeches of the Day, www.votd.com/willk.htm.

DEMAGOGUES AND OTHERS

5.10 Radio address by Father Charles E. Coughlin, 11 November 1934

Father Charles E. Coughlin was born in Ontario, Canada, in 1891. From 1926 until 1966 he served as pastor of the Shrine of the Little Flower in Michigan. He became a radio broadcaster in 1926 and was, at first, a supporter of Roosevelt and the New Deal. His radio broadcasts attracted a huge audience, as many as 30 million people in the mid-1930s, by which stage he had turned against the New Deal, demanding 'social justice' for the dispossessed and downtrodden. A fierce opponent of the banking interest, he demanded inflation to help bring relief to the poor. After the 1936 election he once again swung behind Roosevelt, arguing that the American public had had its say. Coughlin was attacked for anti-Semitism and a change of archbishop in Detroit in 1937 led to his gradual silencing. Nevertheless, he opposed American entry into the Second World War. This led to his final silencing by the Catholic Church, and his magazine ceased publication after it was barred by the mail service for violating the Federal Espionage Act. He died in 1979.

"Increase and multiply" was the command of God – a command that has been sterilized in the heart of every thinking young man who dares not marry because he dares not inflict poverty upon his children.

And this in a nation where the birth rate and the death rate are sparring for supremacy; this in a nation that dares not invite the immigrant to enter because already there is too much unemployment!

Yes, "increase and multiply" was the command which echoed over the flowering fields and the towering forests. It was heard in the sheep-folds and on the pasture-lands. It broke forth in holy emotions as lovers clasped in fond embrace.

"Increase and multiply and I shall kiss your fields with the lips of the sun and water them with the fountains of rain. I will unfold to you the secrets of nature. And I shall teach your nimble fingers to work and labor as I do the wings of a bird to fly."

Oh! how this Sacred Scripture has become perverted as, in the midst of plenty, we struggle to create want – we struggle to create profits – all for the purpose of perpetuating a slavery which has been so often described as the concentration of wealth in the hands of a few!

My friends, the outworn creed of capitalism is done for. The clarion call of communism has been sounded. I can support one as easily as the other. They are both rotten! But it is not necessary to suffer any longer the slings and arrows of modern capitalism any more than it is to surrender our rights to life, to liberty and to the cherished bonds of family to communism.

The high priests of capitalism bid us beware of the radical and call upon us to expel him from our midst. There will be no expulsion of radicals until the causes which breed radicals will first be destroyed!

The apostles of Lenin and Trotsky bid us forsake all rights to private ownership and ask us to surrender our liberty for that mess of pottage labeled "prosperity," while it summons us to worship at the altar where a dictator of flesh and blood is enthroned as our god and the citizens are branded as his slaves.

Away with both of them! But never into the discard with the liberties which we have already won and the economic liberty which we are about to win – or die in the attempt!

My friends, I have spent many hours during these past two weeks – hours, far into the night, reading thousands of letters which have come to my office from the young folks and the old folks of this nation. I believe that in them I possess the greatest human document written within our times.

I am not boasting when I say to you that I know the pulse of the people. I know it better than all your newspaper men. I know it better than do all your industrialists with your paid-for advice. I am not exaggerating when I tell you of their demand for social justice which, like a tidal wave, is sweeping over this nation.

Nor am I happy to think that, through my broadcasts, I have placed myself today in a position to accept the challenge which these letters carry to me – a challenge for me to organize these men and women of all classes not for the protection of property rights as does the American Liberty League; not for the protection of political spoils as do the henchmen of the Republican or Democratic parties. Away with them too!

But, happy or unhappy as I am in my position, I accept the challenge to organize for obtaining, for securing and for protecting the principles of social justice.

To organize for action, if you will! To organize for social united action which will be founded on God-given social truths which belong to Catholic and Protestant, to Jew and Gentile, to black and white, to rich and poor, to industrialist and to laborer.

I realize that I am more or less a voice crying in the wilderness. I realize that the doctrine which I preach is disliked and condemned by the princes of wealth. What care I for that. And, more than all else, I deeply appreciate how limited are my qualifications to launch this organization which shall be known as the National Union for Social Justice

But the die is cast! The word has been spoken! And by it I am prepared either to stand or to fall; to fall, if needs be, and thus, to be remembered as an arrant upstart who succeeded in doing nothing more than stirring up the people.

www.startribune.com/stories/1389/26302.html.

5.11 The basic principles of the National Union for Social Justice

As the Bible had its ten commandments, so Coughlin's National Union for Social Justice had its basic principles.

Many of the principles were unworkable. Based on antagonism towards the wealthy, they seemed to hold out the hope of a better deal for American poor.

1. I believe in liberty of conscience and liberty of education, not permitting the state to dictate either my worship to my God or my chosen avocation in life.

2. I believe that every citizen willing to work and capable of working shall receive a just, living, annual wage which will enable him both to maintain and educate his family according to the standards of American decency.

3. I believe in nationalizing those public resources which by their very nature are too important to be held in control of private individuals.

4. I believe in private ownership of all other property.

5. I believe in upholding the right to private property but in controlling it for the public good.

6. I believe in the abolition of the privately owned Federal Reserve Banking system and in the establishment of a Government owned Central Bank.

7. I believe in rescuing from the hands of private owners the right to coin and regulate the value of money, which right must be restored to Congress where it belongs.

8. I believe that one of the chief duties of this Government owned Central Bank is to maintain the cost of living on an even keel and arrange for the repayment of dollar debts with equal value dollars.

9. I believe in the cost of production plus a fair profit for the farmer.

10. I believe not only in the right of the laboring man to organize in unions but also in the duty of the Government, which that laboring man supports, to protect these organizations against the vested interests of wealth and of intellect.

11. I believe in the recall of all non-productive bonds and therefore in the alleviation of taxation.

12. I believe in the abolition of taxation bonds.

13. I believe in broadening the base of taxation according to the principles of ownership and the capacity to pay.

14. I believe in the simplification of government and the further lifting of crushing taxation from the slender revenues of the laboring class.

15. I believe that, in the event of a war for the defense of our nation and its liberties, there shall be a conscription of wealth as well as a conscription of men.

16. I believe in preferring the sanctity of human rights to the sanctity of property rights; for the chief concern of government shall be for the poor, because, as it is witnessed, the rich have ample means of their own to care for themselves.

Basic Principles of Social Justice Advocated by the National Union for Social Justice, Official Files OF 306/2, Roosevelt Library.

5.12 Radio address by Father Charles E. Coughlin, Station WHBI, Newark, New Jersey, 5 February 1939

As war loomed in Europe Couglin supported the isolationist cause.

France is not a democracy; it is an empire the majority of whose subjects have no voice or vote whatsoever in determining the destinies of the Parisian government …

Nor is Great Britain a democracy in the strict sense of the word. It is an empire, the population of whose imperial units in many instances have little voice or influence in determining or executing the policy of this far-flung domination. The British Isles occupying less than 100,000 square miles with a population of less than 50,000,000 persons, determine the imperial destinies of an empire of some 13,000,000 square miles and 490,000,000 population. Is this democracy? Certainly not.

Both the Empires of France and England stand on a level as far as many of their possessions are concerned with the governments of pagan imperialism. Their subjects pay taxes from their penurious incomes, but these same subjects have no vote in the affairs of empire.

Consider these facts, my fellow Americans, particularly you of the laboring class, when you are fed the spurious propaganda that we Americans must ally ourselves with the democracies of France and Great Britain. The Trust is that in joining with these empires, we are engaged in battling for imperialism. We are engaged in perpetuating the subjugation of India, of Aden, of British Malay, of Borneo, of Kenya, of Uganda, of Tanganyika, of Nyasaland, of Zanzibar, of Somaliland, of Nigeria, the Cameroons, Togoland, Sierra Leone, Djebel, Oceania and dozens of unnamed provinces, islands and territories, the existence of which the ordinary American is unaware.

A military or financial alliance to help fight the battles of Great Britain and France is one designed, I repeat, to prosper an ideology of government which is foreign to our American philosophy. We have no quarrel with either England or France, nor should we have.

If the units of these undemocratic empires desire to pursue in the future, as they have in the past, the policies of imperialism, that is their business, just as much as it is the business of the German or Italian or Russian people to safeguard the structures of Fascism, of Nazism, or of Communism. Our only concern is to maintain free relations with all nations as long as they do not endeavor to impose their ideologies upon us or to use us to protect their own ...

America is not in the blood business, and if she is in it now, it is her business to get out of it. Let our nation be a peaceful nation, permitting other nations to mind their own business and to establish what forms of government please them ...

My friends, let us be Americans and realists, recognizing that our destiny is confined to our America. It is not woven with the destinies of the empires abroad. By fighting for them, we are fighting for neither peace nor democracy, but we will begin fighting for the perpetuation of an obsolete financial slavery, controlled by the Sassoons, Montefiores, the Rothschilds, the Samuels and the litany of those flagless citizens who have obstructed justice, practised usury and used the peoples of the world as their pawns upon the chess board of exploitation. Meanwhile, we must assist the Congress of the United States as they probe into these well suspected foreign relations established by unelected officers; encourage the Senators, write to them, that they in turn will write a neutrality act which cannot be nullified by the stabilisation fund or by any other instrument of law. Encourage your Senators to scuttle the stabilization fund, to cease backing the international bankers and to begin helping American industry, American labor, and American agriculture, which are on bended knee in a country where want exists in the midst of plenty, in a country that has more than 11 billion dollars of gold ... Encourage your Senators to bring an end to all this financial imperialism.

Radio address by Charles E. Coughlin, 5 February 1939, in Official Files OF 306/2, Roosevelt Library.

5.13 Radio address by Huey P. Long, 19 January 1935

Perhaps the most dangerous opponent of the New Deal was the Democrat Huey P. Long (1893–1935). A demagogic speaker, he was elected as Governor of Louisiana in 1928 and proceeded to unleash a range of radical left-wing policies in the state. Elected as a Senator in 1930, Long became disillusioned with the New Deal, which had promised so much, but which he thought delivered so little. He attacked corporate interests and championed the cause of the rural poor. He demanded that the government expropriate the wealth of the rich to give to the poor in his 'Share the Wealth' campaign. Under his plans there would be old age pensions for those over 60 and an annual income for families of $5,000. In the lead-up to the 1936 presidential campaign Long was a source of great worry for the Roosevelt administration. Long himself was confident that he would become President and was prepared to offer Roosevelt the position of Secretary of the Navy in his new administration. However, in September 1935 Long was assassinated. Robert Penn Warren's 1946 Pulitzer Prize winning novel *All the King's Men* is widely regarded as being based on the career of Huey Long, who even today is still fondly remembered in Louisiana.

He rode into the President's office on the platform of redistributing wealth. He has done no such thing and has made no effort to do any such thing since he has been there. There is only one relief that can come to the American people that is of any value whatever, and that is to redistribute wealth by limiting the size of the big men's fortunes and guaranteeing that, beginning at the bottom, every family will have a living and the comforts of life. We can pass laws today providing for education, for old-age pensions, for unemployment insurance, for doles, public buildings, and anything else that we could think of, and still none of them would be worth anything unless we provided the money for them. And the money cannot be provided for them without these things doing twice as much harm as they do good unless that money is scraped off the big piles at the top and spread among the people at the bottom, who have nothing.

Any man with a thimbleful of sense who would be trying to help the poor people today by taxing the poor people so as to give the money back to them, ought to be bored for the hollow horn. Now, Mr. Roosevelt has better sense than that, but he is faced with a proposition. He has made the promise to the people that he will tear down these big fortunes by putting some reasonable limit on them, and he has further promised to build up the little man from the bottom. But he feels he doesn't dare keep that promise; he doesn't dare to keep that promise, and so, what is he doing? He makes every kind of move showing he is for this and for that; that he wants to appropriate a little money – so much for this and so much for that – but when you wind up, you find what he actually does is, that if there is any tax that can be levied on the poor people to give these things back to the poor people, that then he prescribes that kind of cure that never has cured or will cure.

The big interests realize Roosevelt's plan would not cost them anything, which is the same as saying it will be no relief to the poor.

Reproduced in the *Congressional Record*, 23 January 1935.

5.14 Radio address by Huey P. Long, 7 March 1935

Here Huey Long attacks some of the detail of the New Deal and outlines how he would address the economic problems of the nation. Particularly interesting is the way in which he draws parallels between New Deal and Nazi propaganda.

The trouble with the Roosevelt administration is that when their schemes and isms have failed, these things I told them not to do and voted not to do, that they think it will help them to light out on those of us who warned them in the beginning that the tangled messes and noble experiments would not work. The Roosevelt administration has had its way for two years. They have been allowed to set up or knock down anything and everybody. There was one difference between

[Herbert] Hoover and Roosevelt. Hoover could not get the Congress to carry out the schemes he wanted to try. We managed to lick him on a roll call in the United States Senate time after time. But, different with Mr. Roosevelt. He got his plans through Congress. But on cold analysis they were found to be the same things Hoover tried to pass and failed.

The kitchen cabinet that sat in to advise Hoover was not different from the kitchen cabinet which advised Roosevelt. Many of the persons are the same. Many of those in Roosevelt's kitchen cabinet are of the same men or set of men who furnished employees to sit in the kitchen cabinet to advise Hoover.

Maybe you see a little change in the man waiting on the tables, but back in the kitchen the same set of cooks are fixing up the victuals for us that cooked up the mess under Hoover.

Why, do you think this Roosevelt's plan for plowing up cotton, corn, and wheat; and for pouring milk in the river, and for destroying and burying hogs and cattle by the millions, all while people starve and go naked – do you think those plans were the original ideas of this Roosevelt administration? If you do, you are wrong. The whole idea of that kind of thing first came from Hoover's administration. Don't you remember when Mr. Hoover proposed to plow up every fourth row of cotton? We laughed him into scorn. President Roosevelt flayed him for proposing such a thing in the speech which he made from the steps of the capitol in Topeka, Kans.

And so we beat Mr. Hoover on his plan. But when Mr. Roosevelt started on his plan, it was not to plow up every fourth row of cotton as Hoover tried to do. Roosevelt's plan was to plow up every third row of cotton, just one-twelfth more cotton to be plowed up than Hoover proposed. Roosevelt succeeded in his plan.

So it has been that while millions have starved and gone naked; so it has been that while babies have cried and died for milk; so it has been that while people have begged for meat and bread, Mr. Roosevelt's administration has sailed merrily along, plowing under and destroying the things to eat and to wear, with tear-dimmed eyes and hungry souls made to chant for this new deal so that even their starvation dole is not taken away, and meanwhile the food and clothes craved by their bodies and souls go for destruction and ruin. What is it? Is it government? Maybe so. It looks more like St. Vitus dance.

Now, since they sallied forth with General Johnson to start the war on me, let us take a look at this NRA that they opened up around here two years ago. They had parades and Fascist signs just as Hitler, and Mussolini. They started the dictatorship here to regiment business and labor much more than anyone did in Germany or Italy. The only difference was in the sign. Italy's sign of the Fascist was a black shirt. Germany's sign of the Fascist was a swastika. So in America they sidetracked the Stars and Stripes, and the sign of the Blue Eagle was used instead.

And they proceeded with the NRA. Everything from a peanut stand to a power house had to have a separate book of rules and laws to regulate what they did. If a peanut stand started to parch a sack of goobers for sale, they had to be careful to go through the rule book. One slip and he went to jail. A little fellow who pressed a pair of pants went to jail because he charged 5 cents under the price set in the rule book. So they wrote their NRA rule book, codes, laws, etc. They got up over 900 of them. One would be as thick as an unabridged dictionary and as confusing as a study of the stars. It would take 40 lawyers to tell a shoe-shine stand how to operate and be certain he didn't go to jail.

Some people came to me for advice, as a lawyer, on how to run business. I took several days and then couldn't understand it myself. The only thing I could tell them was that it couldn't be much worse in jail than it was out of jail with that kind of thing going on in the country, and so to go on and do the best they could.

The whole thing of Mr. Roosevelt, as run under General Johnson, became such a national scandal that Roosevelt had to let Johnson slide out as the scapegoat. Let them call for an NRA parade tomorrow and you couldn't get enough people to form a funeral march.

It was under this NRA and the other funny alphabetical combinations which followed it that we ran the whole country into a mares nest. The Farleys and Johnsons combed the land with agents, inspectors, supervisors, detectives, secretaries, assistants, etc., all armed with the power to arrest and send to jail whomever they found not living up to some rule in one of these 900 catalogs. One man whose case reached the Supreme Court of the United States was turned loose because they couldn't even find the rule he was supposed to have violated in a search throughout the United States.

And now it is with PWA's, CWA's, NRA's, AAA's, J-UG's, G-IN's, and every other flimsy combination that the country finds its affairs and business tangled to where no one can recognize it. More men are now out of work than ever; the debt of the United States has gone up another $10 billion. There is starvation; there is homelessness; there is misery on every hand and corner, but mind you, in the meantime, Mr. Roosevelt has had his way. He is one man that can't blame any of his troubles on HUEY LONG. He has had his way. Down in my part of the country if any man has the measles he blames that on me; but there is one man that can't blame anything on anybody but himself, and that is Mr. Franklin De-La-No Roosevelt …

I propose:

First. That every big fortune shall be cut down immediately by a capital levy tax to where no one will own more than a few million dollars, as a matter of fact, to where no one can very long own a fortune in excess of about three to four millions of dollars. I propose that the surplus of all the big fortunes, above the few millions to any one person at the most, shall go into the United States ownership. How would we get all these surplus fortunes into the United States Treasury? Not hard to do. We would not do it by making everyone sell what he owned; no. We would send everyone a questionnaire. On that he would list the properties he owns, lands and houses, stocks and bonds, factories and patents, and so on. Every man would place his appraisal on his property, which the Government would review and maybe change on some items. On that appraisal the big fortune holder would say out of what property he would retain the few millions allowed to him, the balance to go to the United States. Say Mr. Henry Ford should allow that he owned all the stock of the Ford Motor Co., worth, say, $2 billion; he could claim, say $4 million of the Ford stock, but $1,996,000,000 would go to the United States. Say the Rockefeller fortune was listed at $10 billion in oil stocks, bank stocks, money, and stores. Each Rockefeller could say whether he wanted his limit in either the money, oil, or bank stocks, but about nine billion and eight hundred million would go to the Government. And so, in this way, the Government of the United States would come into the possession of about two-fifths of its wealth, which on normal values would be worth, say, $165 billion.

Then we would turn to the inventories of the 25 million families of America. All those who showed properties and money clear of debts that were above $5,000 and up to the limit of a few millions would not be touched. But those showing less than $5,000 to the family free of debt would be added to, so that every family would start life again with homestead possessions of at least a home and the comforts needed for a home, including such things as a radio and an automobile. These things would go to every family as a homestead, not to be sold either for debts or taxes or even by consent of the owner except by the consent of the court or Government, and then only on condition that the court hold it to be spent for the purpose of buying another home and comforts thereof.

Such would mean that the $165 billion or more taken from big fortunes would have about $100 billion of it used to provide all with the comforts of home and living. The Government might have to issue warrants for claim and location, or even currency to be retired from such property as was claimed, but all that is a detail not impractical to get these homes into the hands of the people.

So America would start again with millionaires, but no multi-millionaires or billionaires; with some poor, but none too poor to be denied the comforts of life.

Reproduced in the *Congressional Record*, 12 March 1935.

5.15 Long's tactics and the seriousness of his threat in 1936

Businessman James Aloysius Farley ran Roosevelt's campaign for election in 1932 and again in 1936. He was rewarded by being appointed to the Cabinet as Postmaster General. However, he disagreed with Roosevelt's decision to run for a third term in 1940 and resigned from the government. He returned to business and was appointed chairman of one division of the Coca Cola corporation. He died in 1976. Here in the first volume of his autobiography he highlights Long's methods and the concern within the Democratic Party about the impact he might have on the 1936 presidential election.

Day after day during the month of February, Huey took the Senate floor to delight the packed galleries with his threats to "blow the roof off the Capitol" by his sensational expose of the wickedness of the Roosevelt administration. He thrashed his way up and down the aisles, reading excerpts from newspaper articles and bellowing out that what he read was nothing compared to what he was going to prove when the investigation itself got under way. As usually happened under such circumstances, Long's charges made newspaper headlines, and interest in everything else was forgotten temporarily in the expectation of the spicy drama that was to follow ...

We kept a careful eye on what Huey and his political allies ... were attempting to do. Anxious not to be caught napping and desiring an accurate picture of conditions, the Democratic National Committee conducted a secret poll on a national scale during this period to find out if Huey's sales talks for his "share the wealth" program were attracting many customers. The result of that poll, which was kept secret and shown only to a very few people, was surprising in many ways. It indicated that, running on a third party ticket, Long would be able to poll between 3,000,000 to 4,000,000 votes for the Presidency. The poll demonstrated that Huey was doing fairly well at making himself a national figure. His probable support was not confined to Louisiana and near-by-states. On the contrary, he had about as much following in the North as in the South, and he had as strong an appeal in the industrial centers as he did in the rural areas. Even the rock-ribbed Republican state of Maine, where the voters were steeped in conservatism, was ready to contribute to Long's total vote in about the same percentage as other states.

While we realized that polls are often inaccurate and that conditions could change perceptibly before the election actually took place, the size of the Long vote made him a formidable factor. He was head and shoulders stronger than any of the other "Messiahs" who were also gazing wistfully at the White House and wondering what chance they would have to arrive there as the result of a local uprising. It was easy to conceive a situation whereby Long, by polling more than 3,000,000 votes, might have the balance of power in the 1936 election.

James A. Farley, *Behind the Ballots: The Personal History of a Politician* (New York, Harcourt Brace & Co., 1938), pp. 244–50.

5.16 The American Liberty League

The American Liberty League, formed in 1934 under the presidency of businessman and politician Jouett Shouse (1879–

1968), attacked the New Deal for its perceived detrimental effects on American business. In a radio broadcast of 7 September 1934 Shouse highlighted the reasons for the formation of the League.

Announcement of the formation of the American Liberty League was made two weeks ago. That the League has the opportunity to fill a definite need is evident from the flood of responses that has come from every section of the country. Telegrams and letters by the thousands, expressing desire to join and asking for information concerning the League, have been received ...

Equally indicative that the League has struck a chord upon which a vast number of men and women are thinking was the storm of public praise and criticism with which the mere announcement of its organization was greeted. It was front page news in every city in America and virtually all of the newspapers, radio speakers, and other agencies of public opinion followed with editorial comment. All this is the more remarkable when you consider the simple fundamentals for which the League stands.

• First, it proposes to defend and uphold the Constitution of the United States

• Second, it aims to teach the necessity of respect for the rights of persons and property as fundamental to every successful form of government.

• And finally it proposes to teach the duty of government to encourage and protect individual and group initiative and enterprise, to foster the right to work, earn, save and acquire property, and to preserve the ownership and lawful use of property when acquired ...

Some critics have suggested that the American Liberty League places too great an emphasis on property rights. If one thing more than another has been proved by historical experience it is that the denial of property rights has always been the prelude to a denial of human rights. The man who doubts this premise need only trace the course of events in any one of a half dozen European countries during the last decade. The government that begins by coercing property owners ends by coercing labor.

Jouett Shouse Collection, 59M61, University of Kentucky Library.

5.17 The Townsend Plan in brief, 1934

In 1934 California physician Francis E. Townsend put forward a plan, the Old Age Revolving Pensions Plan, under which the federal government would pay $200 a month to everyone over 60 years of age. As well as relieving the poverty of the elderly, the plan would create opportunities for younger workers through enabling the retirement of the old. However, under Townsend's plan there were strings attached to the $200 a month.

Have the National Government enact legislation to the effect that all citizens of the United States – man or woman – over the age of 60 years may retire on a pension of $200 per month on the following conditions:

1. That they engage in no further labor, business or profession for gain.
2. That their past life is free from habitual criminality.
3. That they take oath to, and actually do spend, within the confines of the United States, the entire amount of their pension within thirty days after receiving same.

Have the National Government create the revolving fund by levying a general sales tax; have the rate just high enough to produce the amount necessary to keep the Old Age Revolving Pensions Fund adequate to pay the monthly pensions.

Have the act so drawn that such sales tax can only be used for the Old Age Revolving Pensions Fund.

www.ssa.gov/history/townbrief.html.

5.18 Prosperity for all: Dr F. E. Townsend

The public gave a warm reception to Townsend's plan and Townsend Clubs were set up across the nation to lobby for the implementation of the plan. A national movement backed by an efficient organisation was born. Radio talks by Townsend and his followers were supported by a weekly newspaper. The wave of support for the plan helped to propel Roosevelt into accepting the need for social security legislation.

There are ten million three hundred thousand odd persons in the U.S. above the age of sixty years according to the last census. They are quite uniformly proportioned throughout the population, this proportion, naturally, being greatest in the older settled sections where population is densest.

Two billions of dollars spent monthly in all sections of the country by these old folks would give the entire population of the United States an additional $14 per capita in spending ability each month. Enough to raise the standard of living very materially above the present low level but quite within the nation's ability to provide.

The constantly growing use of power by civilized man (largely electric) is increasing his power to produce the things man must use at an ever decreasing costs. Hence, an ever decreasing number of workers is required in production and an ever increasing number find themselves out of employment. If civilization is to be a blessing instead of a curse a sensible and just provision for their retirement must be devised.

The return to manufacturers in profits tends to increase as power displaces men (since machines are cheaper than men) only up to the point where buying power begins to diminish among the people through lack of paid jobs, thus decreasing market demands. Hence, manufacturers too begin to see the necessity of keeping up the buying power of the people by some such plan as the Old Age Revolving Pensions.

Poverty, once considered a natural curse which the human race was doomed to endure, can and will be abolished in the United States within the next five years never to return. Our country will show the way to other nations and poverty will be driven from the earth. No other construction can be given to the fact that man's ability to produce faster than he can consume is definitely established.

Poverty banished, the incentive to criminal activity will disappear and national, civic and individual standards of fairness and decency will become the natural order of the day.

Prosperity firmly established in America by this simple plan, the peoples of other countries will demand like opportunity and consideration from their governments and similar legislation may be expected to follow. When all civilized people are universally well off and contented there will be an end to warfare. Prosperous and contented people do not go to war.

www.ssa.gov/history/pics/towns11.gif.

5.19 The Townsend Plan: answering the critics

The Townsend plan had many flaws, but it had the attraction of intellectual simplicity. Anyone could understand the plan. In framing the 1935 Social Security Act the Roosevelt administration had to deal with a range of financial and legislative complications that Townsend did not. On 7 May 1936, the *Los-Angeles Post Herald* revealed that even as Townsend was busy predicting the end of the New Deal and its chief architect, the Townsend movement was beginning to break up as a result of in-fighting and concerns over the running of the *Townsend Weekly*.

That our Old Age Revolving Pensions Plan is absurd; that it will break the nation to pay out continuously about one billion six hundred million dollars per month. Yet they loudly applaud the Administration for borrowing ten billion dollars and tossing it out in huge scoopfuls labeled with the various combinations of the alphabet without making any provision for repayment other than that of the same old taxation system already breaking the backs of the taxpayers.

We show how this Old Age Revolving Pension Fund can be obtained from the public, painlessly, each month, put immediately into circulation and returned each month into the same communities whence it originated, insuring prosperous times by volume of circulation rather than by trying to borrow ourselves rich.

They say: That to raise two billion dollars per month from the buying public by means of a universal sales tax would necessitate the raising of prices twenty-five (25) per cent or more. We reply: What of it? Isn't that just what the present Administration is trying to do? The farmers and other large groups require at least one hundred (100) per cent rise in prices before they can be considered at all prosperous. Would it not be better for us to pay five dollars ($5) for a pair of shoes in prosperous times than to pay four in times like these? That is a twenty-five (25) per cent advance.

They say: That two hundred dollars ($200) payment per month to the old folks is too much: that they would not know how to spend such an enormous sum; that they would buy automobiles and slaughter the public with their careless driving; that the younger relatives would live off the old folks and refuse to work; that the young men and women would marry the old folks for a meal ticket; that general debauchery would result from the orgy of spending sure to be indulged in by these frivolous oldsters – and on and on ad nauseum.

We reply: We believe implicitly in the honor and loyalty of all citizens who for 60 years or more have given their best in the perpetuation of the principles of our democratic form of Government. They will only continue this loyalty for the further progression of our country by being true to the reward that the government has provided for their old age, comfort and peace of mind. They will be the protectors of our government and by their knowledge and power of franchise will break up the coercion of political machines whose object is excessive government expense for personal profit. We have no fear for the future of the young American. The finest educational institutions on earth turning out the finest men and women on earth, we believe, will continue to lead this nation to higher aims and greater achievements for a finer and better social existence. Give them the opportunity. Guide them on their way, and there will be discovered new vitality, new energy with progress and prosperity never attained by any nation. There is no other true answer.

They say: It is not fair to the taxpayers to provide all these old people, many of whom have never been able to earn even fifty dollars ($50) per month, with such a sum as two hundred dollars.

We reply: Class legislation in any form of discrimination is odious and un-American. We say, give it to all who apply and qualify without discrimination. Discrimination is wrong and un-democratic. That is just what we are trying to eradicate from our social system. Old folks who have never been able to hold down more than a fifty dollar per month job could now be promoted to the important job of spending two hundred dollars ($200) per month all the rest of their days for the good of the general public, thereby tremendously enhancing their importance and value to society instead of being degraded to the status of worn-out shoes and kicked aside as of no account.

They say: That to ask these old folks to assume the great task of spending two hundred dollars ($200) per month would entail a burdensome task upon them and rush them into early graves with worry.

We reply: Go to the old folks and find out if your apprehensions are justified. Ask them which they would prefer to do, try to spend two hundred dollars per month, or go to the poorhouse – live upon relatives – beg the rest of their days. We say it is quite possible that the old folks would manifest the wit to hire help in spending if they needed to do so. We believe that all, except those who raise this objection, would be able to exhibit such wit.

www.ssa.gov/history/critics.html.

5.20 The American left and the New Deal

> The American left was critically involved with the depression, which offered it the chance to expand, possibly even to stage a revolution, or so some thought. Here Fred Thompson, a member of the Industrial Workers of the World (IWW – 'The Wobblies'), talks to the writer Studs Terkel in the 1960s about how the left viewed the depression, Roosevelt and the New Deal.

Q: In the depths of the Depression, did you hear much talk of revolution?

A: Oh, there was a lot of talk. But there was no anticipation that we were about to take over the works and run it. The IWW felt only an organized working class could do it. A working class that wasn't allowed to eat the food it produced ... that had to go with patches on its ass after it had made too many clothes ... was a working class that could be brow beat. A working class that had to beg for a soup bone wasn't a class that could take this world and run it. They had to organize first. I ran into some ill-informed people who used the word revolution very carelessly – that things were so tough, we were going to have a revolution and so forth. I didn't run into any person who had given serious thought as to how you make one ...

Q: How did the IWW feel about FDR?

A: When he died, I remember an obituary in our paper: "He was hated by those he had helped and loved by those he had harmed." A good many Wobblies felt that was hitting it right on the head. He made a big hullaballoo about what he was gonna do for labor. After he had labor by the tail, he seemed to figure he could disregard it and favor our enemy instead.

Q: What were your feelings towards the New Deal?

A: Here was an economic system that had quit work. The logical remedy would have been for a working class to assert itself: we want at least enough of what we produce so we can keep on working. But you didn't have that kind of labor action. Consequently, the pigs who had been stopping the things from working by their own greed didn't disgorge anything. But certain adjustments were made that allowed people to eat. At the time of Hoover, you could use federal funds to feed animals, but not to feed people. It was up to your neighbors, he said.

Studs Terkel, *Hard Times: An Oral History of the Depression* (London, Allen Lane, 1970), pp. 308–9.

THE SUPREME COURT

5.21 *United States Supreme Court A. L. A. Schechter Poultry Corp.* v. *United States*, decided 27 May 1935

The case against the United States government brought by the Schechter Poultry Corporation was argued before the Supreme Court on 2–3 May 1935. Here the court gives its decision which strikes down the National Recovery Act.

CERTIORARI TO THE CIRCUIT COURT OF APPEALS FOR THE SECOND CIRCUIT

Syllabus

1. Extraordinary conditions, such as an economic crisis, may call for extraordinary remedies, but they cannot create or enlarge constitutional power.

2. Congress is not permitted by the Constitution to abdicate, or to transfer to others, the essential legislative functions with which it is

vested. Art. I, § 1; Art. I, § 8, par. 18. *Panama Refining Co. v. Ryan*, 293 U.S. 388.

3. Congress may leave to selected instrumentalities the making of subordinate rules within prescribed limits, and the determination of facts to which the policy, as declared by Congress, is to apply; but it must itself lay down the policies and establish standards.

4. The delegation of legislative power sought to be made to the President by § 3 of the National Industrial Recovery Act of June 16, 1933, is unconstitutional, and the Act is also unconstitutional, as applied in this case, because it exceeds the power of Congress to regulate interstate commerce and invades the power reserved exclusively to the States.

Supreme Court U.S. 495, Washington, 1935, pp. 528ff.

5.22 Roosevelt's 209th presidential press conference, 31 May 1935

By May 1935 Roosevelt's patience with the Supreme Court had worn thin. Here he tries to prepare the ground for a political offensive against the court.

And so we are facing a very, very great national non-partisan issue. We have got to decide one way or the other. I don't mean this summer or winter or next fall, but over a period, perhaps, of five years or ten years we have got to decide: Whether we are going to relegate to the forty-eight States practically all control over economic conditions – not only State economic conditions but national economic conditions; and along with that whether we are going to relegate to the States all control over social and working conditions throughout the country regardless of whether those conditions have a very definite significance and effect in other States outside of the individual States. That is one side of the picture. The other side of the picture is whether in some way we are going to turn over or restore to – whichever way you choose to put it – turn over or restore to the Federal Government the powers which exist in the national Governments of every other Nation in the world to enact and administer laws that have a bearing on, and general control over, national economic problems and national social problems.

That actually is the biggest question that has come before this country outside of time of war, and it has to be decided. And, as I say, it may take five or ten years.

This N.R.A. decision – if you accept the obiter dicta and all the phraseology of it – seems to be squarely on the side of restoring to the States forty-eight different controls over national economic and social problems. This is not a criticism of the Supreme Court's decision; it is merely pointing out the implications of it.

The Public Papers and Addresses of Franklin D. Roosevelt, Vol. 4 (New York, Random House, 1938), pp. 218–19.

5.23 The Supreme Court strikes down the 1933 Agricultural Adjustment Act, 24 January 1936

The Agricultural Adjustment Act (AAA) had been struck down by the Supreme Court on 24 January as unconstitutional. Roosevelt regarded this as a grave event both in terms of the damage done to the New Deal and also in terms of what he saw as the Court's continuing efforts to sharply limit the scope for the exercise of presidential and federal power.

Memorandum for AAA File January 24, 1936.
It has been well said by a prominent historian that fifty years from now the Supreme Court's AAA decision will, in all probability, be described somewhat as follows:

(1) The decision virtually prohibits the President and the Congress from the right, under modern conditions, to intervene reasonably in the regulation of nation-wide commerce and nation-wide agriculture.

(2) The Supreme Court arrived at this result by selecting from several possible techniques of constitutional interpretation a special technique. The objective of the Court's purpose was to make reasonableness in passing legislation a matter to be settled not by the views of the elected Senate and House of Representatives and not by the views of an elected President but rather by the private, social philosophy of a majority of nine appointed members of the Supreme Court itself.

Elliot Roosevelt (ed.), *The Roosevelt Letters* (London, Harrap, 1952), p. 167.

THE CLERGY

5.24 Successes and failures of the New Deal, 1 October 1935

In 1935 Roosevelt asked the clergymen of America for their professional counsel. Many sent short or long letters expressing their approval or disapproval of the government's policies. Some like James Barrett, minister in Ninety Six, South Carolina, attacked the President over the repeal of prohibition, accusing him of assuming 'the active leadership of the liquor forces in what proved to be a successful effort to deluge the country with drink and its attendant evils'. A few clergy letters, such as this from Greenwood, South Carolina, the neighbouring parish to Ninety Six, attempted to give the President a more balanced assessment.

Its Successes:

(1) The fear complex that had gripped our people and well nigh destroyed the basis … for industry and business is fast being abolished. To see how near we came to disaster, one has but to recall the conditions of the banks of the country when you took office. Your fearless treatment in closing them and the promise of justice that should fall to the lot of "money changers" was the beginning of a new order of things, the full purport of which unfolds as you reveal your plans for our country.

(2) The Home Loan Corporation has saved thousands of homes to their owners, and has established a feeling of security to this class of citizens of untold worth to them and to the country …

(3) Laws safeguarding depositors in the reconstructed banks, and the determination on the part of the government to keep more in touch with its monetary system is of paramount importance and has gone far in restoring a confidence without which there is no basis for business or industry.

(4) NRA together with other types of social legislation have in the

main been beneficial. AAA, CWA, PWA etc. have contributed their share to reconstruction ...

Adverse Results:

(1) Too many and too rapid changes in government relief policies.

(2) Money paid in large salaries to officials and supervisors of relief that ought to go to the ones that are in actual need.

(3) Money spent in temporary transient camps to the detriment of the ones these camps have attracted to them.

(4) Relief stations extending aid in such way that the recipients of it forever lose self respect and man-hood.

(5) The lack of a well defined effort in the matter of a restored budget.

Paul Patton, minister in Greenwood, South Carolina, to Roosevelt, 1 October 1935, President's Personal File PPF 21a, Clergy Letters from South Carolina, Roosevelt Library.

5.25 The African-American and the New Deal in the South, 2 October 1935

Some of the clergy letters to the President in 1935 showed the extent to which the clergy were keen and perceptive critics of New Deal policies. In the application of the New Deal to the South some discrimination against African-Americans was inevitable. Here a Presbytarian minister and teacher of rural sociology and agricultural economics at Clemson Agricultural College tells Roosevelt of his fears.

The efforts of the Federal government to relieve unemployment during the depression have had my admiration and sympathy. I desire, however, to say that I doubt if it has been or will be possible to administer those funds locally without bringing racial and political prejudices to bear. Personally, I do not believe that the Negroes in South Carolina have had, or are likely to receive, their proper share of these funds, or the benefits derived from their dispersing. My observation has been that on roads and other forms of relief-work-employment, the white people are given jobs in greater proportion than their numbers would lead one to expect, and in passing by relief offices I have observed that there are more white people present usually than Negroes. My belief is that the need among the Negroes is as great as among the whites, but they fail frequently to be given opportunity to receive what is justly their due.

W. H. Mills, minister and member of faculty, Clemson Agricultural College, South Carolina, 2 October 1935, President's Personal File PPF 21a, Clergy Letters from South Carolina, Roosevelt Library.

SATIRISTS AND POLEMICISTS

5.26 On Our Way

Satirists were prominent in their attacks on Roosevelt. In 1934 an anti-Roosevelt pamphlet was published entitled *Frankie in Wonderland: With Apologies to Lewis Carroll, the Orignator and pre-historian of the New Deal*. It was dedicated to the 'American Eagle, that noble bird, before it was painted blue and turned into a Soviet Duck'. It made fun of the Roosevelt administration in several ways, including a particularly inventive parody of Lewis Carroll's poem *Jabberwocky*.

T'was brandeis and the brainy coves
Did slyly wallace in the wave,
All ickes were the laborgoves
And the Perkins outgave

Beware the Bankerwock, my son!
The teeth that bite, the claws that snatch!
Beware the Brokerbird and shun
The fumious Stockesnatch!

With his pecora sword in hand
For months the wallstreet foe he sought,
So rested he by the tugwell tree
And smiled awhile in thought.

And as in pinkish thought he stood
The Bankerwock with eyes of flame

Came underwriting through the wood
And burgled as it came.

One, Two! One, Two! and through and through
The richberg blade went snicker snack!
He left it dead and with its head
He came frankfurting back.

"And has thou slain the Bankerwock?
Come to my arms my beamish boy!
Oh NRA, let's all raise pay!"
He chortled in his joy.

T'was brandeis and the brainy coves
Did slyly wallace in the wave
All ickes were the laborgoves
And the perkins outgave.

A. Tory, *Frankie in Wonderland* (New York, E. P. Dutton & Co. Inc., 1934), p. 15.

SPECIFIC FEATURES OF THE NEW DEAL

5.27 The Tennessee Valley Authority and the race problem, April 1934

In this article published by *Opportunity: Journal of Negro Life*, Cranston Clayton, a white writer, argued that the New Deal had failed to address the issue of civil rights and that African-Americans were being denied equal treatment. He further argued that since Reconstruction after the Civil War the issue of race relations had posed a powerful check on the economic development of the South.

In the 40,000 square miles of the Tennessee Valley lying in parts of seven different states are some two million people divided between white and colored according to the ratio roughly of three to one. Negroes are relatively thick in northern Alabama and west Tennessee but are correspondingly scarce in the mountains of Virginia, North

Carolina, and east Tennessee.

The various maladjustments that have existed in the relationship between these two groups since the beginning of the nation has no doubt been the greatest single factor in causing this region, with all its wealth of coal, phosphates and other minerals, with its diversified and abundant plant life, with its climatic advantages, and with its streams and rivers ready to generate an estimated 3,000,000 horse power of energy, to be even at this late day one of the most backward sections, educationally and industriously, of any in the nation. Now the Tennessee Valley Authority comes into this region not merely to build a series of dams and transmission lines, but to "provide for the agricultural and industrial development of said valley" and to foster "an orderly and physical, economic and social development of such areas." How does the TVA with such broad and profound responsibilities propose to deal with the problem of race relations?

As a relief measure or job providing agency, which it really does not purport to be, the TVA has dealt with the Negro more justly than possibly any other one of the New Deal Acts. Certainly more than the NRA for example, which in most cases in the South has either not been applied at all to Negroes or else has simply been the occasion to throw them completely out of work. TVA authorities claim, and I have no facts with which to dispute such claims, that they are employing Negroes according to their proportion of the total population and in all cases are paying them the same wages that whites receive for doing the same work

From *Opportunity: Journal of Negro Life*, Vol. 12, No. 4, April 1934, p. 111.

5.28 The Agricultural Adjustment Act and *Roosevelt Riddles*

New Deal policies towards agriculture attracted particularly strong criticism. Despite the industrial might of the United States, the farmer was still regarded as the heart and soul of America. Any attempt to change agriculture was thus regarded as an assault on American values. To many observers, paying a farmer not to produce crops under the Agricultural Adjustment Act seemed the height of insanity. A 1936 attack on the New Deal entitled *Roosevelt Riddles* gives some impression of the concerns felt by opponents of the administration's farm policies.

71

Q. What was the largest amount paid to any farmer for not growing cotton in 1934?

A. Under one Arkansas contract the AAA paid $115,700.

72

Q. What was the amount of the largest corn-hog contract?

A. AAA paid one corn-hog farming company $157,020, less administrative expenses.

73

Q. Is it true the American farmer has lost his foreign market for grain corn?

A. Practically. In 1932, American farmers sold 7,886,000 bushels of grain corn abroad, but in 1935 only 177,382 were sold abroad ...

75

Q. How much land would be necessary to grow the corn imported from foreign countries last year?

A. About 2,000,000 acres.

76

Q. How much corn was brought into this country from foreign nations in 1935?

A. 43,242,296 bushels, as compared with 106,000 bushels in 1933.

77

Q. Since President Roosevelt was inaugurated, how many pounds of meat products have been imported?

A. Over 240,000,000 pounds ...

93

Q. What is meant by the "Wallace seed racket"?

A. Secretary Wallace is president (1935) of the Hi-Bred Corn Company, Des Moines, Iowa, James W. Wallace, secretary. This company advertises seed corn which will increase the yield of corn per acre by 11 bushels, or more than 25 per cent. Secretary Wallace pays the farmer for plowing under 25 per cent of his corn. The farmer can take some of this money and buy Secretary Wallace's seed corn. If this seed corn does what Secretary Wallace claims, it will increase the yield of the remaining acreage by as much as would have been grown on the land plowed under. The racket is that Secretary Wallace profits by the sale of the seed corn and the farmer grows more corn on three fourths of his land than on his whole farm ...

96

Q. How can the building of huge dams, like those of the TVA, hurt the farmer?

A. Morris Cooke, expert on soil conservation, declares that such dams take the water off the land into the big rivers, thereby contributing to dust storms.

97

Q. What is meant by "nationalization of land"?

A. Many claim the Roosevelt Administration intends to nationalize agriculture by ownership or control of all farmlands. 10,000,000 acres have been bought by the New Deal, and approximately one third of all farm mortgages are now in Federal Land banks ...

99

Q. What did Thomas Jefferson have to say about control of agriculture?

A. He said: "Were we directed from Washington when to sow, and when to reap, we should soon want bread."

Russell Moore, *Roosevelt Riddles* (New York, Doubleday, Doran & Co. Inc., 1936), pp. 74–141.

5.29 Moonlighting on the WPA

One of the major criticisms of the Works Progress Administration was that some of those it employed 'moonlighted' on other jobs. In other words, a large number of those classified as unemployed were in fact engaged in the 'black economy'. This was one area probed by a Senate Special Committee on Unemployment and Relief set up in 1937. Its findings were damning.

For the past year reports have been widespread that Works Progress Administration workers, while employed on the Federal work-relief projects, seek and obtain other employment during the month for which they have been paid out of public funds. An investigation was undertaken to determine the truth with respect to such reports.

In the months of November and December 1937 a group of investigators were sent to the cities of Atlanta, Baltimore, New York, Omaha and Pittsburgh with instructions to go into this subject ...

[As a result of Congress's wording of the Deficiency Appropriations Act of 1936] ... there has developed the possibility of a man employed on a Works Progress Administration project earning the security wage in one-third of the full working hours of a month and being free for the balance of that month. That Works Progress Administration workers have taken advantage of this opportunity is not surprising ...

In the 5 cities mentioned, there were on the Works Progress Administration rolls at the time of the investigation 26,736 workers classified as skilled workers. Of this number, 7982 were interviewed, 5049, or 63 percent, when asked the question admitted that they had other employment ...

A little less than one-fourth (1,036 of 4,312 or 24 percent) were found to be working in outside employment or occupations similar to those at which they were employed by Works Progress Administration, but at a lower hourly rate of pay.

Senate Committee on Unemployment and Relief, 20 April 1938, No. 1625, Harry Hopkins Papers 24, Roosevelt Library.

THE LEGACY OF THE NEW DEAL

5.30 The legacy of the New Deal

Whittaker Chambers was born in 1901 into a middle-class family on Long Island. Veering between the political extremes of the 1920s, after graduating from Columbia in 1924 he supported Republican presidential hopeful Calvin Coolidge before joining the Communist Party in 1925. Until 1938, when he broke with the party over Stalin's purges, he served as a Russian spy infiltrating the American government in the 1930s. He later proclaimed himself as a right-wing Christian and anti-Communist, becoming a writer and editor at the *Time* magazine. In 1948 he was involved in the Hiss Soviet perjury case, successfully bringing charges against Alger Hiss, the head of Carnegie Endowment. A highly controversial figure, who had viewed America's twentieth century from diametrically opposed standpoints, Chambers considered the New Deal to have been nothing short of a revolution.

I saw that the New Deal was only superficially a reform movement. I had to acknowledge the truth of what its more forthright protagonists, sometimes unwarily, sometimes defiantly, averred: the New Deal was a genuine revolution, whose deepest purpose was not simply reform within existing traditions, but a basic change in social, and, above all, the power relationships within the nation. It was not a revolution by violence. It was a revolution by bookkeeping and lawmaking. In so far as it was successful, the power of politics had replaced the power of business. This is the basic power shift of all the revolutions of our time. This shift was the revolution. It was only of incidental interest that the revolution was not complete, that it was made not by tanks and machine guns, but by acts of Congress and decisions of the Supreme Court, or that many of the revolutionists did not know what they were or denied it. But revolution is always an affair of force, whatever forms the force disguises itself in.

Whittaker Chambers, *Witness* (Washington DC, Regnery Gateway, 1980), p. 472.

Chronology of events

1933

2 Feb	The US Congress passes the 21st amendment to the constitution, repealing prohibition.
15 Feb	Assassination attempt on FDR.
4 Mar	Inauguration of FDR as 32nd President of the USA.
5 Mar	Roosevelt summons Congress to a special session and declares a bank holiday beginning on the following day.
9 Mar	Congress opens for a special session to deal with the financial and social crisis.
12 Mar	Roosevelt holds the first of his fireside chats.
5 May	The Tennessee Valley Authority is created by Congress. Congress also passes the Federal Emergency Relief Act and the Agricultural Adjustment Act.
13 Jun	Home Owners Loan Corporation created. It will, over the next three years, help with a million mortgages.
16 Jun	Special session of Congress comes to an end.
2 Nov	Death Valley National Park created.
17 Nov	USA gives diplomatic recognition to the USSR.

1934

31 Jan	Establishment of the Federal Farm Mortgage Company to try to halt the tide of farm foreclosures.
15 Feb	Civil Works Emergency Relief Act signed into law by the President. It seeks to relieve unemployment through civil works.
6 Jun	The Indian Reorganisation Act seeks to give a new deal to first-nation Americans through the encouragement of self-government. Also the Securities and Exchange Commission is formed to police the stock market.
23 Oct	London naval conference to discuss naval armaments

	opens.
11 Nov	In the mid-term elections the Democrats win decisively, holding 69 seats in the Senate to the Republicans' 25. In the House of Representatives they hold 322 seats to the Republicans' 103.
29 Dec	Japan denounces the Washington treaties of 1922 and 1930 which impose limitations on the size of her navy.
23 Dec	London naval conference closes.

1935

16 Mar	Hitler denounces the military clauses in the Treaty of Versailles, promising to restore conscription in Germany.
5 May	Works Progress Administration created by Congress. It will employ two million people in a variety of blue-collar and white-collar jobs. Also the Rural Electrification Administration is created.
27 May	New Deal thrown into chaos by the outcome of *Schechter Poultry Corporation* v. *United States* in the Supreme Court. Sections of the National Industrial Recovery Act are declared unconstitutional.
7 Jul	Wagner Act signed into law. It gives unions rights such as the right to collective bargaining and protection of union members from discrimination.
14 Aug	Social Security Act passed by Congress, creating old age pensions and help for the disabled and unemployed.
10 Sep	Huey Long assassinated in Baton Rouge, Louisiana.
3 Oct	Fascist Italy invades Abyssinia.

1936

6 Jan	In *Butler* v. *United States* the Supreme Court declares sections of the 1933 Agricultural Adjustment Act unconstitutional.
29 Feb	Soil Conservation and Domestic Allotment Act signed into law. It replaces the Agricultural Adjustment Act. In particular it enourages soil conservation through the growing of manure crops.
25 Mar	The USA, Great Britain and France sign the London naval treaty limiting naval arms.
9 May	Italy formally annexes Abyssinia.

19 Jun	"Brown Bomber" Joe Louis loses to Max Schmeling of Germany in a non-title heavyweight boxing contest.
18 Jul	Outbreak of the Spanish Civil War.
1 Aug	Olympic Games opens in Berlin. Black American athlete Jesse Owens wins gold in the 100 and 200 metres, the 4 × 100 metre relay and the long jump.
1 Dec	Opening of the Pan-American Peace Conference held in Buenos Aires at the behest of Roosevelt.
16 Dec	Closing of the Pan-American Peace Conference.

1937

6 Jan	Provisions of the Neutrality Act preventing arms supplies to Spain are renewed.
20 Jan	Roosevelt inaugurated for a second term.
1 Mar	Supreme Court Retirement Act presented to Congress. Under it judges can retire at 70. If they prefer to continue the President is authorised to appoint an extra judge to ease their workload. The plan is later withdrawn after considerable opposition in Congress to 'court packing'.
15 Sep	National Housing Act passed.

1938

Jan	The President asks Congress for massively increased spending on the US Navy.
Feb	Second Agricultural Adjustment Act passed by Congress.
14 Jun	Fair Labor Standards Act is passed by Congress. It creates a minimum wage and a maximum working week of 44 hours.
30 Sep	Munich Agreement signed. Under it, Czechoslovakia is to be divided and Germany allowed to annex the borderlands containing a majority of ethnic Germans.
26 Dec	A pan-American conference declares its opposition to foreign interference in the affairs of the western hemisphere.

1939

4 Jan	Congress votes a massive increase in defence spending.
1 Apr	USA recognises General Franco's government in Spain.

16 Jul	As a result of continuing Japanese attacks in China the USA renounces 1911 trade agreement with Japan.
1 Sep	German forces invade Poland.
3 Sep	Britain and France declare war on Germany.
3 Oct	USA declares its neutrality.

1940

10 May	Germany launches her offensive against the Low Countries.
4 Jun	Operation Dynamo, the evacuation of allied troops from the Dunkirk beaches, is completed. Almost 340,000 British, French and Belgian troops are evacuated.
22 Jun	France signs an armistice with Germany.
5 Jul	Roosevelt bans the shipment to Japan of certain important materials.
13 Aug	The Battle of Britain reaches its peak on so-called Eagle Day (Adler Tag).
3 Sep	USA gives Britain fifty old destroyers in exchange for long leases on British bases in the Caribbean.
Nov	Roosevelt wins an unprecedented third term in the presidential elections.

1941

11 Mar	Lend Lease Bill signed into law.
24 May	German battleship *Bismarck* sinks British battleship HMS *Hood* in the Atlantic. US forces are involved in the hunt for the German vessel.
22 Jun	Germany invades Russia. Lend Lease aid is extended to Russia.
31 Oct	Destroyer USS *Reuben James* sunk by German submarine while escorting British convoy. 115 crewmembers are killed.
13 Nov	Congress amends the Neutrality Act to allow its merchant ships to enter the declared war zone and to be armed.
7 Dec	Japanese attack US naval base at Pearl Harbor.
11 Dec	Germany declares war on the USA.

Guide to further reading

Roosevelt

Davis, K. S., *F.D.R.*, 5 vols (Vol. 1, New York, Putnam, 1971; Vols 2–5, New York, Random House, 1985–2000).

Evans, H., *Hidden Campaign: FDR's Health and the Election of 1944* (Armonk NY, M. E. Sharpe, 2002).

Freidel, F., *Franklin D. Roosevelt*, 4 vols (Boston, Little Brown, 1952–73).

Gallagher, H., *FDR's Splendid Deception: The Moving Story of Roosevelt's Massive Disability and the Intense Efforts to Conceal it From the Public* (Clearwater FL, Vandamere Press, 1994).

Maney, P., *The Roosevelt Presence: A Biography of Franklin Delano Roosevelt* (New York, Twayne, 1992).

Morgan, T., *F.D.R.: A Biography* (London, Grafton, 1985).

Perkins, F., *The Roosevelt I Knew* (New York, Viking, 1946).

Roosevelt, F.D., *Looking Forward* (New York, John Day, 1933).

Ryan, Halford Ross, *Franklin D. Roosevelt's Rhetorical Presidency* (Westport CT, Greenwood Press, 1988).

Tugwell, R., *The Democratic Roosevelt: A Biography of Franklin D. Roosevelt* (New York, Doubleday, 1957).

General overviews of the New Deal and its critics

Adams, David K., *Franklin D. Roosevelt and the New Deal* (London, Historical Association, 1979).

Badger, Anthony J., *The New Deal: The Depression Years, 1933–40* (London, Macmillan, and New York, Hill and Wang, 1989).

Best, Gary Dean, *Pride, Prejudice, and Politics: Roosevelt Versus Recovery, 1933–1938* (New York, Praeger, 1991).

Biles, Roger, *A New Deal for the American People* (DeKalb, Northern Illinois University Press, 1991).

Brinkley, Alan, *The End of Reform: New Deal Liberalism in Recession and War* (New York, Knopf, 1995).

Burns, James MacGregor, *Roosevelt: The Lion and the Fox* (New York, Harcourt Brace, and London, Secker and Warburg, 1956).

Conkin, Paul Keith, *The New Deal* (New York, Crowell, 1967).

Freidel, Frank, *FDR: Launching the New Deal* (Boston, Little Brown, 1973).

Hawley, Ellis W., *The New Deal and the Problem of Monopoly: A Study in Economic Ambivalence* (Princeton, Princeton University Press, 1966).

Leuchtenburg, William E., *Franklin D. Roosevelt and the New Deal, 1932–1940* (New York, Harper, 1963).

Nash, G. D., *The Crucial Era: The Great Depression and World War II 1929–1945* (New York, St Martins Press, 1992).

Patterson, James T., *Congressional Conservatism and the New Deal: The Growth of the Conservative Coalition in Congress, 1933–1939* (Lexington, University Press of Kentucky, 1967).

Romasco, Albert U., *The Politics of Recovery: Roosevelt's New Deal* (New York, Oxford University Press, 1983).

Schlesinger, Arthur M., Jr, *The Crisis of the Old Order, 1919–1933* (Boston, Houghton Mifflin, and London, Heinemann, 1957).

Schlesinger, Arthur M., Jr, *The Coming of the New Deal* (Boston, Houghton Mifflin, 1958; London, Heinemann, 1960).

Schlesinger, Arthur M., Jr, *The Politics of Upheaval* (Boston, Houghton Mifflin, 1960; London, Heinemann, 1961).

Schwarz, Jordan A., *The New Dealers: Power Politics in the Age of Roosevelt* (New York, Knopf, 1993).

Sitkoff, A., *Fifty Years Later: The New Deal Evaluated* (New York, Knopf, 1985).

Watkins, T. H., *The Great Depression: American in the 1930s* (Boston, Little Brown, 1993).

Wolfskill, George and Hudson, John A., *All But the People: FDR and His Critics, 1933–1939* (New York, Macmillan, 1969).

The New Dealers

Ferrell, Robert H., *FDR's Quiet Confidant: The Autobiography of Frank C. Walker* (Boulder, University Press of Colorado, 1997).

Hopkins, June, *Harry Hopkins: Sudden Hero, Brash Reformer* (New York, St Martin's Press, 1999).

Irons, Peter H., *The New Deal Lawyers* (Princeton, Princeton University Press, 1993).

Ohl, John, *Hugh S. Johnson and the New Deal* (Illinois, Northern Illinois University Press, 1985).

Pasachoff, Naomi, *Frances Perkins: Champion of the New Deal* (Oxford, Oxford University Press Children's Books, 2000).

Anti-New Dealers

Brinkley, A., *Voices of Protest: Huey Long, Father Coughlin and the Great Depression* (New York, Knopf, 1982).

Garrett, Garet and Ramsey, Bruce (eds), *Salvos Against the New Deal* (Idaho, Caxton Press, 2002).

The New Deal and American culture

Contreras, Belisario R., *Tradition and Innovation in New Deal Art* (Lewisburg, Bucknell University Press, 1984).

Regional and local studies of the New Deal

Argersinger, Jo Ann, *Toward a New Deal in Baltimore: People and Government in the Great Depression* (Chapel Hill, University of North Carolina Press, 1988).

Biles, Roger, *The South and the New Deal* (Louisville, University of Kentucky Press, 1994).

Forrest, Suzanne and Debuys, William, *The Preservation of the Village: New Mexico's Hispanics and the New Deal* (Albuquerque, University of New Mexico Press, 1998).

Hayes, Jack Irby, *South Carolina and the New Deal* (Columbia, University of South Carolina Press, 2001).

Holmes, Michael S., *The New Deal in Georgia: An Administrative*

History (Westport CT, Greenwood Press, 1975).
Thomas, Jerry Bruce, *An Appalachian New Deal: West Virginia in the Great Depression* (Louisville, University of Kentucky Press, 1998).

American politics and constitution in the era of the New Deal

Adams, David K., 'The New Deal and the Vital Center: A Continuing Struggle for Liberalism', in Herbert D. Rosenbaum and Elizabeth Bartelme (eds), *Franklin D. Roosevelt: The Man, the Myth, the Era, 1882–1945* (Westport CT, Greenwood Press, 1987).
Allswang, John M., *The New Deal and American Politics: A Study in Political Change* (New York, Wiley, 1978).
Kelly, Alfred H. and Harbison, Winfred A., *The American Constitution: Its Origins and Development* (New York, Norton, 1948; 7th edition, with Herman Belz, 2 vols, 1991).
Patterson, James T., *Congressional Conservatism and the New Deal: The Growth of the Conservative Alliance in Congress, 1933–1939* (Lexington, University Press of Kentucky, 1967).
Patterson, James T., *The New Deal and the States: Federalism in Transition* (Princeton, Princeton University Press, 1969).
Schlesinger, Arthur M., Jr (general editor), *History of US Political Parties, Vol. 3: 1910–1945: From Square Deal to New Deal* (New York, Chelsea House, 1973).
Weiss, Nancy J., *Farewell to the Party of Lincoln: Black Politics in the Age of FDR* (Princeton, Princeton University Press, 1983).

The social and economic impact of the depression and New Deal

Badger, Anthony J., *The New Deal: The Depression Years, 1933–40* (London, Macmillan, and New York, Hill and Wang, 1989).
Bernstein, Irving, *A Caring Society: The New Deal, the Worker, and the Great Depression: A History of the American Worker, 1933–1941* (Boston, Houghton Mifflin, 1985).
Bernstein Michael A., *The Great Depression: Delayed Recovery and Economic Change in America, 1929–1939* (Cambridge and New York, Cambridge University Press, 1987).

Brock, William R., *Welfare, Democracy and the New Deal* (Cambridge, Cambridge University Press, 2002).
Chandler, Lester V., *America's Greatest Depression 1929–1941* (New York, Harper, 1970).
Cooney, Terry A., *Balancing Acts: American Thought and Culture in the 1930s* (New York, Twayne, 1995).
Fearon, Peter, *War, Prosperity and Depression: The US Economy 1917–45* (Deddington, Oxfordshire, Philip Allan, 1987).
Friedman, Milton and Schwartz, Anna Jacobson, *A Monetary History of the United States, 1867–1960* (Princeton, Princeton University Press, 1963).
Gordon, Colin, *New Deals: Business, Labor, and Politics in America, 1920–1935* (Cambridge and New York, Cambridge University Press, 1994).
Gregory, James N., *American Exodus: The Dust Bowl Migration and Okie Culture in California* (New York, Oxford University Press, 1989).
Hawley, Ellis W., *The New Deal and the Problem of Monopoly: A Study in Economic Ambivalence* (Princeton, Princeton University Press, 1966).
Romasco, Albert U., *The Politics of Recovery: Roosevelt's New Deal* (New York, Oxford University Press, 1983).
Saloutos, Theodore, *The American Farmer and the New Deal* (Ames, Iowa State University Press, 1982).
Singleton, Jeff, *The American Dole: Unemployment Relief and the Welfare State in the Great Depression* (Westport CT, Greenwood Press, 2000).
Sitkoff, Harvard, *A New Deal for Blacks* (Oxford, Oxford University Press, 1981).
Ware, Susan, *Beyond Suffrage: Women in the New Deal* (Cambridge MA, Harvard University Press, 1981).
Weinstein, Michael M., *Recovery and Redistribution under the NIRA* (Amsterdam, North Holland Publishing, 1980).
William, Joe, *From a Raw Deal to a New Deal: African-Americans, 1929–45* (Oxford, Oxford University Press, 1996).

Foreign policy

Dallek, R., *Franklin D. Roosevelt and American Foreign Policy, 1932–1945* (Oxford, Oxford University Press, 1979).

Divine, R. A., *The Reluctant Belligerent* (New York, John Wiley & Sons, 1965).

McKercher, B. J. C., *Transition of Power: Britain's Loss of Global Pre-Eminence to the United States 1930–1945* (Cambridge, Cambridge University Press, 1999).

Documentary and bibliographic sources

Cohen, Robert, *Dear Mrs Roosevelt: Letters from Children of the Great Depression* (Chapel Hill, University of North Carolina Press, 2002).

Foreign Relations of the United States, 1932–1941.

Ickes, Harold L., *The Secret Diary of Harold L. Ickes*, 3 vols (London, Simon and Schuster, 1954).

Kyvig, David E. and Blasio, Mary-Ann, *New Day/New Deal: A Bibliography of the Great American Depression, 1929–1941* (Westport CT, Greenwood Press, 1988).

McElvaine, Robert S., *The Depression and the New Deal: A History in Documents* (Oxford, Oxford University Press Children's Books, 2000).

McJimsey, G., *Documentary History of the Franklin D. Roosevelt Presidency* (Washington, University Publications of America, 2001).

Nixon, E. B., *Franklin D. Roosevelt and Conservation 1911–1945*, 2 vols (New York, National Archives and Records Administration, 1957).

Pollenberg, Richard, *The Era of Franklin Roosevelt: A Brief History with Documents* (Basingstoke, Palgrave, 2000).

Rijn, G. Van, *Roosevelt's Blues: African American Blues and Gospel Songs on FDR* (Jackson, University Press of Mississippi, 1997).

Walch, Timothy and Miller, Dwight M. (eds), *Herbert Hoover and Franklin D. Roosevelt: A Documentary History* (Westport CT, Greenwood Press, 1998).

Index

Index